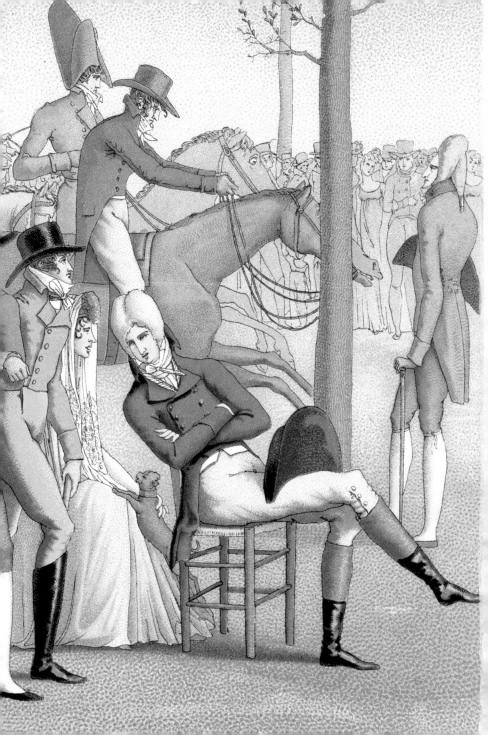

AUGUSTE
RACINET

1825–1893

LE COSTUME

HISTORIQUE.

CINQ CENTS PLANCHES,

TROIS CENTS EN COULEURS, OR ET ARGENT,

DEUX CENTS EN CAMAÏEU.

TYPES PRINCIPAUX DU VÊTEMENT ET DE LA PARURE

RAPPROCHÉS DE CEUX DE L'INTÉRIEUR DE L'HABITATION DANS TOUS LES TEMPS ET CHEZ TOUS LES PEUPLES,
AVEC DE NOMBREUX DÉTAILS
SUR LE MOBILIER, LES ARMES, LES OBJETS USUELS, LES MOYENS DE TRANSPORT, ETC.

RECUEIL PUBLIÉ SOUS LA DIRECTION DE

M. A. RACINET,

AUTEUR DE L'ORNEMENT POLYCHROME,

AVEC DES NOTICES EXPLICATIVES, UNE INTRODUCTION GÉNÉRALE, DES TABLES ET UN GLOSSAIRE.

PARIS,

LIBRAIRIE DE FIRMIN-DIDOT ET CIE,

IMPRIMEURS DE L'INSTITUT,

56, RUE JACOB, 56.

1888.

AUGUSTE RACINET

1825–1893

THE COSTUME HISTORY
FROM ANCIENT TIMES TO THE 19TH CENTURY
ALL PLATES IN COLOUR

TASCHEN
Bibliotheca Universalis

Françoise Tétart-Vittu

Auguste Racinet's "Le Costume historique": A Monumental 19th-Century Achievement

Françoise Tétart-Vittu

AUGUSTE RACINET'S
"LE COSTUME HISTORIQUE"

'Our fathers handed down to us not just a knowledge of their persons but of the headwear, arms and other ornaments that they loved in their own lifetimes. The only way in which we can properly acknowledge this benefit is by doing the same for our descendants.' Jean de La Bruyère (Les Caractères, *De la mode, 15*)

This is the challenge thrown down by La Bruyère. And the man who rose to it was one of the most audacious of the 19th century's scholar-artists. By transforming La Bruyère's 'benefit' into imagery, he ensured that a vast historical cavalcade of peoples of this earth might pass before everyone's eyes. Auguste Racinet's prestigious work on historical costume, which he completed one hundred and fifteen years ago, is justly celebrated. In its wealth of information and minutely detailed drawings, it was the first epitome of costume history to be published in France, and its scale has never been equalled. The study of costume had previously featured in manuals of archaeology as a sub-category of the study of arms; Racinet constitutes the vital link between this approach and the history of civilian costume, at the time an underdeveloped discipline in France.

Racinet shared with a number of French artists the stance he adopted in a controversy that raged for over a decade (1864–1875). This concerned the relation between liberal and industrial arts; Racinet stood alongside the collectors and scholars who founded the Union centrale des Arts décoratifs and the artists who contributed to the publications commissioned by two ministries, the Ministère de l'Instruction and the Ministère des Beaux-Arts — works published by major official houses such as Firmin-Didot.

The bookseller René Colas, author of the first *Bibliographie générale du Costume* (1933), describes Racinet's work as 'the most important general collection on the subject of costume: the documents were taken from earlier published series and original drawings from public collections'.

Albert Charles Auguste Racinet was born in Paris on 20 July 1825. His career was representative of a group of 19th-century industrial draughtsmen, teachers of technical drawing and factory studio managers who helped to diffuse the most significant motifs of the decorative arts of the time. Like many of these men, he had learnt his trade from his father; Racinet senior (also christened Charles Auguste Racinet) was a lithographic printer. The younger Charles Auguste subsequently completed the Ville de Paris drawing course. Represented at the Salon 1849–1874 as a painter, he in fact exhibited nothing but reproductions of ancient documents from manuscripts in the Bibliothèque nationale,

A MONUMENTAL
19TH-CENTURY ACHIEVEMENT

archaeological subjects and projects for stained glass windows. The musée Draguignan still possesses some Racinet paintings of scenes from the life of Charles VI and Jacques Cœur.

His expertise in artistic reproduction naturally led Racinet towards teaching and participation in scholarly works: collections, dictionaries and manuals of architecture and interior decoration. In collaborating on the plates of a work by the painter Ferdinand Séré and the man of letters Charles Louandre — its projected title was *Histoire du Costume et de l'Ameublement au Moyen-Âge* — he was, it seems, simply following in his father's footsteps. As a result of Séré's unexpected death, the lithographer, bookseller and publisher Hangard-Maugé returned to the project somewhat later, when he drew on Séré's work for the four volumes of *Arts Somptuaires, Histoire du costume et de l'ameublement et des arts et industries qui s'y rattachent*, published in 1858. He did so with the assistance of a painter 'expert in archaeological studies', Claudius Ciappori. Part of Séré's project had, however, been published as early as 1847–1851 by the famous Paul Lacroix (known as 'Bibliophile Jacob'), in the volume *Le Moyen Âge et la Renaissance, histoire et description des mœurs et des usages, du commerce et de l'industrie, des sciences, des arts, des littératures et des beaux-arts en Europe*. This was an official State publication, and Lacroix followed it in 1852 with ten volumes of *Costumes historiques de la France d'après les monuments les plus authentiques ... précédé de l'histoire de la vie privée des français depuis l'origine de la monarchie jusqu'à nos jours*. The names of the Racinets senior and junior appear on certain plates of both of these works, signed 'Séré et A. Racinet del. et lith.' or 'Racinet père del.'. In the distribution of labour, the Racinets had, it seems, been principally assigned the didactic plates.

The young Auguste Racinet's participation in works of this kind marked the starting point of his career in scholarly art publishing. This career is summarised in the administrative dossier compiled when he was named a Chevalier de la Légion d'Honneur on 5 August 1878, at which time the publication of his *Costume historique* was already 'in progress'. The report reminds us that Racinet, 'draughtsman and publicist', was not merely the author of *Ornement Polychrome*, translated into English under the title *Polychromatic Ornament* as well as into German, but artistic director of various sets of engravings, such as *La Céramique japonaise*, a colour publication in English and French, *La Collection archaéologique du Prince Pierre Saltykoff*, *Le XVIIIe siècle* by Paul Lacroix, and *L'Iconographie de la Sainte Vierge* by Abbé Meynard. Also cited is his work on typographical illustrations to Apuleius's *Golden Ass*, and on the first printed editions of *Moyen Âge et la Renaissance* and *Arts Somptuaires* by Séré and Louandre, and Engelmann's *L'Institution de l'ordre du Saint Esprit*. The dossier further refers to the reports that Racinet drafted as Secretary to the Drawing Schools Jury for the exhibitions at the Union Centrale, 1874–1876. On his death on 29 October 1893 at Montfort-L'Amaury, near Paris, he was famous above all for his two essential works: *Polychromatic Ornament, comprising upwards of two thousand specimens ... in historical order and in a form suitable for practical use,* published in 1869, which went to a second edition in 1885–1887, and *Le Costume historique,* whose sixth volume, containing the introductions and contents, completed the work in 1888.

This work of vulgarisation was an exemplary product of the editorial policy of the great publisher Ambroise Firmin-Didot (1790–1876), printer to the Institut de France. Firmin-Didot, it will be remembered, was a distinguished Hellenist, elected member of the Académie des Inscriptions et Belles-Lettres in 1872, and a collector of manuscripts and rare books. The publishing house that he developed was that of his uncle Pierre Didot (1761–1853), who had himself published the celebrated *Voyages pittoresques et romantiques en France* by Baron Isidore Justin Séverin Taylor, on which many illustrators had worked; its 685 numbers appeared over the period 1820–1878. Ambroise Didot published a series of archaeological works on Egypt, Greece, Pompeii, and so on, to which Auguste Racinet constantly refers. These were the principal source for his famous *Polychromatic Ornament,* a practical collection put together with the avowed intention of 'rendering major services to our industrial arts'. In this he was at one with the artistic preoccupations of his contemporaries in the years 1845 to 1890. He belonged to the generation trained by Neo-classical artists in the ambit of Percier and Fontaine, influenced by the Schinkel tendency and supported by architects such as Hittorf and, later, Viollet-le-Duc. This scholarly renaissance in Hellenistic art was not, in their view, simply a matter of imitating classical antiquity; they thought of it as underpinning a new start in the decorative arts. A better understanding of past epochs would, they thought, make it possible to attain beauty in the present day. This sense of the past was gradually enlarged during the second half of the 19th century to include the Middle Ages and the Renaissance; as a consequence, it was often criticised for its eclecticism, since the turn of the century was marked by its 'ambition for truth', as Roger Marx put it in his preface (15 October 1891) to Arsène Alexandre's *Histoire de l'art décoratif du XVIe siècle à nos jours.* Racinet placed his archaeological art at the service of the decorative arts at a time when polychromy was central to architectural innovation. Jakob Ignaz Hittorf's *L'Architecture polychrome chez les Grecs* had appeared in 1851, and in 1854 he published his projects for a temple to the Muses and a Pompeiian villa, projects created for Napoléon III, who was himself a collector enamoured of classical antiquity. At the same time, Viollet-le-Duc, as Inspecteur des Monuments historiques et des cultes, was encouraging forms of restoration and decoration very close to the styles of ornament tabulated by Racinet. One example of this is the Romanesque and Gothic decorations composed by the architect Charles Joly-Leterme (1805–1885) for the châteaux of the Saumur region.

Polychromy came to be applied in all areas of the arts, notably in the lithography that was Racinet's own speciality. This was the technique that he adopted for the superlative plates of *Le Costume historique*. In so doing, he fulfilled the wishes of Ambroise Didot, expert for printing of the jury of the 1851 Great Exhibition in London, who had 'seen nothing so beautiful as the lithochromatic products of the Austrian Royal Printing Works', and sought a Frenchman who could work to the same standard. The technique was particularly suited to the reproduction of illuminated manuscripts, and Racinet had been initiated into the art of chromolithography in the ambit of Hangard-Maugé.

For this group of archaeologically inspired architects, costume was a prime component of the culture of antiquity, a point which all of them emphasise in their prefaces. Viollet-le-Duc gave it a scientific dimension in his *Dictionnaire raisonné du mobilier français de l'époque carlovingienne à la Renaissance* (1858–1875). He covered clothes, jewellery and ornamental objects in volumes III and IV of this work, his sense of detail driving him to add dressmaking patterns for the Italian Renaissance. Volumes V and VI of this work were meanwhile devoted to arms and their use.

General histories of costume were more and more frequently attempted, and over the course of time the period studied crept forwards to include the late 18th century. Thus whereas in 1827–1829, Camille Bonnard and Paul Mercuri's *Costumes ecclésiastiques et militaires* had confined itself to classical antiquity and the Middle Ages, after 1858, scholarly interest in later centuries began to extend to the very early 19th century. This interest was not unique to France: in 1852, Carl Becker published a work equivalent to Lacroix's, the *Kunstwerke und Geräthschaften des Mittelalters und der Renaissance*. Becker's enterprise was continued in 1859–1863 by Jacob Heinrich von Hefner-Alteneck (1811–1903), whose principal fame was as an art historian; he was Keeper of the National Museum of Bavaria from 1868. In 1840–1854, he published *Trachten des christlichen Mittelalters* in Frankfurt — a French translation was published in Mannheim — and followed this with the ten volumes of his *Trachten,*

Kunstwerke und Geräthschaften vom frühen Mittelalter bis Ende des achtzehnten Jahrhunderts mit gleichzeitigen Originalen. This appeared over the years 1879–1889, at the same time as Racinet's history, and a French translation followed soon after (1880–1897).

Such historical endeavours acquired particular prominence at the World Exhibitions in the section entitled Retrospective Museum, whose conception was like that of the museums that grew up in so many towns during the 19th century. Having noted a certain poverty of invention in the decorative arts during the Great Exhibition of 1851, a group of artists in 1858 founded the Société du progrès de l'Art industriel, which in 1864 became the Union centrale des Beaux-Arts appliqués à l'industrie. Fascinated by the example of the new South Kensington Museum, which had opened during the London World Exhibition of 1862, the Union centrale in 1865 presented a historical exhibition of art objects and furniture, divided into the categories ancient, medieval, renaissance and 'modern' (17th–18th centuries), along with a large section of oriental art.

The oriental arms of the Marquis of Hertford and the manuscripts of Ambroise Firmin-Didot were much admired, but textiles were barely represented and clothing not at all. The Union centrale subsequently elected to concentrate on a single theme, and the 1869 exhibition on oriental art was a considerable success. War, however, intervened, with its attendant turmoil, and it was not until 1874 that the Union organised its fourth exhibition, which took the form of a museum of costume history. This was in perfect accord with the spirit of the time. Clothing ancient and modern had been taken up by literature and the visual arts. From Gérôme to Tissot and Meissonnier to Roybet, painting was responding not merely to the essays of Baudelaire and the Goncourt brothers but to works contemporary with the exhibition, such as Mallarmé's *La Dernière mode* (late 1874) and Charles Blanc's *L'Art dans la parure et dans le vêtement* (1875). The interest in costume was not confined to the artistic world. The wider public had flocked to see the display of Swedish costumes in the geographical section of the 1867 World Exhibition and the historical clothes from the Musée des Souverains presented in Paris and Versailles.

The Union centrale's 1874 exhibition enjoyed the patronage of conservators such as Edmond du Sommerard and collectors like Dutuit and Baron Double, along with the Marquis de Chennevières and the distinguished painter Léon Gérôme, a member of the Institut and an advocate of a return to classical painting. The executive committee included the manager of the Gobelins, Darcel, the scholar Bonnafé, Régnier, stage-director at the Comédie-Française, and the painters Lechevallier, Chevignard and Racinet. This was no small enterprise. No fewer than 255 owners lent items for the exhibition, and an impressive number of garments, textiles, pictures and objects went on show in order 'to create as complete as possible a sequence of historical documents of the sumptuary arts and to provide manufacturers with numerous elements for study and comparison'. Even today, one is struck by the historical importance of the Louvre tapestries and pictures lent for the show and distributed through the ten large halls. They hung above cases filled with a host of objects provided by famous collectors such as Spitzer, Wallace, the Ephrussi cousins, and the Rothschilds. The textile samples from the Dupont-Auberville collection, the shoes lent by Jules Jacquemart, the oriental furniture sent by Albert Goupil, and the manuscripts and book-bindings from the Firmin-Didot collection were particularly admired.

Nor was the pedagogical side of things neglected. The Ministère de l'Instruction publique had sent prints of seals and memorial slabs made by the Director of Archives. Also exhibited were the patterns of the classical costumes used by Heuzey in his course on Greek costume at the École des Beaux-Arts. Historical monuments were represented in the form of chromolithographic reproductions of frescoes, and the theatre by the drawings made 'on the basis of authentic and historical documents drawn from his collection' by the stage-designer Lacoste for the costumes of two plays presented at the théâtre du Châtelet: *Déluge* and *Théodoros et Ismaïla*. And finally a library was created featuring all recent works published on the subject, and decorated with tapestries and 'artist's proofs' of Jules Jacquemart's *costume portraits* made after pictures, arms and jewellery published in the *Gazette des Beaux-Arts*.

All this underlines how Racinet and Firmin-Didot's work was the perfect follow-up to this exhibition, making available the knowledge contributed by the bringing together of the many complementary 'documents' constituted by the exhibits. But though the Union centrale had demonstrated the existence of a strong interest in every aspect of costume, its founders differed widely in their perspectives. This became clear in April 1875, when the Union centrale established its library and museum in the place des Vosges. Both of these institutions were open to workers leaving their factories and studios of an evening, and admission was free. Certain of the collectors and administrators of the Union had had in mind a quite different and more elitist goal, that of the creation of a museum of decorative arts. The result was the founding in 1877 of a parallel organisation under the instigation of the Marquis de Chennevières: the Société du Musée des Arts décoratifs. The two associations finally united in 1879 to form the Union centrale des Arts décoratifs, which ultimately became the Musée des Arts décoratifs located in the pavillon de Marsan at the Louvre. This transformation of the Société into a veritable museum primarily answered the purposes of rich collectors — potential donors to the new museum — and the many famous painters of the time who sold their 'costume' paintings world-wide.

For in the years 1840–1880, the taste for painting in the Dutch style, which sat so well with 16th–17th century furniture, was diffused by the many 'artisans of art' who had been inspired by Lacroix and Racinet's volumes, by Gérôme's drawing course published by Goupil and by the documentation offered by the Union centrale. Their clients liked to research these periods; they collected original objects, bought 'reconstitutions of ancient works' in porcelain from the famous Parisian manufacturer Samson, or, like Ferdinand de Rothschild, commissioned imitations of objects and jewellery of the 16th century. This mixture of the authentic and the reconstituted, widely used in the repair or replacement of panelling in the great houses of Europe and the East Coast of the United States, was also practised in relation to textiles and costumes. Falling in love with the exotic, collectors sometimes ornamented their Turkish salons with oriental clothes; landowners invented a lineage for themselves that featured ancestors in armour or historical robes. Painters needing authentic items to copy possessed their own collections of costumes, which they strongly preferred to the photos of costumed models sold by certain photographers. Many of these authentic pieces, not all of them unmodified, have since entered museums, of which they were often the original exhibits and point of departure. Examples include the painter Lucas's costumes at the Museum of London, Stibbert's in Florence, Escosura's in Reggio di Emilia, and those of Flameng, Roybet and Leloir in Paris. Certain artists were rich enough to commission costumes from specialist tailors who researched them in scholarly works such as Racinet's. Thus Roybet, who painted scenes *à la* Frans Hals, had suitable costumes and shoes made for him by a Flemish craftsman named Henri Clootens. At this time, the streets around the École des Beaux-Arts contained shops specialising in the sale of costumes of greater or lesser antiquity to painters and theatre wardrobes. This clientele was, as it were, tailor-made for Racinet, and it was not the only one.

A Monumental 19ᵀᴴ-century Achievement

For couturiers, too, Racinet was a mine of information, at a time when costume balls were all the rage in high society. One of the most famous couturiers of the time, Jean Philippe Worth, himself a painter and collector of historical costumes, sought and perhaps found inspiration in Racinet's plates for the stylish and fantastical evening wear that he designed. Fashion-journal editors seeking to provide their readership with engravings of fancy-dress for the carnival could also have recourse to his volumes. *La Mode illustrée*, which Firmin-Didot began publishing in 1862, had one of the highest subscriptions among such magazines. Its patterns and engravings were sold on to other press groups, notably to Franz Lipperheide's *Modenwelt* in Berlin. Lipperheide was at the time in the process of creating (with this wife Frieda, herself a collector of textiles and embroidery), the first and one of the greatest specialist libraries of the literature of costume; it now forms part of the Berlin Kunstbibliothek.

The publication of Racinet's work triggered that of rival works, such as those of Weiss and Hottenroth, and the republication of earlier works such as those of Lacroix and Jacquemin. It also inspired a work of the very early 20ᵗʰ century, Roger-Miles' *Comment discerner les styles du VIIIᵉ au XIXᵉ siècle*, with 2,000 line-engraving reproductions; this was a sort of abridgement of Racinet's work on civilian costume in France and paved the way for the work of the following generation, that of Maurice Maindron and Maurice Leloir.

These men were not, however, entirely uncritical of Racinet's efforts; they criticised him for having done the work of a painter by reproducing, for the most part, line drawings. Consequently, in 1903, they planned the creation of a *Dictionnaire du Costume du Moyen-Âge au XIXᵉ siècle*, conceived along Viollet-le-Duc lines; his was their presiding spirit. This was to be a general history of costume in five volumes, with historical notes and illustrations drawn after originals by the painter Maurice Leloir, to be completed by a dictionary that would include patterns. Leloir had illustrated editions of Molière and Alexandre Dumas, and was not satisfied with merely graphical evidence; he was determined to study the surviving costumes. In 1907, Maindron and Leloir, with the military painter Édouard Detaille, founded the Société de l'Histoire du Costume, whose goal was the creation of a costume museum. This goal was prefigured in an exhibition held in 1909 in the Louvre's pavillon de Marsan, a sort of avatar of the 1874 exhibition that Racinet had seen. But the deaths of first Maindron and then Detaille, followed by the outbreak of the First World War, delayed the projected dictionary, and Leloir's 17th- and 18th-century volumes were published only in 1935–1939. The *Dictionnaire du Costume* appeared posthumously in 1951; it was reprinted in 1992 and remains an authoritative source for costume history.

Racinet's work is, then, not only a documentary treasure-trove covering more than two thousand years of costume. From a historical perspective, as we have seen, it casts valuable light on the history of museums, the applied arts, and the changing notions of what constitutes a work of art. For the 21st-century reader, it further offers a chance to reconstruct ancient times, an exercise of memory and imagination that has its own charms. It is to just such a sedentary voyage through time and place that the reader is hereby invited.

TO THE READER Racinet's *Le Costume historique* is in two closely linked but radically different parts: the 473 plates reproduced here (Racinet considered certain of them double plates, and numbered them 1–500), and the long text that accompanies them. The latter offers a commentary on the illustrations, detailing now items of clothing, now a jewel or ornament. Racinet often complements this information with more general considerations and anecdotes illuminating the character and customs of a community. The original version of this text runs to nearly 1,300 pages and would, if reproduced without abridgement, have constituted much too large a volume. But it seemed important to give the reader some idea of its contents, were it only in fragmentary form, and we have therefore selected a few segments and certain extracts from these long commentaries.

We should, however, warn the reader about two disconcerting aspects of Racinet's text. The first of these is his style, which is typical of the late-19th-century scholarly or academic author; it abounds in circumlocution, periphrasis and lengthy digression. It can therefore be difficult to follow, especially since elements of Racinet's vocabulary can nowadays seem a little old-fashioned. The second aspect calls for a more extensive elucidation. Racinet now and then turns aside from description of clothing and ornament to conduct assessments of the characteristics of specific ethnic groups. Here a nation with a long history of civilisation is deemed worthy of consideration, there the sole interest of a so-called degenerate people is the particularity of its adornments. The ideology implicit in these remarks is not easy to stomach. We should, however, temper our ire. Racinet belongs to a period in which this ideology was suddenly reinforced; the late 19th century was precisely the epoch when France, like other European nations, was pursuing a policy of conquest known as colonisation. The wide range of authors that Racinet consulted when undertaking his panorama of national and ethnic customs included very disparate sources, such as Latin writers and the narratives of explorers now forgotten. But the sources that he synthesises with such brio were almost invariably European.

Today we are aware that the very notion of racism is intrinsic to European culture and was strongly re-activated by the colonial enterprise. Let there be no mistake, this work dates from the period when the West dreamed of establishing an indefinite reign over the entire world. In comparison with the goal of bringing illumination to one and all, massacres, deportations and the enslavement of entire populations were considered a small price to pay. And of course, the true goal of these conquests was the capture of natural resources and the opening of new markets for European trade.

But when we read Racinet attentively, we cannot but perceive his openness of mind. The notion of constituting a sort of general archive of costume, including in a single work all times, places, epochs, forms and tastes — the very idea of demonstrating the eclecticism of the world's cultures — takes its place in a vast project tending to emphasise the extraordinary diversity of humankind. And this in itself, whatever is alleged to the contrary, runs counter to what we now call racism. The reader should therefore treat certain of Racinet's remarks with indulgence, bearing in mind that if he was, in ideological terms, an unadulterated product of his time, he was also a man attracted by those myriad customs that constitute the wealth of human history.

I
THE ANCIENT WORLD

Egyptian · Assyrian · Hebraic · Asian

The Egyptian chariot carried two men (pls. 1, 2): an elite warrior, who wielded the bow, the javelin and the axe, and a subordinate who took charge of the reins and the single shield that served to protect them both. The soldiers accompanying the chariot carry a shield covering the body from waist to head, a spear in the right hand and a short axe in the left. Their white tunic is belted at the waist with a knotted cloth whose ends hang loose.

The ancient Egyptians divided humankind into four families: Egyptians (Retu, men *par excellence*), Blacks (Nahsi), Asians (Aamu), and the white-skinned people of the North. The ancient Egyptian was of a race in all respects similar to the current inhabitants of Nubia, and was, for the most part, tall and slender. He had broad, powerful shoulders, prominent pectorals and a muscular arm ending in a long, slender hand. His hips were narrow, and his legs wiry; his feet were long and thin, and flattened by going barefoot. His head was often too large for his body; his forehead slightly low, his nose short and round, his eyes large and wide open, his cheeks flat, his lips thick but not protuberant.

Furniture (pl. 5) was made in ordinary or rare and exotic wood, and gilded and incised metals. Wood was inlaid with ivory and ebony. Chairs and armchairs were decorated, covered in rich fabrics of plain, brocaded, embroidered or painted linen, cotton or silk. In antiquity, vases formed the most beautiful and richest part of the furnishings. Vases of various forms were made from alabaster, glass or semi-precious stone. This picturesque view of an inner courtyard (pl. 9) is a reconstitution of an Egyptian house such as it appeared in the 14th century B.C.

The civilisation of Asia was born on the banks of the Tigris and Euphrates, and rose to glory in the Ninevite and Babylonian empires, which seem to have been far more extensive than that of the Egyptians. The Assyrians perfumed their jet-black beards and hair, and wove them with gold thread or covered them with powdered gold. Unfortunately, their sculptures do not show the various classes present in Assyrian society.

Among the Hebrews, it is clear that the establishment of the priesthood can be traced back to Moses; he alone could have introduced so many Egyptian elements. We know that Moses selected the servants of the sanctuary exclusively from the tribe of Levi. He divided the children of this tribe into two classes: *Cohanim* or priests, and mere Levites. The costume of the simple priests comprised four items (pl. 13): breeches, a tunic, a belt and a tall bonnet. In addition, the grand priest wore a violet sleeveless outer tunic, and a shorter garment, the *ephod*, woven of linen intertwined with purple, violet, crimson and gold thread. The grand priest wore the pectoral or *rational* (*hoshen*) over the *ephod*. The third part of the Levite's costume was a belt, *abnet*.

The Latin poets refer to the inhabitants of ancient Asia as Parthians, Persians and Medes, apparently without distinction; for them, these groups seemed to have formed a single entity. As to the Amazons, this mythical race of woman warriors came, it is said, from the Caucasus in Asia Minor. During the reign of Theseus, they invaded Attica. The Amazons' garment covered the entire body, with the exception of the left side, which was left naked to the breast.

1 · **MILITARY COSTUME** of Ramses the Great (Sesostris). Combat chariot of the Pharaohs and harness. Royal standard and guards. Egyptian burning incense. Headdresses in hair, metal, leather and cloth.

2 · **MILITARY COSTUMES,** Egyptian and the other human families represented in ancient paintings: Blacks, Asians (Tyrians, Trojans, Bactrians) and the white-skinned people of the North. Combat chariots, decoration of harness. Man at arms and his driver or squire. Egyptian national military uniform. *Klaft* and the striped *calasiris*. Bronze helmet. Linen cuirass. Shields. Bow, javelins, battle-axe, mace and dagger. Staff engraved with hieroglyphs, emblem of command. *Uraeus*, emblem of sovereignty. Hair offering to the gods. The fate of the vanquished. Negro with thick lips, dyed red hair and large earrings. Simultaneous use of arms made of hard wood, flexible wood, bone, bronze, iron and flint.

3 · **CIVILIAN COSTUMES.** Seated Egyptians; Egyptian woman kneeling. Mandora player. Ramses II Meryamun. Curled and plaited hair and wigs. Face-painting; eye lotion; skin-tinting, henna; unguents for the body. The *klaft* or *claft*, the national headdress, and the tight bonnets. Cotton, linen and woollen garments, and transparent muslin. Bracelets, necklaces, and glass and metal headbands. *Oskh*, large cape-necklace. *Uraeus*.

PLATE I

24

PLATE 2

PLATE 3

4 · **DIVINE AND RURAL FINERY.** Gods and goddesses, Pharaohs and queens of the Old and New Empire, that is, from Ptolemaic times. Use of feathers and plumage in clothing and headdresses. Person entirely dyed yellow, red-orange, indigo or green. *Shenti*, tied loin-cloth; skirt, with or without braces, for women. Men's light cuirass. Various *klafts*, hood encompassed by plumage of a bird. Large robe used as cloak. Royal apron. Necklaces of several concentric layers, and the *menat*, used as a counterbalance. Garments in precious metals and other materials. Full *pschent*, composed of war helmet and the *atev*, the high mitre flanked by ostrich feathers. Insignia of the ruler: the *nekkekh*, a whip with two lashes; *pedum*, crook; *lituus, uraeus*; long cordon; *ankh*, ansated cross. Cane serving as sceptre for the goddesses. Thrones. Standard of Ramses III.

5 · **FURNITURE.** Beds, divans and thrones. Night and daybeds; stool for access; portable bedhead, the *uol*, used as pillow. Standing mirror. Materials for chairs, armchairs, steps and divans; fabric with which they were covered.

6 · **UTENSILS AND DOMESTIC OBJECTS.** Large harps. Priest-musicians. Black dancing woman. Egyptian slave. Perfume boxes. Unguent containers. Make-up boxes. Hand-mirror. Horn cupping 'glass'. Eye-lotion pot, comb, etc. *Uol*, the portable bedhead.

7 · **DOMESTIC UTENSILS AND CULT OBJECTS.** Amphorae, ewers and jugs. Balsam and other pots of all dimensions, including flacons. Baskets, cups, bags and offertories. Types of slave.

8 · **PALANQUINS AND BOATS.** Royal palanquins: 1. The great *naos*; 2. The little *naos*, under the *umbella* or parasol, with trestles on which it was placed for stops; 3. Sedan-chair with throne-steps, carried on a plank. Porters, long fans and fly-whisks. The long-distance palanquin with parasol. *Cangia* or Nile boat, with single oar, and with sail and oars.

PLATE 4

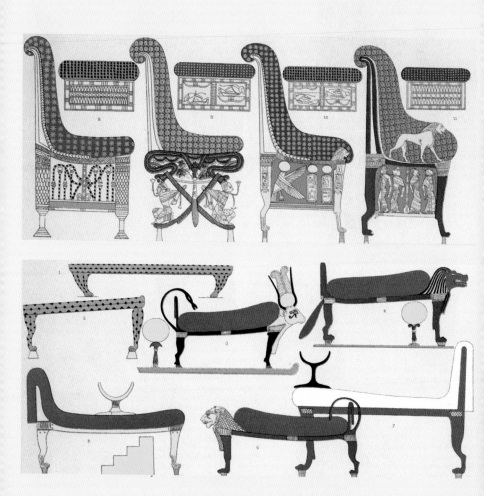

PLATE 5

PLATE 6

29

PLATE 8

31

9 · **INTERNAL COURTYARD** of a private dwelling (c. 14th century B.C.).

10 · **COURT AND MILITARY WEAR. FURNITURE, ARMS AND VARIOUS OBJECTS.** Ruler on the dining couch; the queen on a chair with throne step. Both raise the cup of libation. Their servants wave fly-whisks. Faces painted and made-up; hair curled; hair and beard powdered, sometimes with gold; wigs and hairpieces. Tattoos (stigmata) on forehead and wrists; aromatics and unguents. Headband, robes and fringed coverings. Jewellery. Offering and libation tables; low table; throne in form of stool; incense-burners; matting; fly-whisks. Inlaid furniture; material of the cups. Sword, dagger and quiver. Infantry soldiers armed with large shields and pikes.

11/12 · Kings, queens, lords, soldiers, eunuchs, etc. **GALA AND HUNTING COSTUMES.** Solid wood chariots for hunting large game. Chariot in *tríga* rig, with plumed horses; harness. Tiaras, diadem, bonnets and turban. *Candys*, the Medo-Persian robe; *stole*; tunics; fringed surtout; double belts. King's pectoral, quarter-sandal or Persian shoe. Boots. Laced boots. Padded jerkin as cuirass; long dagger, short sword and baldric. Gauntlet for archery. Bent bow. Fore- and upper-arm bracelets. Sceptre, short staff; parasol, emblem of power; pine cone, symbol of nature's awakening. The psalterions in the hands of the musicians. Hunting with hounds in the *paradisi*. Ruler mounted and wielding the bow followed by his pages. Royal ceremony; greeting by prostration, etc.

PLATE 9

33

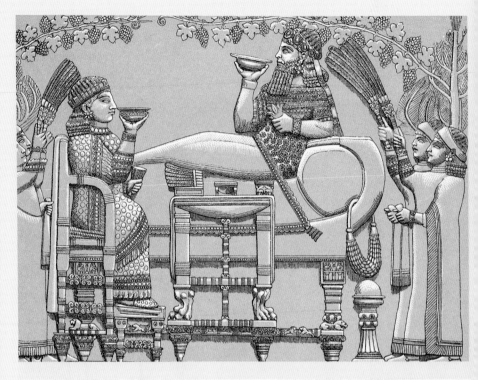

PLATE 10

PLATE II

35

PLATE 13

37

13 · **PRIESTLY VESTMENTS.** Breeches, tunic, belt and tall hat of the simple priest or Levite. *Meil, ephod,* pectoral or rational, *miznefet* (mitre, tiara or turban) of the high or anointed priest. Partial examples taken from Egyptian monuments, to show the parallels between the elements of the Hebrew and Ancient Egyptian priestly costumes.

14 · **COSTUMES, ARMS, FURNITURE AND UTENSILS.** Persian, Parthian, Armenian, Palmyran, Phrygian. The Amazons. Figures from the heroic age and from the Late Roman Empire. Simple tunic, with or without belt; with two belts; with or without sleeves. Over-tunic, with short or no sleeves. Long robe with wide sleeves; half-length robe. Light, short and half-length cloaks. Long, fringed royal cloak. Trunk hose or trousers. *Anaxyrides* and *sarabars.* Bonnets, hoods, mitres and tiaras. Diadems, crowns and headbands. Persian gloves and slippers. Phrygian bonnets. Trojan bow. Battle-axe and martel-defer; shield or *pelta* of the Amazons and their warrior costume. Seats and thrones; fly-whisk.

PLATE 14

39

Greek · Etruscan
Greco-Roman · Roman

One of the difficulties of studying Greek military costume is that the vases almost invariably show only divinities and heroes. There was no prescription or regulation of general character relating to warrior costume. Defensive arms (pl. 15) included the helmet, cuirass, sword-belt, baldric, *cnemides* or greaves, knee-pieces, heel-pieces (these latter used by mounted soldiers with foot-armour and spurs), brassards, shield and *chlamys*. The offensive weapons were: club, spear, long or short sword, dagger or knife at the belt, *harpe* (a sword with a protruding hook), axe and mace; and finally bow, javelins, sling with lead slingshots, and shield. The body of the army probably long continued to use bronze arms.

In civilian life, the Greeks wore the *chlamys* or *chlaine* (pl. 17), a light, short cloak. This was the standard garment worn by young Athenians. The Greeks also used the *pallium*, the large cloak that Homer describes divinities and heroes as wearing. It was oblong in shape, made of wool and fastened at the throat or shoulder by a broach.

Women bathed daily (pl. 18): this was the form of hygiene considered most appropriate for them in the ancient world. They also anointed the entire body with dense, liquid perfumes, pomades and oils. Greek women displayed great variety in the arrangement of their hair (pl. 21). (Men cut theirs short, women grew theirs long.) Veils of light or rich fabrics, fillets of various colours, gold, semi-precious stones, flowers and perfumes were all put to this use. Hair was curled and dyed. Wigs were also worn. The garments worn by Greek women (pls. 19, 20) did not open at the front as ours do. Tailoring had no part in these garments. There were no separate garments to clothe the lower part of the body like the petticoat. The *castula*, which fastened below the breast, came into use quite late as a replacement for the second tunic. The base of the costume was the *chiton*, a tunic of linen or wool. The first item of costume was the inner tunic, worn next to the skin. This short, narrow garment was called the *esophorion*. Tunics were of several kinds; the long one, with its narrow sleeves, was a veritable gown, and entirely closed. The short tunic was put on over the head like a blouse; sleeveless, it covered the shoulders in some measure, and was sometimes belted. The third kind included draped tunics, which were fastened at the shoulders by broaches. The *palla* was a large ceremonial tunic falling to the feet, and consisted of a rectangular piece of cloth whose upper part was partly folded back.

The Greeks ate only an evening meal (pl. 23). The table was long and made of smooth wood. Meat was eaten with the hands. Three courses were served. The first comprised vegetables, oysters, boiled eggs, and liquid foodstuffs made of wine and honey. The second comprised poultry, game and fish. The last: pastries, confectionery and fruit.

All the ancient historians considered the Etruscans to be of Asian origin. The surviving Etruscan monuments in Tuscany are necropoleis, paintings, sculptures, vases, furniture, jewellery and implements of all kinds.

Among the Romans, necklaces were either braided threads of gold or a series of amber, garnet or emerald beads. They could also be made of small pearls, *pâte de verre*, or enamel. At their centre, there was normally a pendant of some kind: flower, animal head, scarab, or gold *bulla*, stamped or incised. The use of rings, as either ornament or signet, goes back to furthest antiquity. In Rome, only senators and *equites* could wear a gold ring. The rings were heavy, since they were solid gold, and were worn on the third finger of the left hand. As luxury spread through Roman society, women too began to wear them. The Romans used intaglios and cameos imported from the East. Miraculous magical powers were often ascribed to rings according either to the stones with which they were set or the manner in which they were made.

The *domus* (pl. 46), the Roman home, was of all but invariable plan. Only the number and distribution of rooms differentiated these buildings. They were divided into two courtyards: the *atrium*, with its services, and the *peristylium*, the body of the building to the rear of the atrium, in which the family lived.

The pictures of legionnaires in plate 36 37 give a clear idea of their equipment. Their offensive arms were the sword, *gladius*, worn on a baldric, the *balteus* or *balteum*. The dagger, *clunaculum*, was worn in an ordinary belt. To this was added the *hasta*, a spear used as either pike or javelin.

Roman clothing (pl. 40) was always grave and severe; this impressive appearance was bestowed by the majestic folds of the toga, a draped garment. The *palla* that Roman women wore folded around them was of similar severity; they also wore a large tunic and a cloak. Married woman wore a large veil. The fabrics of which these garments were made was rich, often bordered with purple or gold. The *toga* was the principal outer garment for the Roman citizen. Romans also wore amulets: images, figures or objects worn to avert malady and spells. Artificial baths were a custom the Romans inherited from the Greeks (pl. 45). The two sexes bathed separately. Baths occupied the remotest part of the private house. They comprised a suite of rooms in which a cold bath was taken, either indoors or out; a warm bath; a steam bath and a hot bath. In the homes of the wealthy, the *gyneceum* had its own bath house. The ancients normally bathed before a late supper. Only the voluptuary bathed after this meal.

Two principles govern shoes (pl. 47): the protection and the reinforcement of the foot. The combination of these two functions resulted in the ancient sandal, that is, the main shoe worn by the Greeks and Romans. Part of the side of the sandal is pierced to accommodate straps that cross on the instep.

15 · MILITARY WEAR. *Nota bene:* The best way of studying the Greek soldier is to see him in action, as he is found in vase paintings; our pls. 15 and 16 show combat poses from paintings. However, the warrior was generally so represented bearing only the principal arms of the heroic age, so this first study must be completed by that of accoutrement, including all the accessories of the warrior costume, which varied over time and according to the nature of the army: line troops or light infantry, and cavalry lightly or heavily armed as their tactical role required. These various arms have been reconstructed by scholars, and can be found in our double plate 25-26. Plate 15 shows: a lightly armed horseman with spear; the *psile* (light infantryman) shooting the Apollonian bow; a warrior not yet fully armed, wearing cuirass, sword, spear, helmet, shield, and *chlamys*; a soldier ornamenting his helmet with painting; various swords and helmets; shields bearing emblems.

16 · MILITARY COSTUMES. War, racing and triumphal chariots. Bridle of horse. Chiefs' helmets. *Pelta.* Chiefs joining battle, carrying the emblazoned shield, with the colours suspended from it, serving as signal for combat; line soldier, kneeling in the front-line of a phalanx, with Boeotian helmet and shield. Soldier in travel costume. War chariots of the heroic age; their harness and use in battle. Armoured horse. Warrior's driver. Ceremonial chariot, with low wheels. Fast chariot, with single driver for four-horse-chariot races in the circus.

17 · MEN'S AND WOMEN'S CLOTHING. HELMETS of various kinds. *Chlamys* or *chloene*, light cloak; *pallium*, large cloak (Homer's *pharos*); light *pallium*. *Poderes*, long robe falling over the feet. *Katastiktos* or *zodiotes*, the multi-coloured robe. The two external belts, *strophion* and *zone*. *Impilia*, felt shoe covering the calves. Leg-guards worn for walking. The Thessalian hat hung over the shoulders, as travellers wore it. The staff of the heralds; the *caduceus*, emblem of the messenger. Helmets for chiefs with rounded crest or in the shape of a Phrygian cap. Helmets with fixed visor of exotic appearance, also used by gladiators (see double plate, 36-37).

PLATE 15

PLATE 16

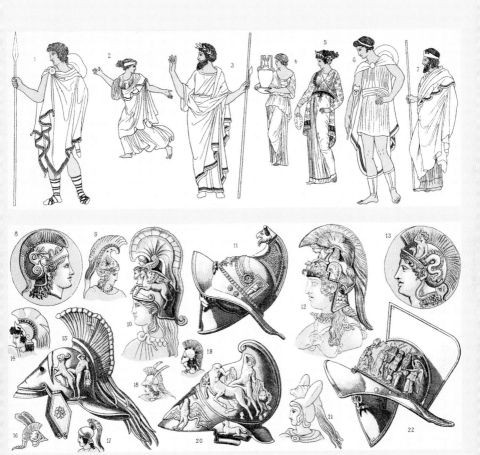

PLATE 17

47

18 · **WOMEN'S DRESS,** beginning with the washing of the body. Elements of costume and objects used therein. Intimate ablution; bath followed by unguents. Electuaries and recipients; toilet water. Hair and hair customs; prejudices in respect of it; dyes; *sapo* or soap to give it lustre; curling. Wigs, powders and perfumes. Light and transparent cloth, veils, scarves, tunics. *Kredemnon*, or floating veil. Fillets. *Strophion*, belt fixed below the breasts; *zone*, waist belt; *anamaschalister*, which passed under the armpits and over a shoulder (for the breast-band worn next to the skin, see the following plate). Basins, chairs, hand mirrors, jewel boxes, the *pyxis* or jewel casket. Types of *flabellum*, fixed fan, and *umbella*, the parasol or *chirophorion*. Lady and her serving woman.

19 · Components of **WOMEN'S COSTUME,** from the most intimate outward. Breast-band or breast-binding, worn below the breast. The shirt, the *esophorion*. Tunics and *chitons*. The *castula*, skirt fastening above the breast. Ionian tunic, long dress with sleeves, worn without belt. Short tunic, like the Ionian, in the style of a woman's blouse, but without sleeves. Dorian tunic, coming down to the knees and belted at the hips. Light tunics barely covering the waist. The *palla*, large formal tunic; *anabole diplois* and *hemidiplois*, double or simple.

20 · **WOMEN'S CLOTHING.** *Palla* or *peplos*, from long *palla* to *palla succincta*, and various *pallulae*. *Chlamydion*, the small *chlamys*. *Chloene*. *Tunica talaris*; *poderes* tunic. *Paryphes*, embroidered, transparent tunic. Light embroidered cloak, belonging to the *pharos* family. Short cape. Long tunic in Dorian style, and *chitoniskos* of the same family. Hairstyles, necklaces and *periscelides*, leg-rings.

PLATE 18

49

PLATE 19

PLATE 20

51

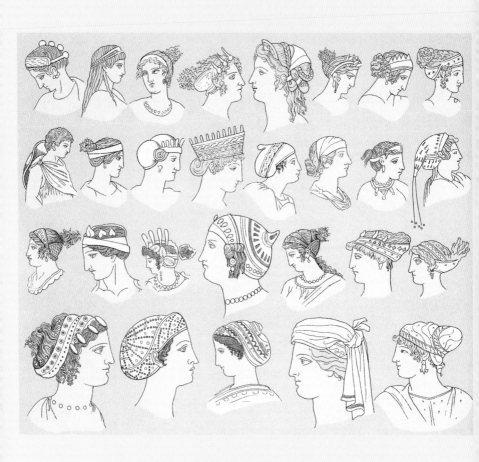

PLATE 21

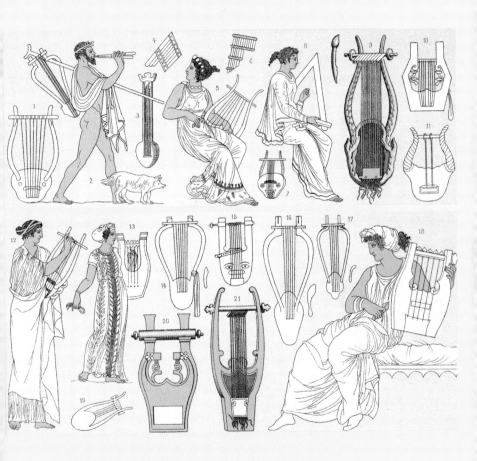

PLATE 22

53

21 · **HAIRSTYLES** of women and young men. Veils, fillets, bonnets, diadem, crown and hat. Wigs and hairpieces. Dying and curling of hair, hair cut off during mourning. *Nimbus; sphendone; cecryphale* or net also called *opisthosphendone, vesica* or bladder; *mitella* or little mitre. *Petasus,* hat. *Strophion,* diadem. *Entrixon, penike* and *procomion,* hairpieces. *Triglenoi* or *triottideis,* drop earrings. Golden cicadas and sequins or *drachmai* hung from movable rings.

22 · **MUSICAL INSTRUMENTS AND TYPES OF MUSICIAN.** Lyres and lutes; harp, *trigone; cithara,* double-flute, *syrinx.* Ambulant musician, singer and dancer. *Psalteria,* professional woman musician, who sang and danced at banquets. Coloured embroidered dress, transparent like Tarentine dresses.

23 · **FURNITURE AND UTENSILS FOR MEALS AND BANQUETS,** and how they were used. *Triclinium;* draped beds; table with drawers. Preparations for the meal; the place of honour; place of women, when admitted. The three courses and the *acroama,* (auditory) entertainment. Vases, *crater, capis, hydria. Kantharos,* goblet with two handles, cups and *rhytons.* Bread basket; glasses, bags, etc. Guests. Serving woman and woman musician.

24 · **INDOOR AND URBAN COSTUME,** exactly as worn, here by Tanagran women. *Chiton* or talaric tunic, intimate robe, long chemise. *Peplos* or *himation. Kalyptra,* light cloak, veil and shawl. Yellow shoes with red soles. Hair dyed and powdered. Faces painted. Thessalian *kausia,* straw hat. Lotus-leaf fan. Figurine.

25/26 · **MILITARY WEAR. CIVILIAN FINERY.** The mythical woman warrior and huntress. Purples, dyes. Soldiers, by arm and rank: chief, *hoplite, peltast,* horseman, *phalangite,* archer; victorious warrior. Character of the various arms; how they were wielded; their resemblance with those of the heroic age; their improvements in historic times. Military march; tactics of the *phalanx.*

DEFENSIVE WEAPONS: 1. Cuirass: brigandine covered with small bronze plates; solid metal cuirass with hinges; surcoat of crossed, doubled and felted cloth; jerkin in leather reinforced by a breast-piece in bronze made of a series of disks; tegulated cuirass, composed of bronze scales covering leather; bronze breastplate on a hide jerkin; leather brigandine. 2. Extension of the cuirass: leather apron or straps. 3. Belt: strong leather strap or hammered bronze. 4. Helmets: with round or low crest, movable visor and beaver, fan-shaped crest; high-domed, with open-work metal crest, horsehair crest, floating tail; Boeotian helmet, with broad cheek-pieces and fixed nasal, and crook-shaped crest, with floating horsehair tail; Etruscan helmet, conical in form, with large antennae, floating or cascading crest; large healm or Minerva helmet, with mobile visor or fixed visor representing the features of the upper face; curved and Phrygian-cap helmet; helmet with plume-holder for feathers; plain metal cap and helmet surmounted by an animal head; triumphal helmet, and finally the leather headdress (replacing the helmet), worn with a long neck-protector. 5. Straps of the cuirass and shoulder-pieces, sometimes extended by an upper-arm arm-guard. 6. Bronze thigh-pieces. 7. *Knemídes* or greaves in bronze, made in tin and laced to a legging. Demi-*knemíd* or heel-piece. Leather greaves. 8. *Krepídes*, sandals with thongs; red soles for the chiefs; in hobnailed wood for foot-soldiers, with spurs for the horsemen. 9. Shields, from the *aspís*, the large Argian shield, round and convex; wooden shield, covered in bronze plates; brass shield, and wooden shield reinforced with cross-pieces, up to those in the *pelta* style, that is, a lattice-work of osier covered with leather. Shield strap or guige for bearing the shield; large enarme through which the arm fits; main dagger, and cords offering further daggers should occasion require. 10. *Chlamys*, cloak rolled around the arm to replace the shield if need be.

OFFENSIVE WEAPONS: 1. Short sword and long sword. Scabbards for these weapons and baldrics for carrying them. 2. Axe, with iron blade and pointed heel. 3. Mace, in bronze. 4. Pikes, spears, javelins; *amentum*, or leather strap for throwing these arms. 5. Long pike and long spears; *contus* and the Macedonian *sarisa*. 6. *Umbo* of the shield. 7. Bow, arrows; quiver and the three ways of wearing it. 8. Hand and feet protected for battle. The *aegis* of the mythical Amazon belongs to the defensive category, and the gymnastics represented by the huntress were the initial preparation of the warrior. Combat ruses; trophy of the victorious soldier. Colour of clothes, in general; dyeing of cloth and leathers of the war harness. Marine purple and plant purple.

CIVILIAN FINERY: Greeks from the time of the Ptolemies, embalmed in the Egyptian manner. Men and women's costumes. Tunics; robe with sleeves; apron-width belt; strips of precious metals sown into the cloths. Bare feet; shoe of plant-fibres. Diadems and necklaces, including the *torque*; profusion of jewels; braids of precious metals and earring pendants.

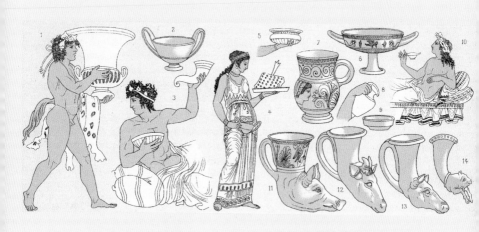

PLATE 24

57

27/28 · Main room of a **RICH ATHENIAN HOUSE,** in the 5th century B.C. Dining room, furnished as *triclinium*, comprising antechamber, reception room, and rest or siesta room. In the centre, the family room, and the porter at his post, at the entrance (see the Greek-style *atrium*, pl. 33).

29 · MILITARY AND OTHER COSTUMES. VARIOUS CHARIOTS. Pleated and festooned tunics. Laced Tyrrhenian shoe. Bandage-style leggings. *Petasus.* Winged helmet of *Hades* (Pluto). Pointed Thracian helmet. Men bearded. Labourer's forked staff, the *bidens.* Messenger's *caduceus.* War chariot in *triga* harness. Travel chariot drawn by a *quadriga.*

30 · PLEATED DRESSES OF THE WOMEN. MALE HAIRSTYLE with knotted chignon. Solemn procession. Light chariot with *quadriga.*

31 · ORNAMENTAL OBJECTS. ORNAMENTS IN PRECIOUS METALS. JEWELLERY. Crowns, necklaces, earring pendants, rings, bracelets, fibulae, fasteners, buckles, hairpins, buttons and amulets. Aiguillette tabs in precious metals, seals and children's toys. Embossed gold, amber, succinite (yellow amber), rock crystal, stones and clay. Beliefs and prejudices about jewels and their substances. Wreath of golden leaves, mark of high rank in women or a military decoration.

32 · **CEREMONIAL SEATS,** thrones; ordinary seats, with seated Greeks. Definition of thrones; their general appearance. *Solium* of the earliest Roman; footstool, or stool serving this purpose, *threnys* and *suppedaneum.* Chairs and folding chairs, wooden stools and benches: *bisellium, klismos, diphros. Deinos* or *delnos,* the basin in which the guest or traveller's feet were washed. Severe costume of the unmarried Greek woman; Greek slave with hair cut short and Ionian robe. Style of bonnet worn by the manumitted Roman.

33 · **ATRIUM** of the Greek-style **POMPEIIAN HOUSE.** *Atrium tuscanium; tetrastylum, displuviatum, testudinatum* and *Corinthian. Tablinum* or *tabulinum. Alae,* the wings. *Armarium,* the library. *Hospitium* and *ergastulum. Atriensis,* the slave in charge of the atrium; *dispensator,* the slave in charge of the shop. *Imagines majorum,* etc. *Peristylium,* internal courtyard; its *impluvium.* Upper storey, used by women. Bedrooms; dining room or *triclinium; oecus* or *cyzicenus* room, a summer room mainly used for banquets. *Lararium* or *sacrarium,* chapel of the domestic deities. *Pinakotheka,* gallery of paintings. *Venereum,* boudoir with licentious paintings. Construction materials. Decoration of internal walls; paintings on plaster, wood or glass. Glass in the furniture, on the walls and ceilings.

PLATE 29

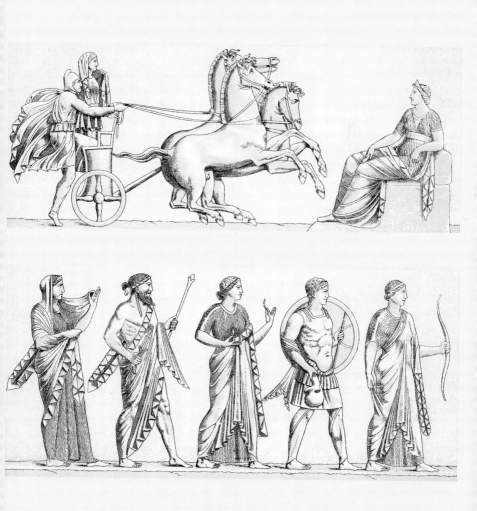

PLATE 30

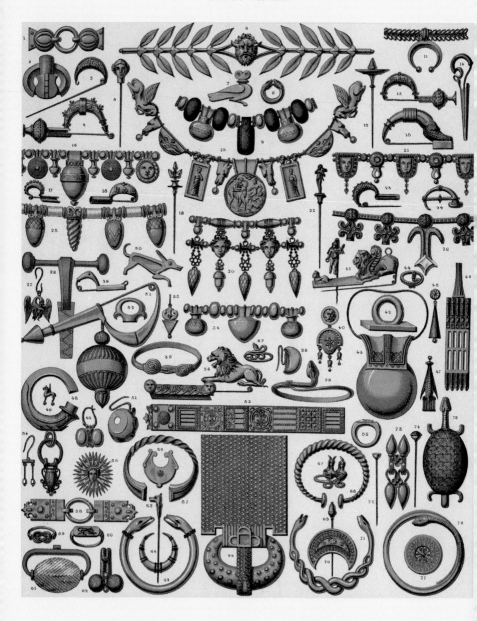

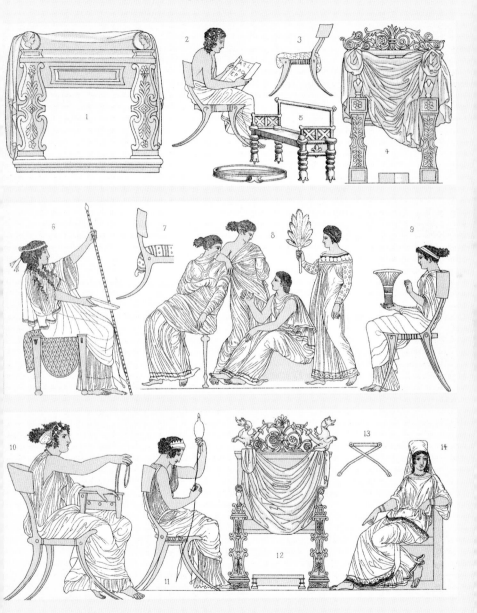

PLATE 32

67

34 · MILITARY COSTUMES. The legionnaire of the Empire. Officers, soldiers, and standard-bearers. Troops marching; foot-soldiers in combat, and resting in camp. Composition of the Roman legion. Only Roman citizens admitted to the army. Defensive arms. Helmet, *cassis*; soldier's cuirass or *lorica*; surcoat, extended or not by leather straps. Shields, *scutum* and *pelta*. Offensive arms. Sword, *gladius*; dagger, *clunaculum*; spear or dart, *hasta*. Equipment. Tunics, *subarmale* and *tunicula*; breeches, *bracae*, *feminalia* or *femoralia*; scarf, *focale*; shoes, *caligae*. Cloaks, *paludamentum*, *sagum* and *sagulum*. Campaign equipment and net containing provisions carried by the soldier, etc. (On these personal effects, arms, and parts of the costume, see double plate 36 37.)

35 · MILITARY INSIGNIA of the Roman Republic and Empire. *Manipulus*, eagle, *concordia*, *draco*, *vexillum*, *flammeum* and *labarum*. *Signifer*, *aquilifer*, *imaginarius*: standard-bearers. The earliest Roman standards. Their nature, depending on the division of the legion into *cohortes*, and subdivision of the cohorts into *maniples*. Eagle, main standard of the legion. Images of the emperors were attached to them, and the cult of the emperor's image. The particular symbols added to the standard to distinguish one corps from another. *Vexillum*, the sign of the cavalry, standard or flag; and the *flammula*. *Labarum*, the Imperial standard. *Draco* or dragon, the barbarian standard, which became the cohort standard for the Romans. The extended right hand, and its various meanings. The removal of standard ornaments as a sign of mourning.

36/37 · MILITARY UNIFORM AND FENCING WEAR. Soldiers and gladiators. Republican and Imperial periods. Early legionnaire, *triarius*; legionnaire of the Imperial period equipped for active service, *impeditus*. *Eques*, cavalryman. Centurion. Military tribune, wearing *phalerae*, boss-shaped decorations. General in command, *imperator*. Legion's standard borne by the *aquilifer*, cohort's by the *signifer*. *Vexillarius*, cavalry standard-bearer. Variety of military uniforms worn in eastern and western regions. Infantryman shouldering arms. Cavalryman charging with spear (for a cavalryman using the sword in combat, see pl. 40, no. 6). Types of legion eagles, and a Victory bearing the cavalry *vexillum*. *Circus combatants: mirmillo, thrax, hoplomachus, retiarius, pinnirapus, essedarii, andabatae, dimachoeri, catervarii, fiscales* or *caesariani, auctorates* and *rudiarii*.

LINE INFANTRY of the Roman legion: *triarii*, *hastati* and *principes*. Bronze helmet of the veterans; their surcoat: woollen *subarmale* and shoulder-pieces. Bronze breast-plate. Bronze sword, its handle, scabbard and baldric. Belt with bronze buckles. Iron *knemides* (greaves). Spear or *pilum*. *Parma* or round shield. *Crepidae* (sandals). The same infantryman, heavily armed, during the Empire, marching on active service: *impeditus*. Iron helmet, *cassis*, the ring for hanging it on the side of the chest. Cuirass, *lorica*, made of bands of steel. The shield, *scutum*. Painting and bronze ornaments on *scutum*. The sword, *gladius*, with Iberian iron blade. Scabbard, *vagina*; baldric, *balteus*, for carrying it. Privation of scabbard, a punishment. *Pilum*, spear with long point. Woollen *subarmale*. Breeches, *femoralia*; scarf, *focale*; *caligae*, hobnailed footware. Effects carried by the *impeditus*: short cloak, *sagulum*, rolled up and carried on a staff with goatskin waterbottle, a leather bag, a scoop and an iron pot, and net for bread and meat. *Expeditus*, his effects carried on carts.

EQUES, CAVALRYMAN. Surcoat in the form of dalmatic, leather and mail. Sword and baldric. *Parma*, shield. The long *lancea*. *Caligae* and spurs.

THE CENTURION. Silver-crested helmet, with feather *crista*. His *bucculae*, beavers. *Subarmale* and breeches. Surcoat and lambrequins. Cuirass and articulated shoulder-pieces. Belt with hanging straps. Baldric embroidered with silver. Half-brodequin, *campagus*. *Vitis*, commander's baton.

THE MILITARY TRIBUNE OR PHALERATUS. Golden helmet. Surcoat with double row of lambrequins. Sword-belt, *cinctorium*. Celto-Iberian sword. *Parazonium*, short sword. Senior officer's *caligae*, fully enclosing ankle-boot. Military decorations: *phalerae* and *torques*.

THE COMMANDER-IN-CHIEF, IMPERATOR AND CAESAR IMPERATOR. Gilded helmet, with *crista* of purple feathers. Surcoat extended by a triple row of lambrequins. Belt and sword-belt. Sword with gilded blade. *Parazonium*. Commander's baton. *Paludamentum*, large military cloak. Footwear: high, closed brodequin, purple like his clothing. Distinguishing signs of the supreme commander.

THE SIGNIFER, INFANTRY STANDARD-BEARER. Bronze *cassis* covered by a wild beast's head. Red *subarmale*, breeches and *sagum*. Cuirass. *lorica squamata*. *Gladius, balteus* and *caligae*. The eagle of the legion. The *signum* of the cohort and maniples.

THE VEXILLARIUS, CAVALRY STANDARD-BEARER. His arms and the nature of the *vexillum*.

THE GLADIATORS. *Mirmillo*, with openwork helmet; arm-piece of articulated plates of iron; straight sword. Straps, belt and sword-belt. Pleated *campestra* (loin-cloth). Asymmetrical leg-wear: the bronze *knemis* (greave), one *calceus*, one *caliga*. *Scutum*. *Thrax* (Thracian). Closed helmet. *Ocreae*, high bronze greaves. Laced open-ended brodequins. *Sica*, the 'Thracian' sword. Iron gauntlet on the hand holding the weapon; shield, *parma threcidjica*. *Retiarius* with his net (*rete*) and *fuscina* or *tridens*. Bronze shoulder-piece and mail sleeve, etc. The origins of gladiatorial combat. Its religious character. The different circus combatants: *essedarii, andabatae, dimachoeri, catervarii. Fiscales* or *caeesariani*, and *rudiarius*.

THE EAGLES OF THE LEGIONS. Their varied appearance. Their prestige. *Pinea* or pine-cone, at the top of the *signum*. Personifications of Rome, bearing the head of a horned animal, or helmets whose shapes bespeak their Phrygian origin. Roman military chief, wearing the Egyptian *klafi*.

38 · RELIGIOUS CEREMONIES. Sacrifices and offerings. Purification of a camp, *suovetaurilia*. Martialis; *augurale*. *Camillus*; *spondaules*, playing the double flute. *Victimarii* and *immolatus*. Sacred *vitta*, the bull's tasselled fillet; *serta*, garland of pig. *Flamen*; *popa*, his axe, *scena* or *scaena*; *dolabra*. *Cultrarius*. *Popa* and *cultrarius* wear *limus*, skirt, *succinctus* when short. *Libium*, cake. *Ara* or altar. Form and materials. *Ara thuricrema*. *Ignispicium*, divination by observation of fire.

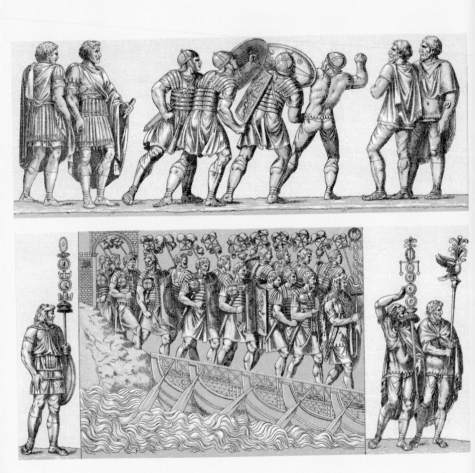

PLATE 34

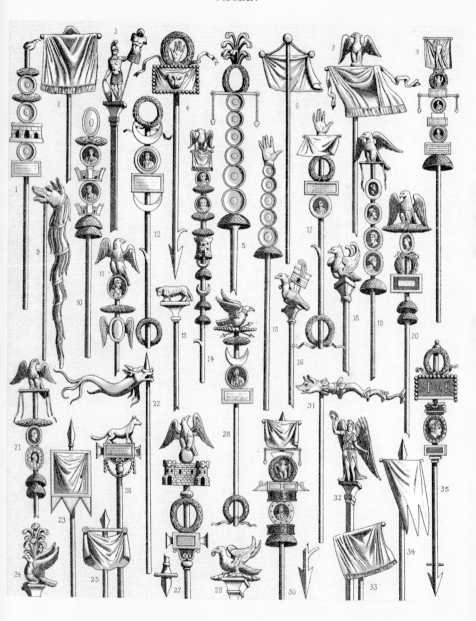

PLATE 35

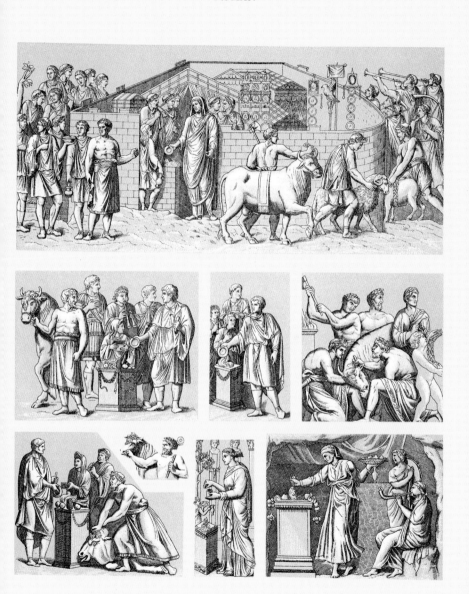

PLATE 38

75

39 · **CULT OBJECTS AND INSTRUMENTS OF SACRIFICE.** Tripods; incense box, *acerra*; *thuribulum*, censer; *praefericulum*, vase for sacred wine. Holy water stoup. *Paterae*. *Pullarius* cage. Augur's baton. Aspersorium. *Malleus*, mallet. Axes, *acieres* and *secures*. Sacrificial knives (for cutting the victim's throat). Butchering knives (for cutting up the victim): *securis* and *dolabra*; *secespita*, butcher's steel. *Simpulum* or spoon. Forks and spatulas. Incense spoons. *Lituus* (trumpet) and *tympanum*.

40 · **CIVILIAN COSTUMES** of the imperial period. Horseman using sword in combat. Togas. *Toga restricta, toga rotonda* or *fusa*. *Praetexte*, named for the purple band bordering it. *Toga pura*, or *virilis*. *Toga picta* or *palmata*, toga worn for triumphs. *Toga rasa, togae vitreae* (transparent) and *toga trita*. *Togatus* and *togatulus*. *Candidatus*. *Velatus*, veiled by the toga. *Cinctus gabinus*, toga belted in the manner of the Gabii. Toga as privilege of the Roman citizen. Arrangement of its folds: the double *sinus*, the *balteus* and the *umbo*. Toga as ornament of the marriage bed. Severe appearance given by the veiled toga. The orator at the senate rostrum, his inviolable right to speak there. Dark colours of the mourning toga. *Togata*, of women, courtesans in particular. Tunic worn with the toga. *Clavus angustus* and *angusticlave*. *Colobium* or short tunic. Breeches or shorts, *feminalia* or *femoralia*; *fasciae*, bands wound around the leg, and *sudarium*, cravat or handkerchief. *Calceus*, closed shoe. Socks and stockings. *Domestica vestis*, indoor wear; the *synthesina*. *Pallium* or *palla*: different from the Greek. *Stola*, woman's dress; its varieties; worn over the top of the inner tunic. Two belts. The *instita*; the train of a dress. Various shoes, from the fully enclosing shoe with thin sole to the high-soled Greek sandal. The *pallium* worn by the Roman *matrona*. Dyed natural hair; wigs, etc.

41 · **HAIRSTYLES**; wigs; bonnets; fillet and diadem. *Causia*, sailor's hat. Wig, *caliendrum*.

PLATE 39

77

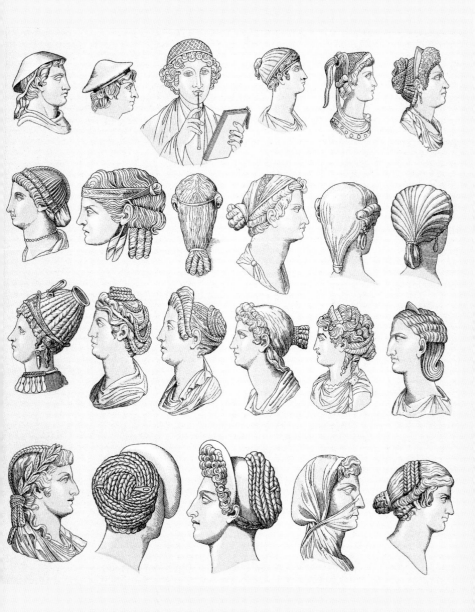

PLATE 41

79

42 · **AMULETS AND TALISMANS:** *abraxas. Probra, servatoria, amolimenta* and *praefiscini. Abracadabra.* Credulousness in their regard and the inclusion of the stones or metals of which these amulets were made in ornamental wear, such as necklaces, hairstyles and rings.

43 · **MUSICAL INSTRUMENTS:** wind, strings, and percussion. 1. *Tibiae: avena, fistula* (flute); *tibia gingrina* (fife); *tibia longa; tibiae pares* (pair of flutes); *tibiae conjunctae* (double flute); *tibiae impares* (unequal diameter). *Tibia abliqua* (forked flute); *tibia utricularis* (bagpipe). Trumpets made from horn, shells, or brass. *Cornu* (large circular horn). 2. *Monocords; dicord; trigonum;* lyre, harp and *cithara.* 3. *Cymbalum; tintinnabulum;* bells. *Tympanum:* drum and *crotalium.*

44 · **FURNITURE** and household objects. Curule chair. Wooden bedframe. Low table. Cupboard or sideboard. Freestanding safe. Key and padlock. Recipient.

45 · **PRIVATE BATHS.** Utensils of the *alipili,* depilators and *aliptes,* who used *strigiles.* Oils, essences, unguents and perfumes. *Gausape,* bath robe. Example of successive phases of steam bath, as represented in antiquity. *Frigidarium,* cold bath room; *tepidarium* for warm bath; *caldarium,* sweating-room; *labrum* or bathroom, in which immersion occurred, accompanied by *aliptes,* depilators, *tractores* (masseurs) and *unctores. Hypocaustum,* for heating water before its distribution. *Laconicum* for raising the temperature of the sweating-room; *clipeus* for adjusting it. *Strigiles,* strigils; *guttus,* scraper. Depilator's tongs. Flacons and bottles. Basins for partial immersion.

46 · Representative rich Etrusco-Greek building. **INTERIOR OF THE PALACE.** Military and maritime trophies. Altars, tripods and tables for offerings to the Lares.

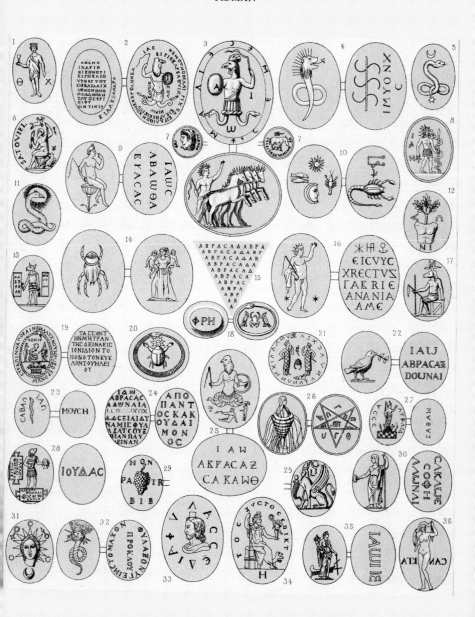

PLATE 42

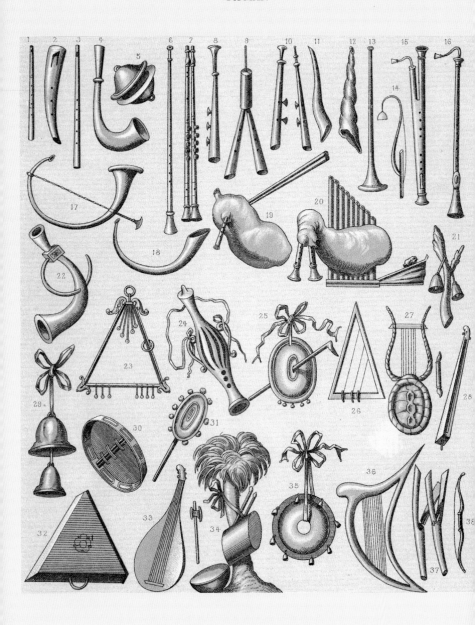

PLATE 43

PLATE 44

83

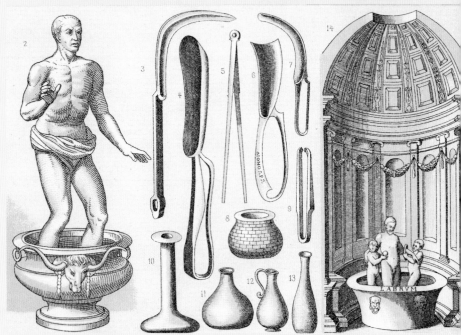

PLATE 46

Barbarian Europe:
Barbarians · Scandinavians · Celts

The men who appear in these plates are by no means contemporary one with another. The warriors armed with bronze are of the same family as those that destroyed the Roman Empire. Celts, Gauls, Germans or
Teutons, Slavs or Sarmatians, Scythians, Finns and Tartars, all of them Asian, reappear during the great 4th–5th century barbarian invasion of the North under the names Visigoths, Suevians, Alans, Vandals, Burgundians, Franks, Huns, Heruli and Rugians.

The others belong to the quaternary period and the race called Cro-Magnon man, whose main centre of population was Europe. The 'ages' of stone, bronze and iron are not in fact ages; although traces of the use of stone for arms and tools exist in almost every country in the world, these traces do not at all relate to the same periods. Currently the most fruitful field of study for these highly prehistoric periods is in northern Europe, in Denmark and Sweden. The most ancient objects of this age are not polished. Relics of the second stone age, that of polished stone, abound in Sweden. The polishing tools found in great quantities are large blocks of sandstone with one or two polishing faces. The Scandinavians of the Stone Age (pl. 50) not only made tools indispensable to the elementary needs of life, but imparted to them the greatest possible elegance. The amber commonly found on the shores of the Baltic was used to create ornaments. The Stone Age Scandinavian cooked food in pots hung over the fire.

The use of metals — bronze and gold — must have produced a higher degree of civilisation. The most common tool was a kind of axe or chisel known as the *celt*. The art of writing runes, the ancient graphic characters of Scandinavia, coincided with the beginning of the Iron Age, during which the Northern peoples gained a knowledge not only of iron but of glass, ivory, silver, lead, and bronze alloyed with zinc; they learnt to mint coins, solder and gild.

During the Iron Age, clothing was made of wool. The cloth was a kind of damask, often with a chequered pattern. The items of clothing included a long tunic, breeches belted at the waist and a woollen cloak with fringed lower edge. Footwear was a kind of decorated leather sandal. Ornament during the early Bronze Age consisted of the elegant spirals and zigzag lines visible on diadems. It is clear that a host of monuments, coins, arms, bronze and glass vases, and *objets d'art* found on Swedish soil came from Roman workshops, and that, from the earliest centuries A. D., the Scandinavians enjoyed constant relations with the principal people of Europe, the Romans. Food, generally presented on plain wooden plates, was cut with the knives that everyone wore in their belts; spoons were made of wood, horn or bone. No spoon of silver has been found dating from pagan times, though there were drinking cups in glass and bronze, the earliest of them being of Roman production. During Viking times, the vase was more common than the horn as a vessel for drinking.

The Gauls (pl. 56 57) descended from the Gaels and the second branch of the Cymry, and were in a state of military decadence two or three centuries before the Christian era. The development of personality and individual independence made the Gauls entirely refractory to discipline. Caesar divided Gaul into three parts: one inhabited by the Belgae, the second by the Aquitani, and the third by those who called themselves Celts, though the Romans called them *Galli*, Gauls.

47 · SHOES, from the most primitive to the liturgical sandals of the Popes, and the ceremonial shoes of Charlemagne. Egyptian, Persian, Gaulish, Hun and Lombard; mainly Greek and Roman, with the fashions and uses. *Carbatinae;* simple sandal, *crepida, baxea, solea, caligo, gallica, campagus, sandalium, soccus, socellus, socculus, cothurna,* more or less open shoes. Closed shoes: *ocrea, pero, calceus, mulleus; phoecasium, udo, odonia, odonaria; udones,* slippers and socks. *Sycionia, lakonikai* or *amycleides, peribarides, persikai, pantophellos,* etc. *Sculponeae* (clogs), *solea* used by slaves; what *barefoot* should be understood to mean in relation to *gypsati* and *cretati.* The footware of the free man. *Ligula,* fastening of the *crepidae,* worn by the citizen. Special laws, related to class, determining the nature of Roman footwear. Materials and colour of shoes. *Cordwain* work, *aluta.* Hobnailed soles. Extraordinary luxury exhibited in shoes. Thick soles used by Roman women to increase their height. Kissing of chief's leg and foot, among the Franks. Kissing the Pope's toe (slipper), etc.

48/49 · THE PRIMITIVE INHABITANTS OF EUROPE, fossile types, from the earliest troglodytes to the inhabitants of the earliest lake villages, in which we find the earliest rudiments of civilisation, well before all historic civilisations. The meeting of the earliest men with paleontological monsters. The human races, differing in appearance and intellectual capacity, superposed in geological layers. Prehistoric chronometry, or the chronology of the use of arms and tools in hard wood and bone, shaped flint and polished stone. Fur clothing; worked leather; wool, hemp and linen. Ornaments made from pebbles, shells, animal teeth, etc. The white-skinned warriors whose families destroyed the Roman Empire, and which the Greco-Latins generally termed Barbarians. Bronze and Iron Ages. Iberians or Slavs, Rasenes or Etruscans. Illyrians or Thracians. Gauls, Celts and Kymris (Cimbri). Germans or Teutons. Scythians; Sarmatians; Scandinavians and Franks, the Merovingians (on these and the Gauls, see double pl. 56/57). Period of bronze arms, and period of iron arms. Details of ornament, military uniform and finery, analysed for each figure. Isolated examples of Gaulish or Celtic bronze arms. Cuirasses, axes including the *Celtic* axe; dagger, and sword-grip with bronze blade. Iron weapons of Merovingian kind: *framée* (spear), *angon* (variety of pike), straight sword, *scamasaxe* (short sword); *francisque* (battle-axe) and circular shield.

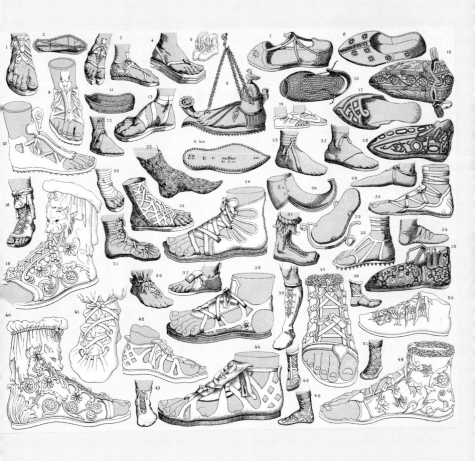

PLATE 47

91

50 · **ARMS, TOOLS, UTENSILS, COSTUMES** and customs of the Stone, Bronze and Iron Ages. From the Stone Age: Shaped flint and polished stones. Axes, spear- and arrowheads, dagger, knife, axe, hammer, scrapers, polishers, gouge, saw; clay vases, bone fishhook, amber bead. Time of the dolmens (megalithic tombs). From the Bronze Age: Dagger; *celt* (axe) with wooden handle in socket, sword, spearhead; hanging vase. Woman's costume, apparently that of the women warriors of *Skoldmor*, the virgins of the shield. *Tumuli*, cairns. From the Iron Age: Scandinavian warrior of the earliest Iron Age. Large clinker-built boat, without deck, propelled by oars. Relief figures from the late Iron Age.

51 · **ORNAMENTS** of the Celtico-Scandinavians of the Bronze Age. Diadems, necklaces, rings, fibulae, needles, buttons, comb, and various objects in bronze from the earliest age and the second period. Concerning the beginning of the Bronze Age in Scandinavia.

52 · **OBJECTS IN GENERAL USE;** fastenings and buckles. Bronze and Iron ages. Fibulae, broaches, fasteners, buckles, and fragment of a reliquary.

53 · **ORNAMENTS,** fasteners, buckles, etc. **FUNERARY CUSTOMS.** Early period of Iron Age. Diadems, necklaces, bracelets, annular pendants, fibulae, buckles made of gold, gold-plated silver, bronze and iron. Bronze bridle of a horse's bit. Aglets of bronze straps. Charger, its harness and the very war-chariot buried alongside the chief. Similarly, a warrior in his ship. The inhabitant of the *tumulus, hogbon,* sitting on a chair in the burial chamber.

54 · **ARMS, DECORATIVE OBJECTS AND UTENSILS** from the Iron Age. Early, middle and late Iron Age. Spear- and arrowheads; swords and sword pommels; scabbards and chapes; spurs; stirrup, shield *umbo*; fittings of scabbard opening; fibulae, made with gold, silver, bronze, iron, solid gold, inlaid silver, gilded bronze, enchased garnets, ivory, bone and inlays. Spoons in elk horn.

PLATE 50

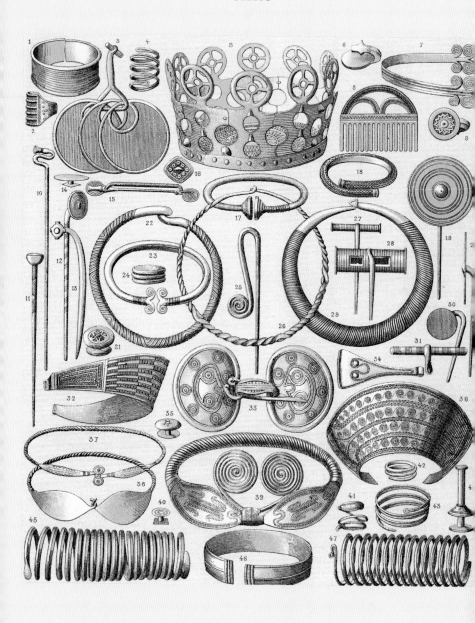

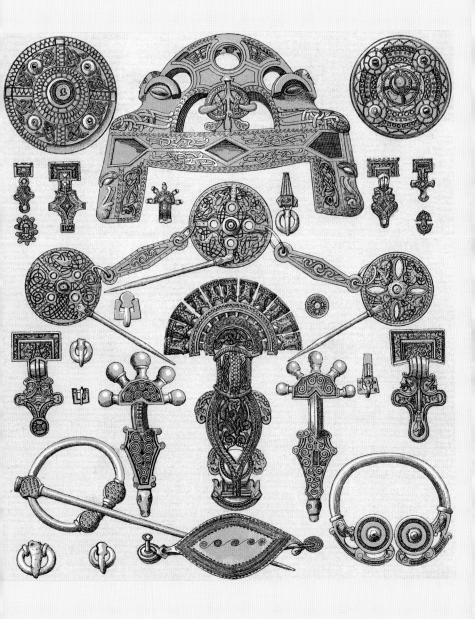

PLATE 52

97

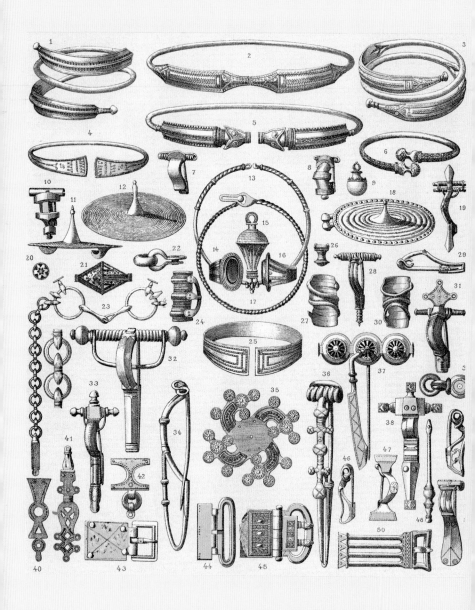

PLATE 54

99

55 · ORNAMENTS AND VARIOUS OBJECTS. Middle and late Iron Age. Necklaces, *bracteates*, bracelets, annular, pendants. Fibulae, needles, buckles. Pendants. Beads, openwork jewels, etc. The hammer of Thor, tin. Key, and trousseau of keys carried by the mistress of a Scandinavian household. Diadem-style ornament. Tweezers and ear-pick in bronze. Tweezers used instead of razor. Elk-horn comb. *Sjokonungar*, kings of the sea, as the Vikings called themselves.

56/57 · INHABITANTS OF GAUL before the Roman conquest, and at the time of Julius Caesar. Merovingian chief and Frankish soldier. Chiefs, warriors, peasants, labourers and soldiers. Women. Weapon-tool in stone; defensive and offensive weapons in bronze; iron weapons.

MEN'S CLOTHING. *Saie* or belted smock, monochrome or, like the *vergata*, a *saie* in the colours of the war of independence, striped. *Braie*, long, closed breeches. *Carcacalla* or *palla gallica*, a tunic with full-length sleeves. *Bardocucullus*, a hooded cloak, or reduced version of this (see *bardocucullus*, large cloak used by the ancient Bretons, pl. 425, Scotland). Cape worn as shawl; *sagum*, short cloak of the Roman soldier. Clothing generally woollen, sometimes decorated with Limousin stripes. Closed shoes and short laced boots. *Pileus* of Phrygian form or fur hat. In everyday clothing, hair loose or confined by a fillet wound one or more times around the head and knotted on one side.

WOMEN'S CLOTHING. Two tunics, one on top of another, the overtunic sleeved. Dresses of varying length, apron. Bodice; cloak or *pallium*. Closed shoe. *Bulga*, wallet serving as small handbag. Hair loose, or knotted in a corymb shape or wrapped in a rolled neckerchief. For ornament, hairnet, fillet or tiara. Hair powdered, cheeks rouged, eyebrows tinted, make-up. Example of the warrior hairstyle, *arcantodon*, chief of a hundred heads; similarly for the simple soldier. Armed soldiers and peasants without protective garments.

WARRIORS more or less completely armed **FROM THE BRONZE AGE**: helmets, cuirasses, greaves, shields, sword, dagger, spear and axe. Horsemen charging; harness of their horses. National symbol, the golden boar, as mace. Example of cock in fighting position. Gaulish Warriors of the Iron Age, from the time of Vercingétorix. Soldier armed for combat. The horned helmet, with *rouelle* crest. Shield with *umbo*; iron-bladed sword. Soldier carrying a *carnyx* (war trump), a bronze loud-hailer that also served as a club. Iron helmet under the fur hat. Gaulish chief carrying the war standard. Winged helmet, gilded bronze with floating 'tail' bordered by the wings of a bird of prey. Coat of mail or brigandine reinforced with bronze; breeches. Chariot or pair of wheels, with spur and saw-bladed scythe, for use in battle. Celtiberian helmet. Defeated warrior, hands tied behind his back, stripped of his arms and his clothes; *saie* among the victor's trophies. Individual independence of the Gauls. Belgae, Aquitanians and Celts. Primitive *Gaels*, tattooed or wearing woad. *C'hlan* and tribe. Distribution of the Gallo-Kymris race, shepherds, hunters, farmers, industrialists and traders. Military tactics. Magnificence of their costumes and their chiefs'

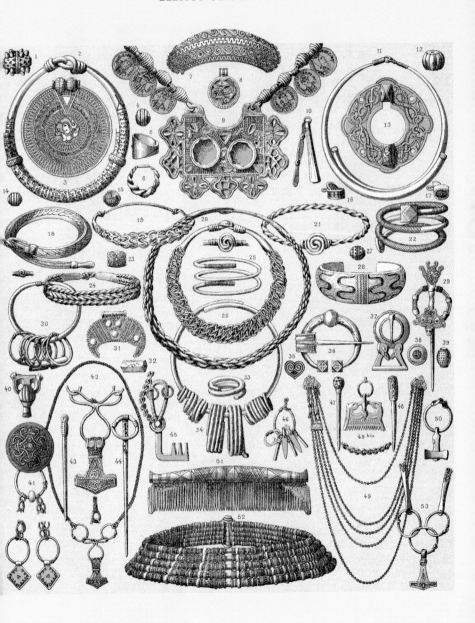

PLATE 55

101

Gaulish

arms; prodigality. Extravagance of meals. Crowds of devoted clients. Passion for wine. Child's first sight, the bronze sword. Round table, the table of equality. Altars of the Druids. The cost of the Romanising of Gaul. (For military decorations and ornaments, and for Gaulish jewellery, see the two plates, 58 and 59.)

FRANKS-SALIANS. Merovingian chief, horseman; and Frankish infantryman. Horseman: short tunic, skirt and cloak. Foot soldier: short tunic, tight shorts or breeches. For both, footwear with a thick sole, cross-ties high on the leg. Horseman's spur. Chief's helmet, a cap of leather and bronze. Bareheaded soldier, protected only by his plaited hair. Protective wear. Furred pelt replacing cuirass; small round shield with pointed centre. Weapons: sword hanging from baldric, *scamasaxe*, *framée*, *angon*, and *francisque*, axe and battle-axe. Details of chief's necklace, of his swordhandle decorated with cloisonné enamel, and of the precious metalwork of the soldier's baldric. (Concerning arms, see the double plate 48-49, and for precious metalwork and jewellery, pl. 58.)

58 · FORGED AND PRECIOUS METAL ORNAMENTS. Jewellery. Modern

embroidery of Celtic character. *Torques*, military necklaces. *Rouelles*, neck ornaments. Bracelets, fastenings, fibulae, needles and aglets. Buckles and plates of the sword-belt. Various ornaments: keys, masterkey. Eagle, a military decoration, of the *phalerae pectorales* family. Gold; silver; chased and engraved bronze; gilded and enamelled bronze; glass beads simulating stones, set as cabochons or inlaid. Cloisonné enamels. Breton embroidery.

59 · BRITANNI OF THE ROMAN OCCUPATION. Gallic nations: Celts or *Gom-*

ers (*Kimbr* or *Cimri*, *Gumiri*, *Kymri*, *Cimbri*). Irishman or Caledonian (*Scoti* and *Picti*) or Albanian. Warrior naked, with tattoo or woad applied in pastel form. Winter costume of the inhabitants of the island of Irne, Ireland. Military costume of Britons, chiefs, and foot and mounted soldiers. Officer in Romanised costume. Inhabitant of the Cassiterides, the Isles of Scilly. Druid judges, women and priestesses. *Galli*, priests of Cybele in Rome. *Brehons*, the ancient laws of Ireland, and the military chiefs, the *Dal Ríata* kings. Fighting dogs of the Breton armies; military tactics. Arms of metal, bronze and iron, and also of stone. Earthenware club. *Copar*, metal for making swords. Metal threads in spiral form. Woollen cloth, and brightly coloured cloths like those of Scottish tartans, with the colours of the *clan*. (See Scottish costumes, pls. 425, 426 and 427, forming a historical sequence up to modern times.)

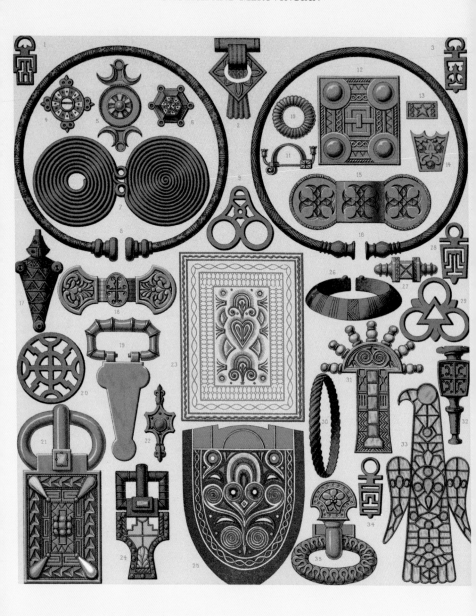

PLATE 59

II
THE 19TH CENTURY BEYOND THE BORDERS OF EUROPE

Oceania

The populations disseminated across the lands broken into infinitesimal particles by the South Seas present three of the primordial forms of human existence. The Alfurus are mountain or forest people who depend on hunting and river-fishing. The Papus, who live mainly on fish from the sea, have become very astute navigators. The Australians are a wandering people, and live on their vast continent at the mercy of chance encounters, hunting and fishing. All of these have, of their own making, only the use of wood, stone, fishbones and sharp stones. There are few if any relations between the many branches of the Papu family (pl. 60 61). Isolation on the major islands of the Pacific has maintained them in a state of profound barbarity. Some of them are swarthy brown in colour, others blacker than the very Ethiopians. Their hair is very black, neither straight nor frizzy, but woolly, fairly fine and very curly. In general, they go all but naked. A tight belt passing between the legs and a loin-cloth in the form of a little apron, called *maro* by the Polynesians, is all the homage they pay to modesty.

The South Sea Islands constitute a maritime world that is greater in extent than the whole of the rest of the world; they have been described as a 'sprinkling of islands'. The Oceanians presented here pertain to 1. the yellow-skinned Asian family, 2. the Oceanian branch, and 3. the Malayo-Polynesians (a mixture of the yellow-and brown-skinned races).

Tattooing is perceived above all as decorating nudity. In its most general sense, the tattoo invariably signifies the tribe to which the individual belongs. Tattooing by incision runs the gamut from pricking with a needle to penetration of the skin by a chisel-blade or even a series of teeth.

OCEANIA

60/61 · **BLACKS.** Alfurus, Papus and Australians, Kanaks, Nuku-Hivians. Costume and toilette, arms and military ornaments. Wood and Stone Ages, still current.

FIJIAN. Hair curled and dyed; comb to ornament it; stave piercing ear. Necklaces of shells, animal teeth, and jaws of small species. Belt in *tapa* (paper mulberry-bark cloth); war-club, barbed spear.

NATIVE OF THE NEW HEBRIDES (VANUATU). Wooden helmet; pectoral in woven reeds; saw-bladed sword; barbed spear with many spikes.

AROSSIAN (SOLOMON ISLANDS). Aglets and ring in pierced nose. Black teeth and scarlet lips as a result of betel use; unkempt hair, divided and dyed; comb decorated with tassels and feathers; forehead decoration; necklace of human teeth; gorget; belt and bracelets of shells. Wrought shells, pierced and polished, acting as beads in ornamental wear and as a currency; plant-fibre cloth, rich apron and garters; bow, assegai and war-club, poisoned darts in barbed wood and bone, whose head remains in the wound. Fortified village; traps on approach routes. Ambushes and surprise attacks. The skirt of the dancers; ceremonial war-club, exclusively male choreography. Condition of women. Nudity of unmarried woman. The Arossian woman and the flying fox bat that she carries in her hair.

NATIVE OF THE ADMIRALTY ISLANDS. Hair dyed red, white or yellow; comb with cock feathers; painted face, presenting a white or red mask; tattoos; forehead, nose and ear ornaments. Shell necklace; *humerus* hung from the neck; bracelets; apron of fine *tapa*; bow, sling, club. Knife with obsidian blade carried in belt. Communication of friendly intent.

PAPUS FROM NEW GUINEA AND NEIGHBOURING ISLANDS. Papu-mafor, a fashionable Papu, and a Papu with woollen garment. Papu-mafor: undyed hair, comb and bouquet of feathers; man-shaped amulet at the neck. Bracelets, diversity of their materials, their accumulation. Belt bearing betel box. *Peda*, sabre-cleaver, both weapon and tool; flexible bow, barbed arrows. Shield decorated with human hair. Fashionable Papu: hair vertical, dyed russet, powdered white; war comb. Diadem of feathers and oblique headband; face painted red. Batons through nose and ear. Fringed belt. Necklace of sperm-whale teeth and large shell necklace; mobile bracelet, decorated with a human jaw. Wooden truncheon and serpentine club; stone battle-axe. Spear with barbed bone head. Light arrow also used as small hammer. Papu in woollen garment, from an ancient civilisation: bag-shaped garment with openings for head and arms, hemispheric hat, rich baldric bearing a straight sabre. Strong spear. Wooden shield with inlays. Bracelets and long pendant earrings.

KANAKS OF NEW CALEDONIA. Sketch of their society. The two races: blue-black and chocolate-coloured. Piece of *tapa*, maintained by a belt, only habitual clothing; way in which *tapa*, paper mulberry-bark cloth, is made. What the Kanak thinks of shirts and trousers, which he likes to possess but not wear. Use he makes of woollen blanket, and its value to him. Huts, hive-shaped and built with straw, surmounted by trophies. The ingenious resistance of the huts to high winds. Women belonging to the tribe; women living together. Necklace of betrothal, the only indication of marriage. Women with shaved heads, dressed only in a cord belt, smoking pipes as they work on the land. Chiefs, *Aou* or *Alikirs*, and their subjects, *Tambuet*. *Takata*, priest, sorcerer and doctor. *Pilou-pilou*: character of this exemplary tribal festivity, with its spectacle of war. Appear-

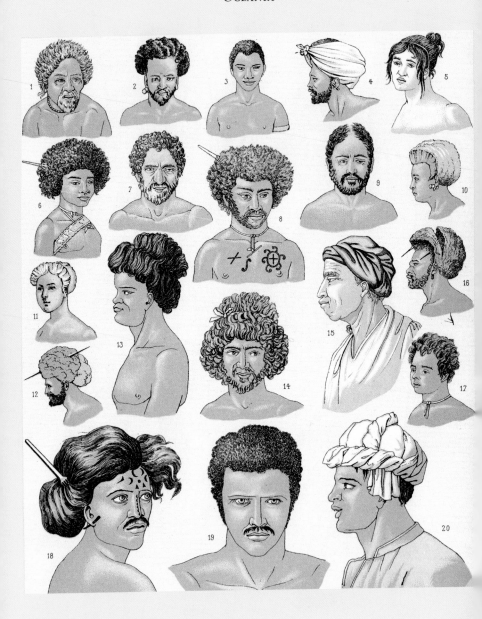

PLATE 62

ance of combatants governed by personal taste; *moinheau* completing their costume. War mask, *dangat*, that makes the man who wears it seem gigantic. Dance and chants set off by this hideous apparition culminating in cannibal frenzy. Beginning of open hostilities, the challenge. Vestiges of ancient civilisation. Sling, assegais; short wooden tomahawk, chief's tomahawk comprising an axe in polished jadeite. *Cagu*, mace resembling a pick-axe. Among the insignia of the chief, little-finger-ring of left hand, *tillet*. Vampire bat or flying fox; its hair, dyed red, is used to make braids and tassels. The value of these braids, which are a medium of exchange. Women sold for a nail; the more beautiful the woman, the larger the nail. Tomahawk, or axe, inseparable companion of the native; on expeditions, the gourd and a provision bag. Traditional mimicking of astonishment among these peoples.

AUSTRALIAN. Land unproductive and not cultivated by the nomads. Nomad families moving in search of food. Women beasts of burden. *Dura*, branch bivouac taking only minutes to construct. Sacrifice of last-born children. Harsh punishment of women, including mutilation when the child that the father wished to conserve dies. Australian aborigine can no longer read the writing left by his ancestors. Physical and moral degradation caused by remoteness from seashore. Ordeals by which youth passes to attain manly status, *wilyalkinyis*. *Manka* or tattoo required for war-rior status in the tribe. Bone or reed passed through the septum of the nose. Body painted red and white. Body rubbed with oil, which accumulates; one incisor pulled out in youth. Short cloak of kangaroo skin. Long spear in hard wood, smooth but barbed. Javelins and assegais, thrown with the aid of the *vummera*. Boomerang; tomahawk. Shield in wood or bark; axes in shaped stone. Little net sack containing the ingredients for body paint and dry wood tinder set on fire through friction. Savage instincts inevitably emerge at puberty. Danger inflicted when they are dressed in European fashion, and fatal consequences when they wear shoes, shirt or overcoat.

NATIVES OF THE MARQUESAS. Nuku-Hivian chiefs in military costume. Tatooed from head to foot. Large headdress with cock feathers; diadems, aglets, cheek appendices, gorget, leg-rings and bracelets, often made of the hair of victims. *Tapa* loin-cloth, sometimes a little apron in animal-skin. Large *tapa* cloak. Nacreous shell as pendant. Shark-tooth necklace; half of an enemy skull used as drinking vessel. As sign of chief's status, fan of woven reed, with handle. Tomahawk, long spear and javelins. War trump.

62 · **HEADDRESSES** of Papua New Guinea and the Fiji islands. Hair becomes the prin-cipal object of ornament among peoples who wear few or no clothes. Need for ornament, the sociable instinct. Arrangement of hair varies all the more given the differences between Melanesia and Polynesia. (Among the examples included in this plate, there often appears a sort of large pin, the handle of the bamboo comb with which the hair is decorated; the comb can be seen in isola-tion in pl. 66.)

63/64/65/66 · **MALAY ARCHIPELAGO, MICRONESIA, MELANESIA, POLYNESIA.** Costumes and ornaments, arms and utensils; customs. Tattoos and the function-ing of *moko*, the incised and powder-dyed tattoo, the *tatau* of the New Zealanders.

OCEANIA

PERSONS DEPICTED: Malays from Java and Borneo. Dayas or Dayaks, Binuas of Singapore, various Dayas in hunting and war costumes. Karens or Chinese and Parsees from Borneo. Timorese from Roti island, in the Moluccas. Indios from the Philippines. Hawaiian warrior and women dancer (fragment) from the Hawaiian islands. Papus, Alfurus and Turajas from the Celebes (Sulawesi) islands, among them Catholic Alfurus, men and women, in formal attire. Bourgeois militia-man of Tondano (Sulawesi) in 1828, and soldier from the Gunong-Tello bay — a nest of pirates.

ISOLATED ITEMS: Hairstyles and men and women's hats (Micro- and Melanesia). Conical hat from the Caroline islands. *Saraus* of the Guebians, used as sunscreens. Helmets of the Hawaiians. War hat of a Moluccan sultan. Hat of a Solomon island warrior, and that of the Marquesas; one made from the skin of a fruit used by the Papus. Shoes. Sandal in palm frond (Micronesia, Melanesia). Sandal in straw and creole mule from the Philippines. Belts in vegetable fibre, shells and grains (Sulawesi); decorated with rings of shells (Caroline islands). Cuirass or surcoat in coconut fibre (Sulawesi). Necklaces from the Caroline islands. Neck ornaments from the Solomon islands. Head ornament from the Marquesas, and comb from Tongatapu (Tonga islands). Ear pendants from the Solomon islands. Fly whisk from the Hawiian islands. Wooden pipe carved in the Marquesas. Tattooing comb, or *moko* comb from Tahiti; coconut-wood spoon, from the Moluccas; earthenware bottle wrapped in husks; the large calabash used as vase by the Tahitians; *oho*, a six-foot long spatula used for ploughing. Arms. Stone mace from the Mariana islands. Sling, wooden spear blade, quiver and drum from Papua; varieties of *kris*, the Malay dagger, the arm and its scabbard. *Kampilan* or axe from Borneo. *Klevan* or *klervang* from Sumatra, and its scabbard with fastening for hanging up the weapon.

DAYAKS. ORANG-UTAN, THE MAN OF THE EARTH [MAN OF THE FOREST], THE BINUA FROM SINGAPORE, who lives in the depths of the jungle and has only wooden weapons. *Sipet, sumpit* or *sumpitan*, blowpipe, with its little poisoned arrows; pike, sword and shield (*tavalang*). For clothing: apron, a skull-cap-style helmet decorated with leopard skin and feathers, a broad knee-band with ties for the hunter who must wait in ambush for his game. Feathers fitted to the short blowpipe to facilitate aiming. Gentle customs of the Binua. Light-skinned Dayak, tattooed with *moko*. Hair brought up in a chignon with a headband. Dayak, hair similarly arranged, carrying a cuirass made of hurdles. Dayak headhunter in warrior costume. Tight dalmatic used as cuirass; long blowpipe with spearhead and sight in the form of a blade. At his feet: *ottat*, bucket or basket used for carrying the freshly removed head. Triumphal return with *ottat* to the tribe. Treatment and fate of the victim's head. Long-drawn-out ambushes of headhunter: his virtuosity at decapitation. Religious superstition involved in this sanguinary passion. Sacaran headhunters, who have attained living conditions superior to those of their neighbours, and possess remarkable industries. Dayak women from the Biaju family, one of the most civilised in Borneo. Cotton garments, and headdress of woven straw. Little painted wooden pannier used for gathering provisions. Dayaks of the plains and the fishermen, who differ at least in skin-colour. Mutual aversion and hostility in which they live. Fortified, entrenched villages; houses built on tall wooden stilts; three movable ladders for access to the dwellings. Prejudices of the young Dayak girl, to whom her suitor must show at least one enemy head.

PLATE 65

NATIVE OF BORNEO, IN WARRIOR COSTUME. Cuirass in the form of tight dalmatic made of several pieces. Closed woven case for blowpipe arrows. Necklace and bracelets made of tiger or leopard claws. Reed helmet.

MALAY FROM BORNEO. Hat like an upturned wash-bowl; Cut-out robe and broad belt with ends hanging. *Krís* with undulating blade, and spearhead.

JAVANESE. Man and woman, dressed in long, broad trousers of Indo-Persian origin.

The main items of **MALAY COSTUME:** *saroeng, sarung, sarong, sahrung* or *sahrong; kolambi; sabuk, jarit; sikapan; cabay, shelana, sembug* and *kuluk.* Physical beauty according to traditional prejudices. Flat noses found throughout Malay Archipelago. Teeth blackened by a varnish; filed back to the root, in Sumatra; hidden by setting them in a gold plate, among the Lampungs. *Siri*-chewing, common to both sexes, maintaining the blackness of teeth. In the Caroline islands, ears elongated by lower-lobe piercing, so that the ear almost reaches the shoulder. Yellow skin-coloration passing for beauty; nobles and ladies procuring this colour through henna and turmeric.

JAVANESE WOMAN eating earth, *ampo*, to prevent plumpness. Betel chewed by men, women and children. The red handkerchief at the shoulder of certain Creoles, which becomes part of the costume. The betel chewed by the chief passed to the subordinate as a sign of benevolence. Lovers exchanging their betel.

KAREN OR BORNEO CHINESE, and the native women whom he marries on a temporary basis. The man in his everyday wear; the Dayak woman in her habitual costume.

PARSEE FROM BORNEO. Hindu costume.

TIMORESE WOMAN from the Lesghian race, in the Moluccas. Costume showing off the figure, made of cotton in bright colours and silk interwoven with gold thread. Loin-cloth the only garment worn indoors; breasts covered on the arrival of a stranger. Beauty of the Lesghian women gives them queenly privileges. Husband of inferior origin is at her mercy, as he can be sold into slavery by his father-in-law's family.

INDIOS FROM THE PHILIPPINES, Carayos, Lutas or Lubanis, in warrior costume. Armour, called mail but in fact made from vegetable fibre. Usefulness of the back-plate, and the use made of it in combat by the pikeman, a man at arms attended by his servants.

PAPUS OF BOTH SEXES, wearing elements of Indo-Malay clothing, more to ornament than to protect their habitual near-nakedness.

WARRIOR OF THE KING'S GUARD, from the **HAWIIAN ISLANDS** (Polynesia). 'Feather' cloak, whose weft is a net; helmet in *íye*, a sort of osier; adze, the emblem of command. Special tattoo, chequers, triangles and diamonds.

Bust of a dancing **WOMAN FROM MAUI ISLAND,** one of the Hawiian Islands. Tattoos on the neck, arms and breast, with little goats around her breasts. Nature of Hawiian dancing. Extreme courtesy expected in upper class women, of receiving visits while lying face-down on a mat.

TATTOOING or engraving of the skin, its probable origin; the advantages to the cutaneous system. South Seas tattoos: a mark of distinction and caste-privilege; means of recognition among tribal brothers, each family having its own design. Tattoo incised and filled with *moko*, and the series of iron teeth making up the tattooing comb (see this adze-shaped object, pl. 66).

Stoicism required to endure the tattooing operation. How the practitioner works, introducing the indelible dye into the bleeding wound with the use of a brush. Considerable time taken for the wounds to heal; further episodes required over the years to tattoo a New Zealander from head to foot. Polynesian *moko* the equivalent of the European nobility's coats of arms. Chief signing a contract for the *moko* design. The homage rendered to the head of the warrior fallen in combat by the enemy, if the head is well tattooed. Those who refuse to be tattooed lack all influence within the tribe. Husbands glory in the decorations incised on the skin of his wife. Not allowed to tattoo all of her face, she has complete liberty for the rest of her body. The variety of drawings mixed with the lines of the tattoos: animal, plant, harvest and fruit, fights and human sacrifices. *Moko* black replaced by indigo in Timor. Polychrome tattoos, a military decoration among the Orong-Matavi. Tattooing practised on child in early youth by its mother. Finally, slaves banned from using *moko* among peoples who make most use of tattooing.

ALFURUS OR TURAJAS FROM SULAWESI. Warrior in ceremonial attire. *Tapa* or mulberry paper, replaced by silk and cotton goods in Gorontalo; Malay sarong, camisole vest, neckerchief rolled around the head as turban; *kampilan*, and shield, *salamako*. Catholic Alfurus, man and woman, in their Sunday best. Two crossed scarves on the man's chest. Enormous cross-shaped comb on the woman's head. These women, dressed in more or less European fashion, but bare-foot. Priest of the idolatrous Alfuru prophesying on the appearance of the entrails of the freshly killed animal. Main chief of the tribe, *kapulabalak*, who combines functions of priest and soothsayer. Greeting by rubbing noses, the *chumik* of the Mariana Islands; mutual kissing, widely practised among the natives, and safe conduct for the stranger so kissed. Complete extinction of the majority of the natives of the South Seas expected in the near future. What Europeans have brought to these island-dwellers.

PLATE 66

119

Africa

Blacks form a majority of the African population. These intermingled peoples are divided by ethnographers into typical families: Guinean (also called Nigritic), Senegambian (including Wolofs, Mandinke and Fulah), Abyssinian, and that of the Bantus or Kaffirs.

The inhabitants of Nubia are skilful, courageous hunters. Nubians trade in slaves, gold powder, ivory, ostrich feathers, rubber, medicinal plants, balms and incense. Nubians are svelte and muscular. They have lively eyes, fine teeth, abundant hair and rarely wear beards. Their clothing is of the simplest: breeches of white cloth and a broad piece of white wool bordered with red. A curved dagger is worn in the belt. The five Nubians represented here (pl. 69) are those forming part of the troupe exhibited in 1877 in Paris at the Jardin d'acclimatation where they had set up a tent.

Most inhabitants of Timbuctu belong to the negroid race. Thanks to their relations with the Moors and Arabs, the costume of these natives presents certain of the characteristics found in the towns of Mediterranean Africa.

A group of peoples found in the eastern Sudan is known as the Niamniams. Their name means 'big eaters' and clearly refers to the cannibalism of which they are accused.

The Kaffirs of southern Africa are a handsome race with black, woolly hair. Both sexes show great taste in self-adornment, of which the principal component is tattooing. In Senegal, one finds both whites (Berbers and Arabs) and blacks (Peuls, Malinkes and Wolofs), the latter being native to the area. The national arm is the spear, whose point exhibits a great variety of forms.

The two remaining plates show pipes and cigar-holders used by Africans (pls. 74 and 75). Observers have often been in a position to describe the effect of hemp on smokers, which includes an increase in physical strength. A group of hemp-smokers forms a rather grotesque scene; the result in some cases is a sort of delirium, taking the form of a rapid flow of senseless speech.

67/68 · THE BLACK FAMILIES: Guinean, Senegambian, Sudanese, Abyssinian, and Bantus or Kafirs (Xhosa), represented by 1. Native of the coast of Guinea; 2. Wolof or Peul of Senegal; 3. Pahouin, Mpongwe women and Bakale medicine man from Gabon; 4. Bertas from south of Kordofan, 5. Galla, from the tribes of south Ethiopia; 6. Abyssinian; 7. Basuto or Zulu from Kaffraria.

THE GUINEAN OF THE COAST, belonging to the warrior tribes, using a flintlock; iron weapon like the angled axes of the Ancient Egyptians.

WOLOF AND PEUL CHIEFS. Wolofs, Mandingos (Malinke) and Fulani, the last-named divided into Torodos, Peuls and Toucouleurs. Wolofs, living as a nation, divided into castes, polygamous. Guinea cotton, blue cotton cloth of which their clothes are made. *Koussab*, long sleeve-less shirt. *Tob* or talisman, with infallible protective powers. *Tamaka*, used instead of tabacco. Straw hat, of the kind called *bambarra*; the broad tunic called *boubou*; breeches called *yata*. Habit of rolling up and attaching clothing for walking, hunting and combat. The stratagem of the combatant who disturbs the sand with his hands to envelop himself in a cloud of dust. Peuls, Fuls, Fulbes, Fulani, etc., generally shepherds, camping in straw huts. Hair in little braids under which the rest is maintained in wads, the whole soaked in butter. The smock bound by a cloth wound round the waist. Peul necklace, a large white and blue necklace. Wide use of leather, worked with great skill, and of straw, woven with remarkable taste. Sabre hung from the shoulder; long bow, its arrows frequently poisoned. Archer digging a foxhole in order to shoot without being exposed (for further Senegalese costumes, see pl. 72).

GABONESE, divided into Mpongwe, Shekianis (called Bulus), Bakales, and Fangs or Pahouins: the last-named superior to the others in energy and industry; polygamous, having medicine-men, cannibals trading their dead, they are skilled ironworkers. The crossbow, the most dangerous of their weapons, and the terrible poison of its small arrows. Race tattoos; incisors filed to a point. Population always on its guard; villages set out as fortresses, children bearing arms of reduced scale. Mpongwe women. Fichu that does not cover the breasts; piece of cloth replacing tunic or skirt; breeches; belt-necklace carrying *moondahs*, fetishes, and the keys of trunks. Earrings, bracelets, accumulated leg-rings forming greaves; rings on hands and big toes. Hairstyle indicating woman's status, married or not. The disgust that white men elicit in these women, and their expression when they encounter one. *Bakales* who provide the recruits for the school of medicine men, whose students learn a ventriloquism allowing them to pass themselves off as *mediums*. The twofold character of doctor and soothsayer, required to obtain the confidence of the blacks; accoutrements of these 'Levites'. Bakale loin-cloth held up by a beaded belt; use of a sort of red chenille, clusters of beads and bells; necklaces worn conventionally and diagonally, passing under one arm.

BERTAS, PEOPLE OF THE UPPER NILE. Independent negroes, covering them-selves from behind only by an animal skin hung from the belt; for hunting and warfare using only javelin, sword, a short club or tomahawk, and a large shield. Iron necklace, without clasp, such as can be removed from the wearer only by decapitation.

NIGRITIANS-GALLAS, nomadic hunting tribes, divided into hordes, primitive in character, a single chief governing the tribe. Formidable neighbours, scalping their enemies like the American Redskins; skilful forgers of iron, possessing remarkable arms. Slightly more clothed than the Bertas. Hair in natural state, or arranged in long braids, always in a thick coat of butter. Tattooed forehead, skin belt. Silver earring sometimes found. Leopard-skin-headband the mark of the chief. Spears large bow short, straight sword, long club; butchering knife. Shield; necklace of shells. Iron bracelets. Arm-rings indicate the number of enemy warriors killed.

ABYSSINIANS. Constant anarchy of their three principal states, Shoah, Amhara and Tigre. Abyssinian is incapable of remaining a labourer, and, when he takes up arms, is like a medi-eval bandit; his wife accompanies him on expeditions. Beatings inflicted on women of the Negus's entourage. Abyssinians habitually wear a cloak; difficulties consecutive on loss of this garment; use of breeches and a very long piece of cloth worn around the body. *Metab*, a neck cord marking the Christian. Leather sachet for the *gris-gris*.

BASUTOS AND ZULUS OF KAFFIRIA. Basutos, pastoral and agricultural, of an-cient warrior blood, traditionally pastoral; incision on thigh, rendered indelible, and indicating the number of enemies killed in war. *Kobo* or skin cloak; *pukoye*, skin apron; laced greaves; sandals, *lishaaku*. *Phuru*, leather skull-cap. Bouquet of antelope hair, forming a martial decoration on the head. Necklace. Large gorget in bronze, the composition of the bronze being like that of classical times. Shield incorporating a standard on a staff used for pastoral and hunting purposes. Assegais; *tipa* or knife; *thako*, punch or awl, whistle and amulets worn at the neck; club or tomahawk; bow, whose arrows are often poisoned. The Basuto is always armed. The destitution of the Kaffirian deprived of cattle. The conqueror often restores a part of the booty to the enemy: 'one should not let one's enemy die of hunger'. Widespread anointing of body with fatty substances. *Sibilo*, powder, *mukokla*, perfume; *lekaata* passed through the ear. Areas of the head shaven, leaving furrows within the hair. Bracelets in gut or bark; ivory, copper and glass beads.

AMA-ZULUS OR ZULUS. Pastoral and agricultural, but primarily a warrior nation; all soldiers subject to severe discipline. The state, a sort of meeting by selection of the best elements of the race. *Kobo, pukoye*, apron, skin hat. Military bracelet, leg ring. Double leopard-skin adornment of cloak-collar, the mark of the chief; breastplate of the nature of a trophy. Club, assegais, shield with a pole hand-rest. Bow with poison arrowhead, etc. With the exception of chiefs, who are interred with some ceremony, Zulus do not practice burial; the ill are exiled.

69 · **NUBIANS. COSTUMES, ARMS, UTENSILS AND CAMP.** Resemblance of Kenus or Bambaras to ancient Egyptians. Since their hair protects them from sun-stroke, they take great care of it; extreme cleanliness of these people. Cloth pants; broad piece of woollen cloth draped. Leather shoe. Dagger; iron hammer. Bracelet carrying a knife; frequently the Muslim's amulet. Spear with iron-capped base. Long, wide, straight sword, the nation arm *par excellence*; special scabbard. Shield. Low tent or cabin covered with mats, with door-curtains. Ossified hippopotamus head and ostrich eggs ornamenting the entrance to the tent. Parasol for the chief planted in the ground by the tent.

70 · **NATIVES OF TIMBUCTU,** Shilluks, Niamniams, Bazy or Bary (upper Nile). Woman not subject to rape and enjoying considerable liberty in Timbuctu, wearing the *gandoura* with wide sleeves and headscarf. Man wearing the *chechia*, dressed in waistcoat and jacket. **SHIL-LUKS,** pastoral and agricultural tribe; few clothes, protecting the body with a layer of wood ash, or a mixture of cow dung and cow urine. Hair in crest, helmet or fan arrangements, stiffened with clay or glue, etc. Necklaces of shells or pieces of ivory; panther skin for clothing. Spear, curved sabre. **SHIR,** from the White Nile. Cotton mob-cap on hair braided into cords; loin-cloth, necklace and bracelets. Javelin for hunting elephant. **NIAMNIAMS,** eastern Sudan. Tattooed, incisors filed to a point, hair in pigtails or curls. Skull-cap and high hat with plumes. Decorations made from animal teeth. Sole garment, loin-cloth hanging from the belt. Man's codpiece with large fan-shaped tail. Javelins, barbed spear; sabre with curved blade and several points, *trumbash*. **BAZY OR BARY,** from the White Nile. Men entirely naked, hair arranged like that of the Shilluks or Niamniams. Women wear an elegant loin-cloth, decorated with shells and glass beads. Long shield, spear and barbed arrows.

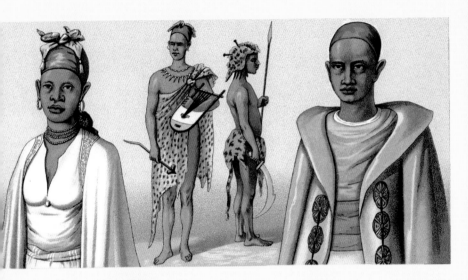

PLATE 70

127

71 · KAFFIRIA, LAND OF THE MAKOLOLO AND OF THE BECHUANAS. BECHUANAS, BESOTHOS, MATABELES, AMAXHOSAS AND AMAZULUS OR ZULUS.

Tattoos, basic ornament for both sexes. Entire body covered in unguent as a prelude to dressing. Climate does not require any clothes, and modesty content with few. Raised tattoo, a convex scar procured by burning the incision made with a lancet. Young girl enduring this to receive ornament; women profusely tattooed. Fatty unguents, used for anointing the head and entire body, a hygienic function become an element of coquetterie. The ultimate elegance for an African: to display oneself shining beneath a layer of *mpafu*, perfumed oil. Vegetable butter, say; highly aromatic pomades and their emanations. Pulling out of one upper, one lower incisor, or these teeth cropped to form a triangular space, a mark of aristocracy in both sexes. Very varied hairstyles. Women's hair a dense mass into which small objects can be stuffed. Hair arrangements requiring several days of work, and lasting for six or more months. The shaven head of the fashionable with braided wigs. *Nkola*, used to dye the hair red. General depilation, armpits excepted. Men and women's eyebrows also shaved. Tattoos and face-paint adjusted; kohl used to enlarge the eye. Skin cloak, form varying, that of men exceedingly small. *Shakal*, covering the sex. Skirt or apron, one behind, one in front. Braided belt to hold them. Smock like a scapular. Fillet veiling the women's breasts, essentially ornamental. The strange rear apron worn by the Nasike women, who do not wear a skirt. Bands of leather rolled around the legs, accumulation of leg-rings. The leather sandal. Necklaces; upper- and fore-arm bracelets all on one arm. Bells worn on dandy's legs. Rings on women's hands and toes. Nose cartilage often pierced, and earlobe split: jewels specially for these openings. Everyone smokes the wooden pipe. Assegais, club, pelt shield, etc. (see the Besotho and Zulu, double plate 67 68).

PLATE 71

72 · COSTUMES OF SENEGAL. The Blacks and the Moors. *Tiedos*, man at arms. *Ferdah*, draped cloak; *tobé*, shirt-like over-garment. *Guinea* and American cloth. *Signores*; high hats; headscarves; pointed turban. Varieties of spear, the national arm (see Wolof and Peul, double plate 67/68).

73 · HOTTENTOTS, KAFFIRS (XHOSAS) AND BECHUANAS; PARTICULARLY THE HOTTENTOT AND BUSHMAN. Physiognomy of the Hottentot, smoked yellow skin-colour, produced by mixed race. *Kross* or *kaross*, animal-pelt cloak, mattress to the sleeper and shroud for the dead. *Kut-kross*, apron of modesty; second apron added to the *kut-kross* and falling over the small of the back, an important element in women's dress. Skin skullcap for winter and rain. Hair rubbed with soot and grease, creating a hat of black mortar in the dog days. Hottentot skill in preparation of skin. The sanitary advantage of anointing the entire body in a grease. The smell of rancid mutton grease and animal butter countered by *buku*, a very strong perfume. The paint with which the Hottentots bedaub their faces. Glass beads and fake pearls among the components of necklaces, bracelets, belts and aprons. Particular care given to the skimpy apron falling over the small of the back, to attract attention to the development of the buttocks, of which the 'Hottentot Venus' is proud. Examples of rich women wearing the *kross* and double-*kross*, man in warrior costume, and of formal wear for the family woman among the Bushmen. Sarah Bartmann, as she could be seen in public in the Paris salons in 1815. Kaffirs and Bechuanas. *Kerri* or *induka*, one of a pair of clubs. The hair of the women arranged to form a platform for carrying burdens such as a large basket, an earthenware recipient, etc. The bear-tooth necklace of a tribal chief. The headband, the 'marriage band' worn by Bechuanas of both sexes.

74 · THE APPARATUS OF THE SMOKER. Pipes, calumets, cigar-holders and accessories. Examples from Kabyle regions, Gabon, Senegal, Hottentot regions, central Africa, Algeria, Madagascar, the Ajan (Zanzibar) coast, the shores of the Red Sea and the banks of the Upper Nile, Abyssinia, Khartoum, and the mouth of the Congo.

75 · CONTINUATION OF PLATE 74. Use of *matokuane*, hemp; the way in which it is smoked, women and men both smoking it, and its effects on physical and moral strength.

DETAIL OF PLATE 71 ›

PLATE 72

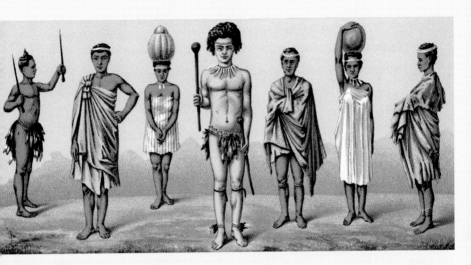

PLATE 73

133

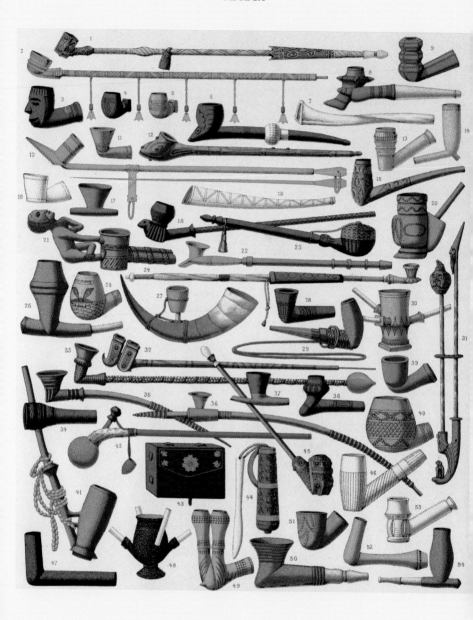

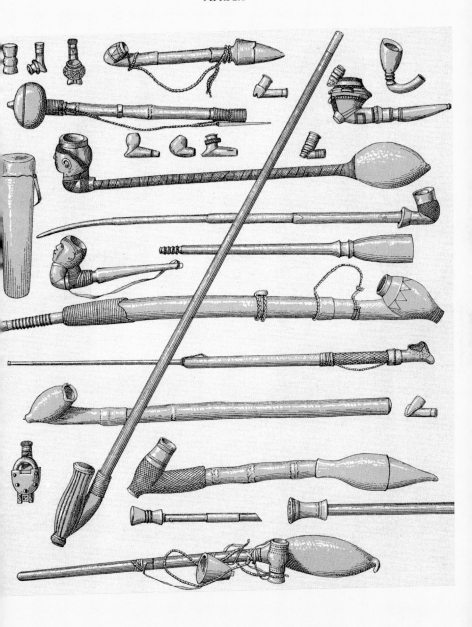

PLATE 75

135

America · Eskimos

The natives of Brazil and Paraguay are divided into three families: the Guaranis, the Caribs and the Botocudos. The Botocudos are still primitive hunters living off nature. Only among the Guaranis, who live in huts, have cultural habits been detected.

The black race forms the majority in the large towns in Brazil, and imparts to the population as a whole its stamp of originality. In the markets, especially, the curious assemblage of different races and different colours can be encompassed in a single glance.

Amerindian Chile is for the most part occupied by the Araucanos, one of the few native peoples of America to have raised itself – under the influence of the Europeans – to some degree of civilisation. The basic population of Chile is constituted by aboriginal Indians, Spanish Creoles, and half-breeds of the two races. This entire population is united in wearing a short cloak, the poncho; this sleeveless dalmatic is the national garment (pl. 78). It is a four-cornered piece of cloth about three ells by two, with an opening for the head in its centre.

The population of Mexico is composed of pure-blooded natives, descendants of the Spanish, and the categories of mixed-blood. The natives in their turn are divided into *cacique* Indians (Chichimecas or Talascans, and Aztecs) and tributary Indians, in addition to some unsubdued tribes (*Indios bravos*), such as the Mecos, Apaches, Comanches and Lipans.

The natives of North America (pl. 80) are the sad remnants of the greatest hunting people known to history, and they grow fewer with every passing day. The Eskimos are to be found in Lapland and Siberia; on the Kamchatka peninsula and in the Aleutian islands; on the banks of Hudson Bay; in Baffin Bay, in the lakes of Mackenzie and in the Nootka islands. The American Eskimos call themselves *Innu*, which means 'man'. This title seems clearly to refute those fables according to which the Eskimos attributed a strange origin to their race, believing themselves to be descended from the apes.

76 · **NATIVES FROM BRAZIL AND PARAGUAY:** Guaranis, Caribs, Botocudos, Camacan-Mongoyos, Puris. Nomads on the march; the carrying of children. Family baggage. Feather hat, *charo. Barbote, botoque, ñimato.* Ear ornament, *huma. Giucan, tacanhoba, tacanioba, kiranaika.* Women's apron. Puri hammock; hut made of leaves, *cuari.* Trophy: desiccated head of enemy. Knife, chisel, *ororo.* Dance instrument, *kechikeh.* Bow, *bigonia.* War and hunting arrows. Necklaces; string of beads; feathers. Hear worn in crown, or loose. Body-painting: *urucu, genipaba.* Net; utensils; tools; tinder-box, *nomnan;* earthenware cooking pot, marrows, *kekrok;* goblets; loud-hailer, *kunchun cokan;* iron axe, stone axe, *caratu. Pote,* the fire that is never allowed to go out.

77 · **BRAZIL. CHILEAN AMERINDIAN. STATE OF BUENOS AIRES.** The black Muslims of Brazil, the *quitandeiras* of the Mina nation, wearing the turban. The *estado indómito,* the untamed state of Chile. The Araucanians who occupy it; the Peguenches. The Gauchos of the Rio de la Plata pampas. Chilean spur; a primitive cart. Industriousness of Araucanians. Long cloak, *ichella;* broach by which it is fastened, *tupu.* Poncho, cloak and blanket. *Chiripa,* breeches. *Tirador,* load-belt, etc. Knife worn on the back; *lazo, bolas* and *rebenque,* whip.

78 · **CHILEANS, ARAUCANIANS, SPANISH CREOLES AND GUASOS, CROSSBREEDS OF THESE TWO RACES.** Poncho, a sleeveless dalmatic, national garment of ancient origin; its decoration in bands evoking the ornamentation of animal-skin clothing. Hat in the shape of truncated sugarloaf, also indigenous. *Calzoneras* in white canvas; gaiters of serge; *ajotes,* hide sandals, and the spur that fits on top of them or on the bare foot, seen from the right. *Peones,* the pastoral and arable farmers of Chile, Tucumán and Paraguay.

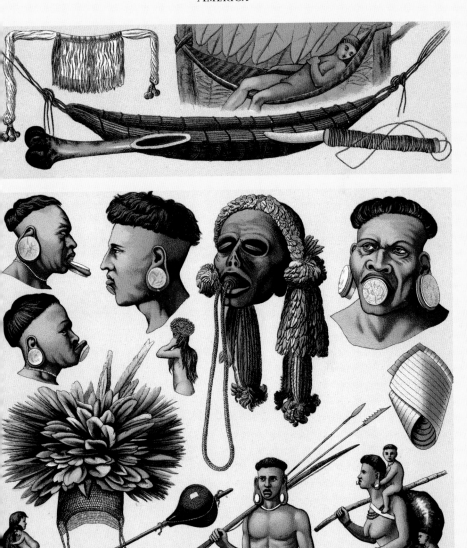

PLATE 76

139

PLATE 77

PLATE 78

79 · NATIVE RACE, CONQUISTADORS AND CROSS-BREEDS. *Indios bravos*, unconquered nomads, represented by Lipan chief dressed for war. Typical accoutrement: diadem of feathers, bison-skin tunic; cylindrical whistle, chieftain's insignia; plumed shield, bow, and reed dart with barbed point. Mexicans of the Spanish race, riding, urban and festive costumes. *Caballeros* and *señoras*. *Sarape*, cloak used by both sexes; *calzoneras*. Hide trousers, open at the side. *Chaparreros*, covering the leg and widening toward the foot. *Toquilla*, hat ribbon for women. *Rebozo*, shawl. *Magua*, underskirt. Little satin slippers worn without stockings. Cross-breeds: mixed-blood woman with bare feet; cobbler; *aguador* or water-carrier, and *léperos*, represented by a parrot-seller.

80 · Examples of YUTES (UTAH), SIOUX OR DACOTAS, CHIPAWAYS, PONKAS, ETC. (Mississipi Basin and Colorado). Costume answering the requirements of horseman, hunter and warrior. Ornaments retaining traditional character. Hide and fur headgear; headscarves; plumes or crowns of feathers; neck-scarf; smock; jacket; cloak; tunic; blanket; trousers; gaiters; garters; mocassins. Apron, a relic of the distant past (loin-cloth). Tomahawk and pipe-axe. The fire (tinder) bag, etc. Flat-heads or Hang-Ears, flattening of the front of the skull practised on children for cosmetic purposes. The peculiar foot-shape produced by the use of mocassins. The sad remains of the greatest hunting people known to history.

81 · THE REDSKINS OF THE STATES OF KANSAS AND NEBRASKA: LAKES, IOWAS, PAWNEES, ETC. Fan, mark of the chief. Sunburst of feathers crowning the headgear. Hide tunic decorated with paintings or embroidery, like the gaiters. Faces painted vermilion and white. Horsemen's trousers. Large cloak. Cotton smock. Necklace of bear teeth and claws. Ornaments made of dollars, piastres, medals and disks of metal; mirror and glass beads. Hide jackets, fringed with hair. Bracelet, a decoration for the brave. The totem, tattooed on the chest of the chief. *Wampum*, primitive mnemonic technique constituted by necklaces and knotted cords of the Redskin outfit.

PLATE 79

PLATE 81

145

82 · INDIANS OF OREGON. THE KILLIMUS OF UPPER CALIFORNIA.

Squaws and *papoose*, the child; portable cradle. Artificial flattening of skull. Hair shaven or braided; beard plucked; bodies painted for ceremonies. Hide clothes. Cotton fabrics. Wickerwork headgear. Embroidery using shells. Necklaces of stones, seeds, shells and glass beads. Headbands. Utensils of reed and osier; woven pottery. Provision nets. Knife carried by men in their hair. Spears, shields, bow, quiver; sabre, for throwing. In many respects, Stone and Wood Age. *Cíbolos*, who use ancient practices like those of the Hindus.

83/84 · HYPERBOREANS. SEA-FISHING PEOPLE.

Costumes. Weapons for hunting and fishing. Canoe, kayak. Sled and equipment. Skate or snowshoe. Interior of winter dwelling; household utensils. Widespread use of walrus bones in arms and tools. Clothes in sealhide for both sexes. Bonnet; headscarf; cloak; hood; sleeved coat; jacket; hunting pockets; breeches with leggings; mittens. Stockings; socks; boots (*kuminias*). Embroidery: woollen braids. Rings; headbands and fillets. Spears; hooks; fishhooks; harpoons; oar. Necklace; muzzles and shoes for sleddogs. The way in which the Kamchadal drive them. Knives; spoons; bags; ladle; tobacco pouch. Kamchadal lamp. Stool. Camp bed. Tent, *teepee*, for summer. Hut into which they crowd in winter. Layers of clothes during the cold season. Adaptation of certain faculties developed by exercise and heredity, according to the places in which man is required to live. Eskimo never idle. Eskimo woman plays a vital role in the family.

PLATE 82

147

CHINA · JAPAN · ASIA

In China, the emperor, the Son of Heaven, is the father of all his subjects, over whom he exercises the supreme authority bestowed on him from above. His garments, his jewels, his sceptre (pl. 85), and in particular his throne and the screen that conceals his august face from the profane gaze, all of these things are invested with a sacred character and venerated even in his absence. The *Li-Ki*, the fourth of the canonical books, recognises the emperor's right to possess up to one hundred and thirty concubines, whose costume is no less accurately prescribed than that of the empress (pl. 86). The mandarins are civil and military administrators, categorised according to the importance of their work and wearing the insignia of their grades. The principal mark of rank is a button placed at the top of the official hat (pl. 87): the substance, size and colour of these buttons vary from that of the first-rank, first-class to that of the seventh-rank mandarin. The official costume comprises a robe embroidered with dragons and serpents. There are prescriptions concerning the colour of clothing. Yellow is the preserve of the emperor, princes of the royal blood, and those whom the emperor has authorised. Red is the colour of the mandarins. Black, blue and violet can be worn by anyone. Finally, etiquette requires that a man must wear his boots and pointed hat when making or receiving a visit, and hold his fan in his hand.

Chinese women are considered inferior to the male, and have no civic status. Their feet are mutilated in childhood, in order to make them a more or less prestigious object of trade. The Chinese adore the air of weakness and indecision imparted by bound feet. When their wives come hobbling along, they compare their walk to the swaying of the willow in the breeze.

The Chinese is the most convenient Asian costume. It is long, ample, hygienic and very diverse. Men wear a long shirt, long breeches, sewn stockings, a long robe, and a wide belt that serves as a pocket and is fastened with a hook. For winter, they don a spencer in cloth or fur, and leg-warmers worn over their breeches. Women's costume is similar in nature. They are enveloped by it from head to foot, so that no hint of their body shape can be discerned. No people so venerates the dead as the Chinese, who therefore bestow a peculiarly solemn character on their funerals.

The historical era of Japan began some six centuries B.C. Japan swam into the ken of Europe as a civilisation complete in itself. However, only in certain coastal towns, recently re-opened to European trade, can one ever meet the Japanese. They are a conquering race.

Their system of government is feudal. Having long rejected foreigners, Japan is today assimilating certain European habits with surprising rapidity.

One thing is certain, the Japanese have attained the greatest perfection in the art of tempering steel. The military profession is held in high esteem in this country. Soldiers belong to the fourth degree of the social hierarchy, and are called *samlai*. Japanese swords are constituted of two short pieces of iron applied on either side of a longer piece of steel that forms the blade. In this way an arm is obtained whose chamfered edge shows swirling shapes known as 'clouds'. Blows from these sabres are dreadful. With a little practice, one can cut off a head with a single blow. A ruined noble will sell all that he possesses rather than part with his two sabres. In the scabbard of the little sabre there is often a needle bearing a particular mark or cipher. When the warrior kills an enemy of distinction, he plants this needle in his head, so as to recognise his victim among the dead after the battle.

The Japanese population is divided into nine castes. The princes or *daimyos*, the nobles, the priests and the military are the four classes that may wear two sabres. The man of letters can wear only one sabre. Tradesmen, artisans, peasants, coolies and sailors constitute the remaining castes and may not bear arms. In short, there are two societies: one armed and privileged, and the other disarmed.

The genius of the Japanese is their aspiration to simplicity. The entire population, men and women, wears the *kirimon* (pl. 99), an open robe; the women's version is slightly longer. This is closed over the chest and belted by a silk scarf. Men's costume further comprises trousers that fit closely over the shin and one or more cassocks, in white cotton for the people and blue-grey silk for the nobility. The trouser worn by the nobles is very wide, very brightly coloured, and quite short, leaving a part of the shin uncovered. During the winter, cotton stockings are worn. The Japanese prefer sombre garments. The inevitable kimono, a long robe with sleeves, is draped, tucked up or fully unfurled, as the requirements of work dictate. Married women, with their plucked eyebrows and teeth blackened by iron filings soaked in saki, do not wear bright or even light-coloured stuffs. Instead of a shirt, women wear a tunic of red silk crêpe. Japanese woman make much use of cosmetics. Lips are rouged, or even gilded.

The Laotian race is reminiscent of the people of north Polynesia. Western Laotians are tattooed from above the shin to the navel. In Borneo, among the Dayaks, it is the woman who has herself tattooed in order to make herself attractive to her lover. Siam is one of the richest kingdoms of the Middle East. Women are honoured in Siam, and enjoy great liberty.

85 · **CEREMONIOUS INDOOR COSTUMES.** emperor, *Thien-Tseu*; empress, *Hoang-Heu*; princess; female attendants, *niutze*; mandarins, *kwans*. Imperial insignia; insignia of senior dignitary. Furniture. Jade sceptre; large necklace, *su-cheu*; five, four or three-clawed dragon; pectoral embroidery, *pu-fu*; peacock feather, *xwa-lin*; crystal globe, *tin-tso* (see pl. 87). Diadems, velvet, precious stones, artificial flowers, crowns, pendants, drop earrings, pins, bracelets. Fan, *talapat*; Hats; silk cravats; over-robe, *ma-cual*, under-robe, *haol*; jacket; muff, *pi-kien*; boots. Thrones, seats, tables, incense-burner, opium-pipe.

86 · **EMPRESS;** second-category wife, her attendant. Furniture, embroidery, fragment of robe. Sceptre, *fong*; *phoenix* hairstyle. Imperial clothes, and their making. Prerogatives of the empress. Four categories of wife: *fu-gin, pin, shi-fu, yu-tsi*. Attendants. Bench with cushion, *kan*; table, *kan-thoo*.

PLATE 85

PLATE 86

87 · **MANDARINS**, great and lesser *kwans*; insignia and official uniform. Tartar lady; Chinese woman. Mounts; mule; Tartar-style saddle. Means of transport; sedan-chair with porters (see pl. 88). Classes of mandarins. Distinctive emblems; red, blue, white, gold buttons; high collar; *pu-fu* pectoral; *xwa-lin*; *lan-lin*; foxtail; red parasol; *wan-min-san*; velvet, satin or fur hat; boots. Summer costume; conical hat; shoes. Women's clothing. Pearl pendants, *fu-kwan*. Bootees with high toes. Fans; pipe; tobacco-pouch. Colours reserved for the emperor, princes of royal blood, old men and mandarins. Rules of etiquette.

88 · **HIGH AND MIDDLE CLASSES, WORKERS.** Wheelbarrow-omnibus. Physiognomy of the yellow-skinned race, the Chinese; condition of Chinese women; a married woman and concubines. Mutilation of feet. Skullcap, winter and summer hats; shirt, robe, spencer, collar, stole, belt, fastening or hook, *yu*; breeches, stockings, slippers, shoes, boots. Hair tied back. Women's hairstyles: hair in tufts, braided, raised Chinese style; authentic; *kaimien* operation, shaving hair above the brow; cushion; artificial flowers; precious stones; feathers. Make-up, beauty-spots. Long nails.

PLATE 87

PLATE 88

89/90 · SHOES; FANS, *talapat*; PENDANT EARRING. MANDARIN, MAN AND WOMAN. TONKIN CHINESE. Popular types: housewife, bourgeois woman, button-seller. Chinese and Tartar ladies; clothing, ornaments, accessories. Hats; hairstyles with pendants. Pants, trousers, chemisette, *han-chaol*, cravat, apron-skirt. *Haol, ma-cual*, jacket, collar; summer fabric, *koppu*; autumn and spring fabric, *siao-kien*; winter fabric, *tuan-tse*; furs, *tael-pi*; belt, stockings; three kinds of shoe, buskin. Smoker's equipment: pipe, pouch. Fan; perfume sachets. Hairpins; *phoenix* hairstyle. *Fong-hoan*, diadems, pads. Nail cases.

91 · HEADDRESSES; ORNAMENTS; HIERARCHICAL INSIGNIA. TALIS-MANS. PERSONAL OBJECTS. Empress's bonnet; pendants; Mongolian headdress; skull-caps; pigtail hairpiece; feather and felt hats. Pins; drop earrings; broaches; bracelets; necklaces; belt buckles; trinkets; jewellery motifs. *Tin-tso. Kao* or *kao-tso*. Lady's bag; comb, pince-nez. Velvet collarpiece.

PLATE 89

161

PLATE 90

PLATE 91

163

92/93 · **FUNERAL OF A RICH CHINESE MAN.** Cortege. Preliminary ceremonies. Emblems of deep mourning: *hyao-i*; the widow's veil; the son's hat, *leang-kwan* and clothes, *mai-i*; his mourning baton, *san-thiang*; the family's sackcloth. Composition of the cortege: burial valets; attributes; musicians; banners; incense-burners; picture of the dead man; the coffin; the catafalque; palanquins; bronzes; provision porters. Funeral banquet. Cemeteries, tombs.

94/95 · **OLD-STYLE (INFANTRY) ARCHER. EQUIPMENT.** Inner and outer clothing and armour. Effects: belts, robe, pants, bonnet, ribbon, jacket, shoes. Protection: rear neck-plate, gauntlets, greaves, braconnière, brassards, ailettes, articulated plates, pansière, dossière, flancard, pauldrons, reinforcing rondels, copper ring. Offensive weapons: dagger, sabre, bow, quiver, arrows, fan (see pl. 96/97).

96/97 · **THE PRIMITIVES, AINUS.** The conquerors: Japanese prince, *daimio*; army general; his mount. *Yakunin*, officer; standard-bearer; guidon-bearer; archer; Yedo fireman. Coolies, *betos*. Warrior and fencing costumes and arms. Helmet with horsehair earpieces, horns, cervelière, gorgerin, mask with moustachios, cuirasses, coats of mail, tassets, pauldron, passe-gardes, ailettes, rear- and vam-braces, gauntlets, genouillères, greaves, sollerets. Vouge, halbard, sabres, scabbard, bow, quiver, arrows; iron fan. Standard, guidon with coat of arms; the banner of the firemen. Chief's cloak, *jinn-baori*. Equipment for horse: bit, reins, chamfron, cuirass, gilded leathers, silk decorations, stirrups. Fencing costume: mask, hood, plastron, tassets, gloves, short boots; bamboo staff; game of Aunt Sally. Clothing: jacket, *fundoshay*, belt, trousers, sandals, shoes. Tattooing and body paint. Shaven skull; hair. Historic era of Japan; civilisation; feudal system; castes; physiognomy of Ainus; Mongolian character of Japanese; constitution and manufacture of armour and arms; *syakfdo*; *sawa* metal. Military condition: samurai, *samlai*; wearing the two sabres; *seppuku*.

98 · **ARTISANS:** porter, carpenter. Two handed sabre; stirrup. Interior objects: *koton* (buffet), chequerboard.

99 · **ARMED AND DISARMED CASTES;** *yakunins*; *lonins*; bourgeois, ladies; pilgrim. Winter and summer costumes; corporate insignia. Felt hat; straw, cuir-bouilli and bamboo hats; *kirimon* or kimono; surcoat with shoulder-pieces; cassock, jerkin, tunics, trousers, sandals, pattens; *guettas*. The outcaste: *Kotsedjikis, Hettas, Christians*.

100 · **CIVILIAN COSTUMES;** means of transport, the *palanquin*.

101 · **WOMENSWEAR;** robes layered one over another; family arms; belt, *obi*; sandals, pattens. Fan, white paper, perfume sachets, *moi-bukooro*. Hairstyles, flowers, ribbons, pins. Parasols.

102 · **BONZES. WOMEN** in urban and indoor clothes. *Shamisen*. Means of transport: *jinrikiska*.

JAPAN

PLATE 100

PLATE 102

103 · **LIFE LIVED ON MATS. WOMEN DRESSING.** Women of the people, women of the nobility; female musicians and their instruments; *kokiu* or *biwa, koto, shamisen.* Civil servant, his two sabres, one an emblem of office. Interior of the house, measurements of the mat; screens, mattresses, bolster, pillow, nightlight. Trestle mirror; toilet case, kettle, tea tray. Cosmetics.

104 · **LIFE INDOORS,** sitting up late by the fire. Family theatricals. Legal wife and *makakes* (concubines), mimes, women musicians, *ghekos; shamisen,* flute, tambourin. Interior objects: screens, blinds, lanterns, *brasero,* kettle, arm-rest.

105 · **GALA COSTUMES, INDOOR AND URBAN COSTUMES;** serving woman, high-class ladies, street salesman. Women's hairstyle. Intimate toilette. Young girls relaxing. Bamboo hat, headscarf; *kirimon;* jacket, jerkin, breeches, quilted cloaks, hood, apron, pattens. Arrangement of hair, hairpins. Hand-held lantern.

106 · **MEANS OF TRANSPORT.** *Norimon* and *cango.* Lord and suite; the Japanese greeting; mobile canteens; *shabinto,* river boat; corporations of porters, coolies. Typical peasant. Hat, cloak.

107 · China, Indo-China, Japan. **TOBACCO AND OPIUM PIPES;** smoker's set; tobacco pouches, holders, lighters, cup, lamp. *Tabacco-bon.*

108 · Laotians. Siamese, Koreans. **CIVIL AND MILITARY CLOTHING;** interpreter, woman guard, mandarins. Rain costume. Theatre costumes. Madras, headband, bonnet, beret; straw, felt, oiled-paper hats; shirt, *languti,* jacket, waistcoat, jerkin, tunic, belt, scarf, shawl, trousers; *fheile-beag,* game bag, shoes, sandals. Gold circles, earring pendants, nail-cases. Laotian tattoos. Polygamy. Siamese customs, *cutting the tuft;* entertainments; Chinese civilisation of Korea.

109 · India, Persia, Java. **SMOKER'S SET,** tray, cup, knife, lamp. Ordinary and water pipes: *hubble-bubble, kalium, hookah.* Cases (see pl. 144).

PLATE 103

177

PLATE 104

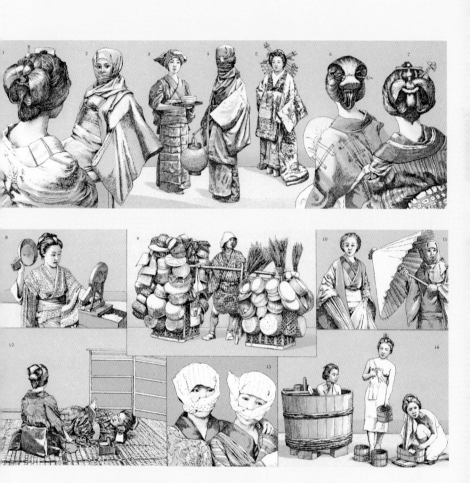

PLATE 105

179

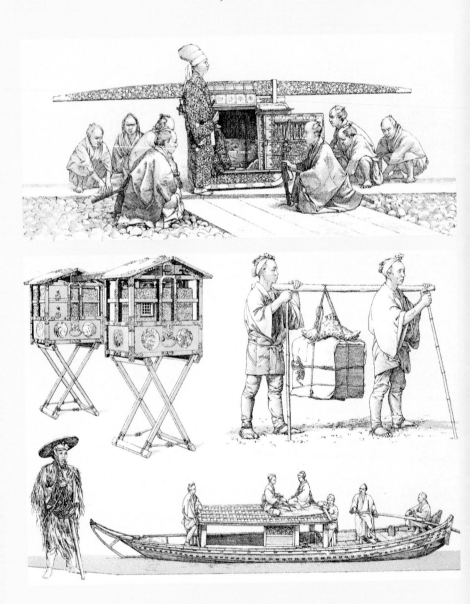

PLATE 106

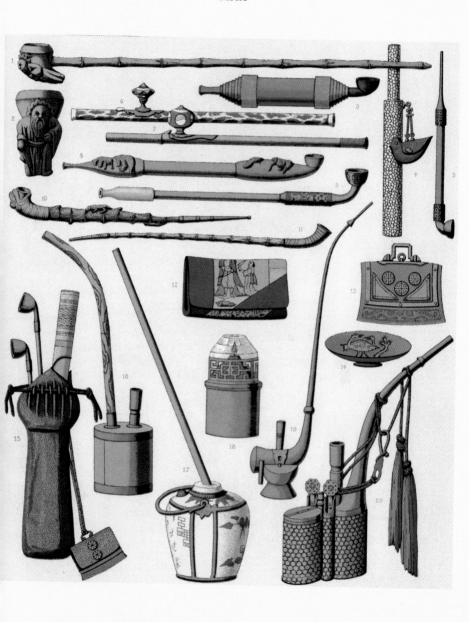

PLATE 107

PLATE 108

PLATE 109

183

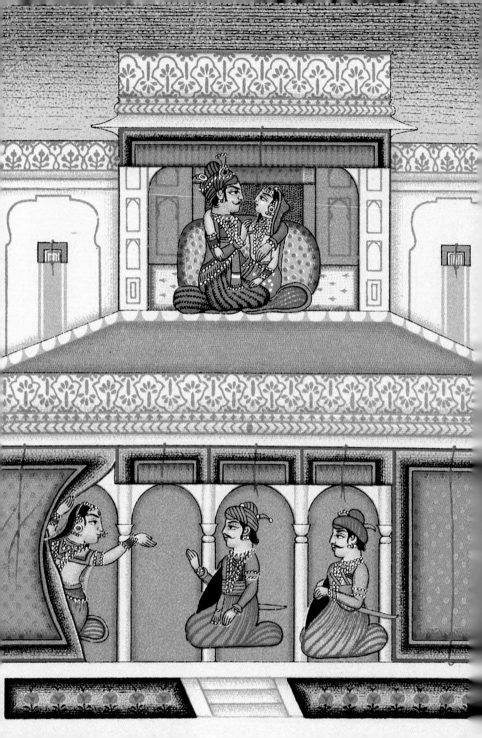

INDIA

The Mogul reigned over the vast Indian empire for more than two hundred years, but the most brilliant period of this dynasty was the 16th century. The court became a byword for its magnificence, and 17th-century European notions of the Great Mogul must have seemed barely if at all exaggerated. Travellers waxed lyrical about the very rich ornamentation of the famous 'peacock throne' (pl. 115). When the king processed with his cortege, he was preceded by two poets singing his praise, and followed by some five or six thousand men with elephants, palanquins and military bands. The Mogul women represented wore veils of incomparably light, smooth, silky muslin. Their gowns were made of light, fine cotton from Dhaka. Their trousers were in embroidered silk, while the cloth of gold hanging from their belts was made in the valley of Kashmir.

Palaces generally comprised small courtyards, sometimes open, more often planted with trees, and surrounded by high buildings. The white stucco of the wall (*chunsīn*) is of very high quality and made from a very specific limestone. Palace rooms are painted with watercolours and sometimes oil. Mogul gardens are mostly symmetrical, with long narrow canals, built of stone and stucco, all leading to the central fountain. Cool retreats are arranged throughout these gardens. Country houses are always coated in white stucco. Floors are covered with a thick carpet. The furniture is all movable.

The Mogul emperors (pl. 119) went to war wearing a gold damask helmet. Their body armour consisted of a short-sleeved jacket with a round skirt made of strongly quilted and stitched silk; this was covered in velvet and decorated with geometrical designs, whose centre is marked by a big button.

In India, Brahmins are an object of veneration to the laity, whose liberality to them is excessive. Most temples are served by Brahmins, and they are responsible for the conduct of ceremonies. Indians burn their dead on a pyre in a lying position. Members of religious orders are cremated in a seated position.

In India, women can leave the house on the slightest pretext. Red predominates in their costumes because it is the colour of joy and happiness, whereas black is ill-omened. There are three classes of dancing girls in India: *devadasas* (devoted to worship), *veshastri, varangana* (who accompany processions) and *cancenis* ('ruined' women, who are summoned to private houses to sing to the accompaniment of an orchestra). Hindu women paint their bodies with saffron powder. Their glistening hair is anointed with walnut oil and put up as a mass or braided into long plaits. The inferior castes are subdivided into trade corporations. Each caste has its own rites and its own costume character.

Plate 128 shows soldiers of the Kashmiri army. The women of Kashmir have a deserved reputation for beauty and are distinguished by the purity and nobility of their features. Vehicles clutter the streets of Bombay. The *hackery* (pl. 131) is one of the few vehicles of Indian origin still to be met with. Though it remains a two-wheeler, its body is not without elegance. It is surmounted by a little roof on four small columns; this shelter is extended by the horizontal canopy. *Ruths*, carts covered with light gilded domes, can also be seen. The functions attributed to the horse and donkey elsewhere, in India fall to the ox.

DETAIL FROM PLATE 117/118 ›

110 · MILITARY CASTE. THE RAJPUTS (CHILDREN OF KINGS). HISTORICAL PORTRAITS. Golden sun jewel, gold ribbon, necklaces, bracelets, pearls, emeralds, rubies, diamonds, belt worked in precious metals. Turban, jacket, scarves, trousers, pyjamas, robe, slippers. *Kunda*, sabre, *khuttar*, dagger (see pls. 120 and 121), shield, rhinoceros skin, guige.

111 · MOGUL EMPERORS. RAJPUT PRINCE, HAWKING. Handkerchief, *sudarium*.

112 · IMPERIAL PRINCE, SHAHZADEH. SOVEREIGN OF DELHI. *Omra*. Garment of honour, *khelat*, cloak of investiture, *kurta*.

113 · PORTRAITS OF SOVEREIGNS. LADIES. Court of the Mogul emperors. Costumes, jewels. Woman's veil, nose ring. Painting of body, saffron. Great reception throne. Parasol.

114 · CLOTHES, IMPERIAL SEATS; ordinary and ceremonial audiences. Lady in highly formal clothing. Costume of fiancée. Gala robe, *raz*. Custom of bare breasts; braided hair, decorated with flowers. Body-painting, saffron and henna; jewels: *tali*, earring pendants, jewelled choker, necklaces, bracelets, rings, crown, apron of the married woman.

PLATE 110

189

PLATE III

PLATE 112

191

PLATE 113

PLATE 114

193

PLATE 115

PLATE 116

195

115 · PORTABLE THRONES OF MOGUL EMPERORS. *Tractavans. Mikdember hauze* and peacock throne. Emperors' cortège. Audiences in the open air; *kutual, cadi, itimad-ud-deulet*.

116 · INTERNAL COURTYARD OF THE SERAGLIO or *mahl* (see pl. 117-118).

117/118 · THE PALACE OF DELIGHTS; terraces of the *mahl*. Building formats: courtyards, gardens, apartments, chambers. The imperial tents: *amka, kargai*. The sovereign and his favourite; female musician; fortune-teller; chief eunuch; example of fakir, *yogi* or *samias*, gymnosophist or gymnasiarch. Essence of rose, *attar gul*.

119 · WARRIOR COSTUMES of the 16th century. *Padishah*. Royal standard; horsemen, infantrymen, harnessing. Royal attributes: aigrette, parasol. Defensive weapons: helmet, camail, jacket, vambraces, cuissarts, genouilleres, shields. Offensive weapons: lance, sabre, arrows, quivers, club. Horse's harnessing: caparison, collar, frontal, bit.

120 · ARMS from India, Nepal, Persia and Turkey. Daggers, *khuttar*, swords, sabres, *kunda, kukri-kora*, matchlock; thrusting weapons; mace.

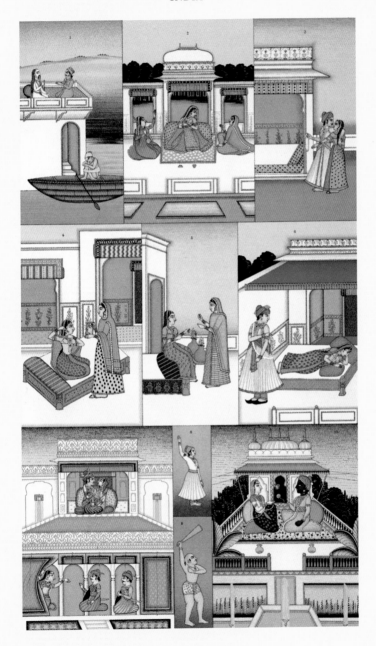

PLATE 119

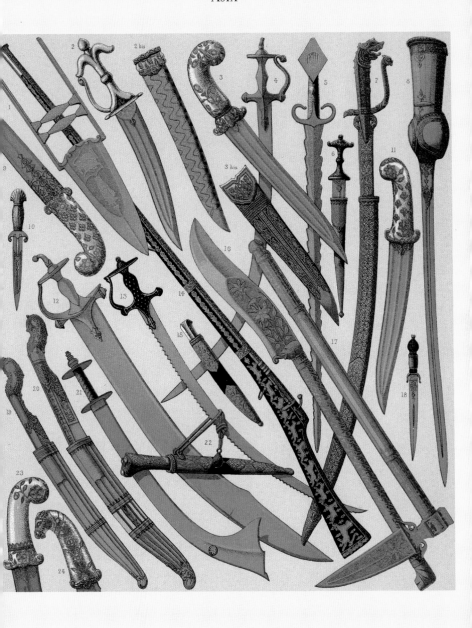

PLATE 120

199

121 · **ARMS AND OTHER OBJECTS:** Helmet, dagger, knife. Mahout's hook, jewels, buttons, broaches, earring, pendants. Shoe, fan, spoons.

122 · **FUNERAL OF A BRAHMIN** (see pl. 123); bearer of the sacred flame. **RAJPUT PRINCES, PATHANS, MARATHAS, BRAHMIN MERCHANT.** Turbans, veil, sari, sacred lock, *shindu,* caste indications, sacred cordon; breeches, *dhoti.*

123 · **ADHERENTS OF VISHNU AND SHIVA, FUNERAL MUSICIANS, MARATHA LADIES. WASHING CASHMERE.** Corset, jacket (*choli*), skirt, scarf, mules. Cadogan-style hairstyle. Nose-ring, *moncauty;* necklace, *taitun;* earring pendants, bracelets, rings. Musical instruments: *phunga* or *tare, matalan, tal, gopijantar, tambura, pukhaway,* cymbals.

124 · **MEANS OF TRANSPORT:** *doli,* and its porters, *bohis;* **GOVERNESS, AYAH, WIFE OF A SOMAR, CASTE OF SUDARS, VAYSIAS. DANCING-GIRLS, NAUTCH-GIRLS.** Headcap; dress of precious materials, *kangra.* Red, symbol of joy; belt, *cummerbund.*

125 · **THE MARRIAGE CAR,** *shaupal.* Fly-scarers, coolies. Standards, betel-carriers, bayadères, musician; trumpets, castanets, bagpipe, *turti* or *turry,* and *matalan.* Categories of **DANC- ING-GIRLS:** *devadeses, nartachis, veshastris, varanganas, suarims;* bayaderes, *cancenis.* Hair anointed, plaited; brassiere, transparent skirt, trousers, scarf; jewels.

PLATE 122

PLATE 123

203

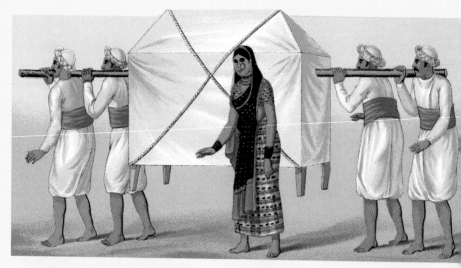

PLATE 124

PLATE 125

126 · HINDUS, MUSLIMS, their FUNERALS. Examples of BRAHMINS. *Shivaists, Vishnuites, Saktites.* Turbans according to caste, sacred thread, string of beads, hairstyles, ferronnière, necklaces, *malla*, shell bracelets, *sunk*, earring pendants. Fan, *punya*. Ablutions, perfumes, emblems, marks of the sect, bodycolouring, ornamental hairstyles. Betel use.

127 · LOWER CASTES, MERCHANTS. MONASTIC ORDERS, MENDI-CANT MONKS. EXAMPLES OF WOMEN, REQUIRED TO CARRY A BURDEN. FUNERAL CEREMONY: *jalledar.* Sandals, pattens, leg-ring, bells. Arm of scales; weights, nets.

128 · RAJPUT SOLDIERS; INDIGENOUS PRINCES, IN CEREMONIAL ATTIRE. KULU MOUNTAIN PEOPLE; MINAS; KASHMIRI NAUTCHNIS, AND their dances. Embroidered bonnets with twisted cords of hair; corselet, tunic, veil, pants, trousers, cloak, *languti*; gaiters, curved shoes. *Moncautys*, broaches, necklaces, pendants.

PLATE 126

207

PLATE 127

PLATE 128

209

129 · NATIVE WOMEN FROM THE MOUNTAINS: ASSAMESE, GARO, KOLI. BAYADÈRES, their jewellery, the frontlet. Women on a pilgrimage. Manipuri woman.

130 · WORKING SQUATTING DOWN. Joiner, Kashmiri engraver, barber, pastry (*mitai*) merchant, Banyan pedlars: *multanis*. Family grinding wheel. Manipuri mountain-people. Gurkhas. Assamese women. Hats, tunic, shirts, *kurtah, angarkah,* trousers, breeches, *janghir.* Head-dresses, woollen braids, breast plaques.

131 · TYPES OF DWELLING: Native house, Marwari merchants' house. Means of transport: inflated animal skins, *sarna*; carts, *hackery, ruths.* Pleasure boats: *murpunky, fyl-t-chiarra.* Fishing boats, traders: *bangle, poluar, gonga, pinass, graab* or *paal.*

PLATE 129

211

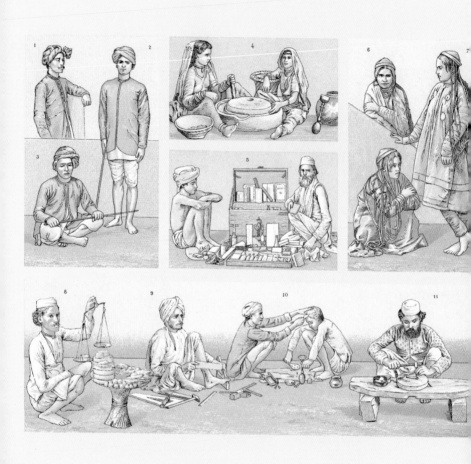

PLATE 130

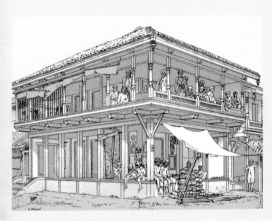

PLATE 131

213

Asia · Persia · Muslims
the Orient · Syria

The native population of the island of Ceylon can be divided into four races: the Veddahs (probably aboriginal), the Singhalese, who came from India, the Malabars (also from India) and the Moors. Singhalese nobles wear a jacket buttoned to the neck in cotton and silk. The *comboye* worn by men and women alike is the item of national costume to which the Ceylonese attach most importance. It is a piece of cloth rolled around the hips like a sheath-dress. Despite the abolition of caste decreed by the English government, the inhabitants of Ceylon still observe traditions regulating the clothing suitable to each class.

The Malay Archipelago includes the Philippines, the Moluccas, Celebes (Sulawesi), Borneo, Sumatra, Java, Timor, and other parts; all these are inhabited by Malays. The Malay dagger, the *kris* (pl. 134) is a thrusting weapon, with straight or undulating blade. It is sometimes poisoned with upas resin.

Orientals are highly proficient at wrapping the turban (pls. 135, 136). The material of a turban is normally a long strip of cloth, sometimes up to fifteen or sixteen foot long, and it takes two people to wrap it correctly. The cloth can be wool, silk or muslin. In India, the size of the turban varies between castes and sects, but its shape changes according to locality. In the rest of the East, certain peoples wear bonnets like the Persian lambskin *cula* or the Kurdish fez.

Persian women leaving the home (pl. 137) put on broad trousers in which the folds of the skirt are entirely enclosed. Their faces are covered by the thick percale of the *rubend*, whose only opening is narrow and covered in textile lattice-work. Coffee is widely served in Persia at all hours (pl. 138). Grounds are twice boiled in a pot with a long handle. Travellers carry coffee grounds mixed with honey. This forms a sort of preserve to which the gourmet adds opium. All the serving women represented have their fingers and toes painted with henna. In Persia, the terms 'dancer' and 'courtesan' are more or less synonymous. The dance (pl. 139) consists of passionate movements and expressions combined with swaying of the neck.

The goldsmith has had more than the jeweller to do with the jewellery seen in plate 140. The Asian artisan is above all an artist: his ornamentation is now severe, now lofty and sumptuous, and sometimes quite splendid, but he does not generally impart the kind of finish customary with European craftsmen.

The rich costume of the Shah's dignitaries (pl. 141) consists of a gold-lamé robe falling to the feet. The headgear of these civil servants is the *kulah*, made of astrakhan: lambskin with short, curly black wool. In Persia, the term mollah (pl. 142) is given to those devoted to the study of jurisprudence, morality and theology. The pipe (pl. 144) is a more or less obligatory part of Persian costume, and widely used by both sexes. Particular care is taken of the pipe, and it is often a resplendent object. The violent sensation imparted by the strong tobacco of Bukhara is very remote from the sweet ecstasy imparted by Shiraz. Women's pipes are more delicate and ornate than those of men. Plate 147 presents the habits of various Eastern Christian religious orders, some of which have since disappeared.

DETAIL FROM PLATE 136 ›

PLATE 132

PLATE 133

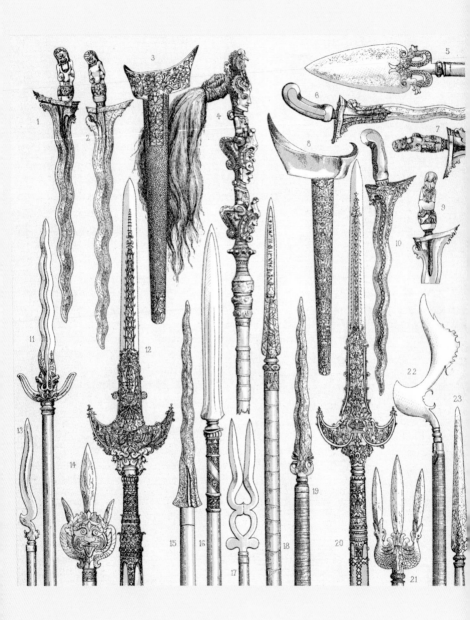

PLATE 134

132 · **SINGHALESE.** Novice. Priest, *kapural*. Jews. Parsee children. Turbans, robes, *sanghati*, *outtavasangho*, *antarawasaka*; surplice, *sadra*, canezou, long jacket, *comboye*, trousers, shoes, slippers. Yataghan, baldric. Earring pendants, necklaces, bracelets. Combs. Parasol, vent-holes. Indigenous population: Veddahs. Sinhalese or Singhalese. Malabars. Moors. Castes: *Kshatriya, Brahman, Vaisya, Sudra.* Outcastes: *pariahs*.

133 · **MALDIVANS. SINGHALESE. KANDIAN. HINDUS:** nobles, lower classes, sailor. Skullcap, beret, hood, headscarf, jacket, belt, sari, sandals. Hair, bun, comb.

134 · Asiatic Archipelago (Malay Archipelago). **OFFENSIVE WEAPONS.** Standard. *Kris, vedung,* javelins, spears, halberd.

PLATE 135

PLATE 136

PLATE 138

135/136 · **HEADGEAR.** Persian. Yazdi. Baktiani. Afghans or Pushtuns. Indians. Parsees. Thugs. Turkomans. Lesghiz. Yliats. Arabs. Kurds. Catholic bishop; dervishes. Turbans, *dulbend, kinkab;* hats, fez, *puskul, cula,* skullcaps. Damascene skullcap, nasal, iron camail. Finery of betrothed woman, earrings, pearls. Hair, 'dog's ears', 'long-wave curling'; beard.

137 · **WOMEN'S COSTUMES.** Ladies of Trebizond and Teheran. *Hyader, rubend* (see pls. 139–147). Yliat women. Meals: *kofta, mash-pullao,* yoghurt.

138 · **HOUSEHOLD SERVICE.** Preparation of coffee, tea, samovar. *Kaleyan; affabeh.* Serving women; *enderum;* dervish; Turkoman betrothed. Colouring of hands, feet, henna.

139 · **DANCING WOMAN, MUSICIANS;** dance of the bee. Tattoos. Musical instruments: *bandyn, dohl, tar, kamanche* or *kemanshesh, zurna* or *zurnay.*

PLATE 139

227

PLATE 140

140 · **ORIENTAL JEWELLERY.** Fastenings, *chaprass*; necklaces, *guerdanlik*; hanging jewellery, pins, buckles, earring pendants; bracelets, *halhal*. Horse harness; hanging ornament.

141 · **SERVICE OF THE SHAH.** Pipe-carrier, *pish-khedmet*; musicians. Popuar industries: water-carrier, *abdari*; preparers of *kaleyans*, *nargilehs*. Indian dervish, *kuskul*. Hat, *kula*; the outer garment, *erkaling*: *caba*, *bagali*, *tikmeh*, *biruni*; *katebi*. Dagger, *kanjar*. Beard customary.

142 · **COSTUMES. TYPES OF SMOKERS.** Mollah; *mirab*, mountain-soldier; *chervadar*, muleteer. Armenians.

PLATE 141

PLATE 142

143 · **THE INTERIOR OF THE HOUSE,** *enderun*; main room, *talar*; furniture. Crystallised order of Ottoman architecture; stalactite vaulting, latticed windows.

144 · **WATER AND ORDINARY PIPES; CIGAR- AND CIGARETTE-HOLDERS** (Turkey, Arabia, Turkestan, Persia, India). *Nargileh, hookah, kalium, kaleyan, ghalian, shibbuk, bukan. Sariel-hookah, chelem.*

145/146 · **MUSLIM PRAYERS.** *Namaz.* Example of muezzin: *Sabah (al-Subh), oilah (al-Zuhr), Akíndy (al-'Asr), Asham (al-Maghrib)* and *Yatzu Namazy (al-'Isha)*; ablutions, *wudu, ghort.* Prostrations: *rak'at, shafi'i; Istigfar, Takbir, Tasbih, Fatiha.* Oriental greeting, *al-salamu'alaykum.*

147 · **CHRISTIAN MONKS AND MEMBERS OF RELIGIOUS ORDERS.** Templars, Carmelites, *Barrés*, Capuchins, Acoemetae or Studiites; orders of the Holy Sepulchre, of Saint Anthony; Armenian, Mingrelian, Georgian and Maronite churchmen. Hat, skullcap, turban, veil, wimple, hood, cloaks (*kappa*), cope, pluvial, tunics, robes, mozzetta; *kurdy, cadeby, rubend*, jacket, breeches, trousers, sandals. Hair, beard.

148 · **MOUNTS;** transport animals; dromedaries and Bactrian camels (see pl. 149).

PLATE 143

233

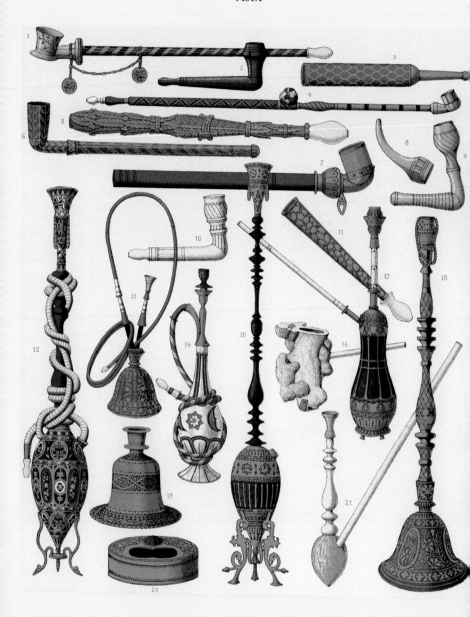

PLATE 147

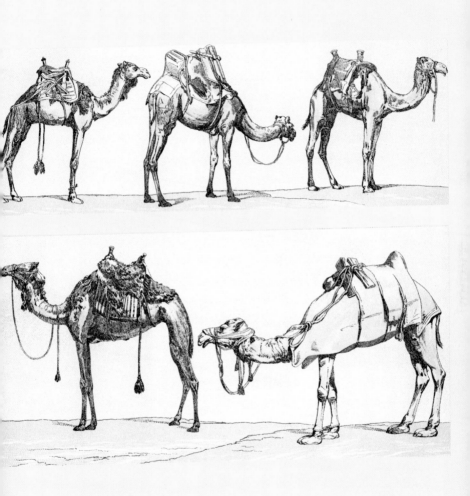

PLATE 148

237

Africa · Moorish

The patient camel, the ship of the desert, bears all burdens, drags the plough, turns the water-wheel, and accompanies the pilgrim. The horse is the friend and companion of the Arab. Arab and Berber saddles are like those of the Turks, soft and comfortable. In Cairo, horses are sometimes ornamented with bizarre coquetry, using henna and other cosmetics.

The Berbers (pl. 150), considered the oldest inhabitants of the African soil, are divided into several branches: the Amazighs in Western Morocco, the Tibus, the Touaregs, and the Kabyles, who inhabit the Atlas mountains. The Kabyles are a brave and industrious people, warriors and traders who prize their nationality above their lives. The Kabyle man wears a *clotte* on his head; he combines it with a woollen shirt, the *derbal*, with or without the woollen belt, and a leather apron. To this can be added the hooded cape, the burnous.

Plate 152–153 shows (amongst other things) two women making *couscous*. Kabyle jewellery (pl. 154) is as severe in its form as in its coral or enamel decoration. Strictly speaking, there is no furniture inside an Arab tent (pl. 155). Life in the tent varies according to its inhabitants' occupation. The shepherd is nomadic and moves his encampment every day. The agricultural labourer lives near his field. Kabyle women of all ages dye their hair; it can never be black enough for them. A mixture of gall, sulphate of antimony and copper pyrites is used, diluted with olive oil, which is then heated to form a paste. Plate 156 shows ten examples of 15th-century Moorish costumes. The costume worn by Jewish women in Algiers (pl. 158) is a heterodox mix of northern European and Oriental fashions. These women do not seek to shine, and their costume sometimes bears this out rather obviously; it is for the most part made of coarse fabrics and lacks the graceful cut exhibited by Moorish women. In Algeria and Tunisia, the inequality of the sexes is noticeable from earliest childhood in the importance accorded to all that concerns boys. There are no such attentions for girls. In ethnographic terms, Algeria and Tunisia both comprise the same categories of people: Berbers, Arabs, Moors, Jews and Blacks from Central Africa.

In towns, the Arab woman of well-off family is always veiled to some extent. The same is true of Moorish women, who rarely leave the house and are never seen in the street without the *beskir* (*sassari*), a sort of *haik* of light cloth which covers the body completely; beneath it the indoor costume, always elegant and rich, is completely invisible. The dress of Jewish women varies from place to place. In the towns of the Barbary States, women's costumes have retained their original form but are no longer made in the pleasantly coloured and silky wool that is one of the most delicate products of Moorish hands. Now a common cloth, generally in blue check, is used. The lower classes constitute the great majority of the people, but among the Arabs these classes do not present as varied a spectacle as they do in Europe. The Saharans (pl. 165) dress with greater care than the inhabitants of the Tell Atlas. Among Arabs and Berbers alike, the signs of wealth are: silk, women's jewellery, heavy leg-rings, bracelets, coral necklaces, plaques. The collective name for these appurtenances is *shebka*.

149 · **THE SHIP OF THE DESERT, HORSE, ASS.** Example of palanquin. Masked Touareg or *Targui*. Egyptian woman. *Jellabahs*. Jackets; *lebni*. Harness, saddles, stirrups; decorated riding animals; henna.

150 · **BERBERS; KABYLES** (see pls. 151–156 inclusive). **ALGERIA. TUNISIA.** Working clothes, warrior costume; harvesters; transporting water, milk; sifting grain; child's hammock; chief; warriors. Woman in ornamental dress (see pls. 155 and 165). Kabyle society; condition of women. *Anaya, sgara*. Rifle; *flissi; yataghan*; baldric, powder-horn, game-bag. Skullcap, hats; *haik*, burnous, hood; *derbal*; belts, tunics, *palla*; greaves, babouches. Brooches, necklaces, leg-rings. Curled, shaven hair. Vases, basins. *Amazighs. Tubus (Tedas)*. Touaregs.

151 · **KABYLE WOMEN, M'ZABITES, MOORISH WOMEN; METAL-WORKERS** (see pl. 152 153). Tunisian Berbers: Kroumer, Ouchetettas. Agricultural work, olive- and fig-picking. *Ichouaoun*, toque, head-cloth, skullcap; tunic, *gandourah*. Ornament, *thibezimin* or *thabezimth*, its pendants, *tisherurin*; earring pendants, *zeruayar*; *ibesimen* (see pls. 154 and 155).

152/153 · **INTERIOR OF GOURBI** (hut). **ITINERANT SILVER- AND GOLD-SMITHS.** Beni-Yeni. **WOMEN WORKING,** the making of *couscous*; production of ceramics. Beni-Aissi. Tattoos. Stable; loft; furniture; utensils, scales, hand-mill, wattle fences, spoons, porringers, burettes, wooden vases, *gaça* (see pl. 154); earthenware vases, amphorae and jars. Constitution of Kabyle village; *dehera*, families, *kharubas, dahman, ukil, amin, taleb*.

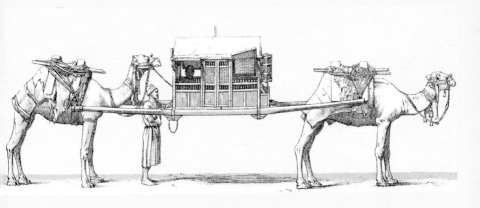

PLATE 149

241

PLATE 150

PLATE 151

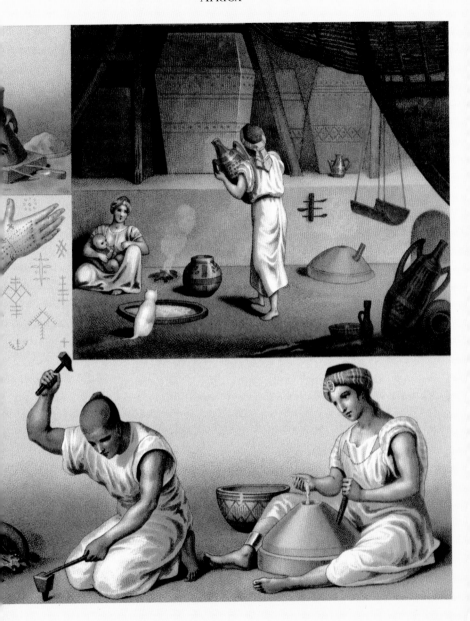

154 · **KABYLE JEWELLERY.** Diadem, *thacebt*; earrings, *kuneis, zeruiyar*; necklaces, *thazath*; broaches, pins, hooks, *ibesímen*; belt, chaplet, jewelled ring; leg-ring, *khatkhal*; jewels in chased and wrought silver, coral worked and plain; enamels, glass beads, shells, cowries (the regional currency); seeds. Characteristics of Berber jewellery, its origins. Gold- and silver-smith tribes, *Beni-Rhab, Beni-Wassif, Beni-Yeni. Beni-Aissi, Beni-Abbez, Flissahs.*

155 · **THE ARAB TENT; NOMAD; SEDENTARY.** Kabyle woman, in ceremonial attire; woman from Biskra; Moorish woman. Within the tent: *feljas*; sacks of provisions, *tellay, meguds*; utensils, water-skins, funnel; *keskes, tabag, guenina, sindukh, guessaa*, handmill, pot; furniture, carpet; esparto mat, *asseyíra*; pillow; *ugada. Douar.* Women's costumes: headgear, *ashuaau-thabeníkt*; handkerchiefs, dresses. Enamel jewellery, circle worked in precious metals, small chains, sequins, necklaces, rings. Make-up, cosmetics, hair-dying, eyebrow-dying, *hadída*, kohl. Vases in *thalakht.*

156 · **COSTUMES OF CHIEFS; THE DIVAN.** *Al-dyonan.* Examples of swords, 15th and 16th century. Turban, *xasia*, scarf, *marlota; albornoz* or burnous; hood, *almofar*; petticoat, *fereje*; half-boots, *borseqís.* Sword, *alfange*, baldric. Cushions, *almohadas.*

157 · **ARABS FROM THE TELL ATLAS, FROM THE TRIBE OF THE DESERT SMELAS;** chief's costume. Berbers, *Chaouía.* Jewesses. Algeria (see pls. 158, 164, 165, and 168). *Chechía*, turban, cord of goat- or camel-hair; feather-hat; *yemeni*, headdress in cotton, veil; *haik*; Ottoman-style clothing, jacket, Tunisian belt, pants, bodices, skirt, breeches, babouches, sandals, *torbaga.* Braided hair. Religious, noble, military tribes: *Djouad, Mehal, Douaouda.* Vassal tribes.

158 · **ALGERIAN POPULATION:** Negro, Vandal Berber; Moorish men and women; Kouloughli women. Headcloths, skullcap, robe, bodice, belt, closed garment (*poenula*), pants, *serual.* Rings, earrings, necklaces, bracelets. Tattooing of face, arm, hand, foot.

PLATE 154

PLATE 155

Plate 156

249

PLATE 158

251

159 · **POPULAR COSTUMES.** Children; merchants; oriental mount. Algeria. Tunisia. (see pls. 160–163). Arab good wishes. Inequality of the sexes; daughter, *telfa*. Algerian, Moorish clothing: *chechia*, hats, *alarakia*, *sarmah*; turban, *jemala*; *kaftan*; *haik*; burnous, *gefara*, *barnus*; waistcoats, *farmela*, *sadria*; *serual*; breeches, *serual-dakelani*; lace, *tuka*; stockings, *kelasset*; shoes, *sebbat*, *babra*; slippers, *rihiyea*, *sebbarla*; flat-soled slip-on shoes, *besmak*; clog, *kabkab*; Arab shoes, *belgha filali*.

160 · **POPULAR COSTUMES** (Algeria, Tunisia): Kabyle, Arab and Jewish women. Skullcap, *ishaun*, turbans, veils, *beskir*, *takreta*, bonnet, *kuffia*; shirt, *shelulha*; tunic, *gandourah*; bodice, dress, belt, apron, light *haik*, *sassari*; cloak (*palla*); babouches. Earrings, necklaces, sequins, bracelets, rings, broaches, *ibesimen*. Mandolin, *durbakka*.

161 · **ARABIC, MOORISH, NEGRO, BEGGAR POPULACE;** *Rumi.* Example of Egyptian *fellaheen.* Handkerchief, headscarf, *saffaka*, *acbeh*; skullcap, *libdeh*; veil, *tarbah*; *borqo*; silk shirt, *jaboli*; jacket, *farmela*; dresses, *jelesh*; *shintian*; *peliçon*, belt, apron. *Guslar.*

162 · **ALGERIAN AND TUNISIAN MOORISH WOMEN, INDOOR WEAR; ARAB CHIEF, BEGGAR CHILDREN, FELLAH AS PORTER. SPAHI, PEASANT WOMEN.** Native costumes: amulets, virtues of topaz (*yagut-astar*), of the red gem (*hajar-ed-dam*), of turquoises, rubies, emeralds diamonds (*elmas*), hematite (*maghnatys*). jade (*yechm*), tiger's-eye (*ayn-el-hor*).

163 · **COSTUMES OF THE LOWER CLASSES:** female beggar, female gleaner, Kabyle woman, Tunisian soldier. *Berranis*, M'zabi fruiterer, oil-seller (*ar'uati*). *Mar'rarba*; Rifian; *Shelauq*; inhabitant of Biskra, Kabyle man, Negro. Arab shepherds, *hall-el-badia*, *rehhala*; urban poor, *haddar*.

PLATE 159

PLATE 161

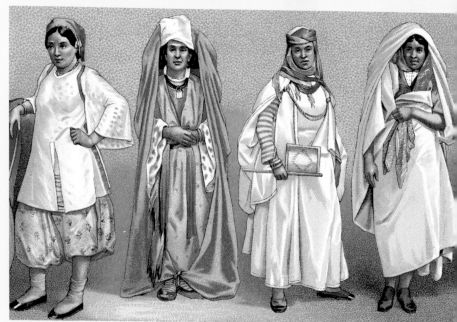

PLATE 163

164 · **POPULATION OF THE ALGERIAN SHORE.** Dancing women, *a'ualem* or *ghawazy*; Moorish woman, urban costume; Moorish country men and country women. Jewess, serving woman, beggars. *Tanbur bulghary. Darabukkeh, rabab.*

165 · **NOMAD AND SEDENTARY WOMEN OF THE SAHARA.** *Lallas* (ladies) from Touggurt and Biskra, from the Beni-Saad and Ouled-Nayil tribes; serving women, outdoor and indoor clothing. *Shebka.* Kabyle mountain-woman, in ceremonial costume. Turban, handkerchiefs, scarf, veil, piece of cloth, *doumasi,* skirt, dress, *malhafa,* cloak, *ghamma*; babouches. Frontal, little chains, earrings, broaches, necklaces, belt, bracelets, rings, neck-chains, talisman, leg-rings. Plaited hairpieces.

166 · **INTERIOR** of a wealthy household in Cairo. The cool or summer salon. Plan of the ground floor of the house. Distribution of the apartments; *mandara.*

167 · **INTERIOR OF A LORDLY RESIDENCE,** 13th and 14th century. Blessing room, *sala de la Barka,* Alhambra Palace.

168 · **MOORISH HOUSE,** courtyard, patio. Ground- and first-floor galleries.

PLATE 164

PLATE 165

PLATE 166

PLATE 168

263

Turkey · byzantine

The turban of the Grand Vizier (pl. 169), like that of the Sultan, is the size of a bushel; it is covered with a piece of muslin. The janissaries, an infantry corps, were founded in 1350 by the Sultan Orkhan to guard the throne and defend the frontiers. The janissaries then wore a white *kukth* or felt bonnet as their insignia. Dervishes wore the *tajh* or 'crown'. In the 18th century, upper-class Turkish ladies changed their furs several times a year (pl. 170). Ermine was the fur of choice for autumn, sable for winter and squirrel for spring. A particularly recherché fashion required that noblewomen cut their hair in a double crescent over the forehead, with the central apex hanging down almost to the bridge of the nose.

The Muslim home is famous for its division into the *selamlik*, the man's side, and the harem, the women's side. The name *harem* is also used collectively of the women of the household. The lady is *hanum*; the young girl *idz*. The house is generally of timber construction. Almost the only item of furniture is the sofa, on which one sits cross-legged, but there are small tables that can be drawn up for snacks or meals (pl. 171). The *tandur* is a rectangular table whose tablecloths reach the floor; on it is placed a copper brazier whose temperature is regulated by the layers of ash in which it is covered. Plate 172-173 shows the interior of the imperial harem. The seraglio, in the time of Süleyman II, contained as many as six thousand people. The title of sultana was reserved for the mother, sisters and daughters of the sultan. The *valideh sultan*, mother of the reigning sultan, enjoys very extensive privileges. She alone can appear unveiled in public. The *cadinns* were the sultan's wives. In defiance of the Koran, which permits only four wives, the sultans took five, until Ibrahim further braved the Koran and took seven. The majority of the harem women were *odah'qs*. The vestibule or *salamlik* (pl. 174) of the sovereign's palace is in fact frequented only by men. It need hardly be said that the room in which we have shown women is a secluded one, like all those of the harem.

It is the custom for Turkish women who leave the house to conceal the wealth that they so complacently display in the home beneath a garment that covers them from head to foot.

Manissa is said to be the greatest cotton market in Asia Minor. The bourgeois of this town (pl. 176) wears an *à la franka* waistcoat over a shirt without cravat. The ladies of Manissa sometimes wear the ancient *fez*, which resembles the *mortier*; it is bordered with a band of gold embroidery. The strange garment exhibited by the Muslim peasant of plate 176 is a white felt overall decorated with bizarre designs.

The principal resource of the Kurds, who live in nomadic hordes, is the product of their herds. Kurdish women's costume is very different from that of Turkoman women (pl. 177). Their short *mintan* of cloth, embroidered with gold at the sleeves and bodice, fits tightly over the upper body. Druse women (pl. 179) have retained a form of headdress that dates back to earliest antiquity: the *tantur*, a hollow horn of silver several feet tall and laden with chased or repoussé ornaments.

Plates 181, 182 and 183 offer various civilian and religious costumes from the time of the Greek emperors, when the Eastern empire was fast coming to a close.

DETAIL FROM PLATE 176 ›

169 · 18th century (see pls. 170–173). **HIGH-RANKING DIGNITARIES.** *'Ulama.* Officers of the court. Hierarchical headgear. *Sherif* of Mecca. *Reis-effendi* or *reis-el-kittab, sadri-az'hem, agha* of the janissaries, *hizlar-agha, silidar-agha. Qadaris.* Sheik, dervish. *Seraglio,* internal officers: *ish-aghassis; tutunjy;* eunuch, *coz-bekji-bashi, dilsiz, tshavush, capuji, capuji-bashi.* Seraglio, external officers: *tshocodars; iskemle-agha, tshantaji, khass-akhorlu.* Turbans: *urf, taj* (see pl. 176), *mudjeweze;* hats, fez, *zarcola, take, takie, yelkem, pashaly-cawuk, uskief;* skullcaps, aigrettes, pelisses; court suit, *ustkurby,* kaftan, *khulat;* Indian shawl; belt, *aba;* trousers, *shalwar;* jackets, *ortacushak, tshepken;* shoes, babouches, boots. Dagger, *khantsher,* knife, *bitshak.*

170 · INDOOR, CITY AND PILGRIMAGE COSTUMES. Egyptian woman, Turkish ladies, slave. Furs; spring and summer garments. Public dancers, *tshenguys.* Veil, *yashmak;* turban, pompon, hat; cloaks, *fereje, ihrams;* collar, *yaka;* robes; shirt; *beurunjuk;* breeches, trunk hose; shawls, waistcoats, *jamadan, yelek;* headgear; jackets. *tshepken, salta; shalwa,* trousers; half-boots, *terliks;* babouches, shoes. Frontal; filigree bouquet, *sergutsh;* buckles, earring pendant, necklaces, *guerdanlik,* chain, *contenance,* belt, clasp, *tshapras,* watches, rings, *khatims.* Arrangement of hair.

171 · RECEPTION ROOM of a Muslim lady; *tandur* (see pl. 172–173). Furniture, *sofa,* corners, *kioshes;* occasional tables. *Tuntun, shibuks. Dundurmas.*

172/173 · INTERIOR OF THE IMPERIAL HAREM. Palace of timber construction. The great hall, apartments, working room, prayer-room, bedroom; internal service. The seraglio. The Sublime Porte, the 'greetings' gate, *Bab-üs-Salam,* the gate of felicity (Salutations). Inhabitants: the chief of the women: *kizlar aghassy; valide-aghassy; shazadeler oghassy; khazinedar aghassy; buink oda aghassy; kutshuk oda aghassy;* the sultana, *valide sultan; khassegui sultan; odalisks, Oustacaddin, guedeklis.*

174 · Internal architecture of the palaces. **HAREM CHAMBER,** 19th century.

175 · 19th century. **COSTUMES OF CONSTANTINOPLE.** Bourgeois ladies, *hanums;* Armenian and Jewish brides; dervish *Bektashi;* porter, *hamal;* water-carrier, *saka; Aivas, Caikji.* Headgear: *kulah, saryk,* fez; veil, *yashmak, telpetshe;* bride's crown. Shirt of boiled silk, *berunjuk.* Cloaks, *hyrka, djubbe, ferdeje,* robes, *entari.* Jackets, *salta, arkalitsh.* Waistcoat, *yelek.* Belts, apron, *futa.* Lace, *oya, bibil.* Trousers, *potur, shalwar.* Stockings, shoes, *yemeni, terliks, pabujs* (see these items of clothing, in the following plates, 176–180). *Teslim tash;* rings, earrings. Use of kohl, hennah, *kermes.* Satchel, *jilbend;* herdsman's horn; porter's crook, *semer;* water-skin of the water-carrier, *kyrba.*

PLATE 169

269

PLATE 171

271

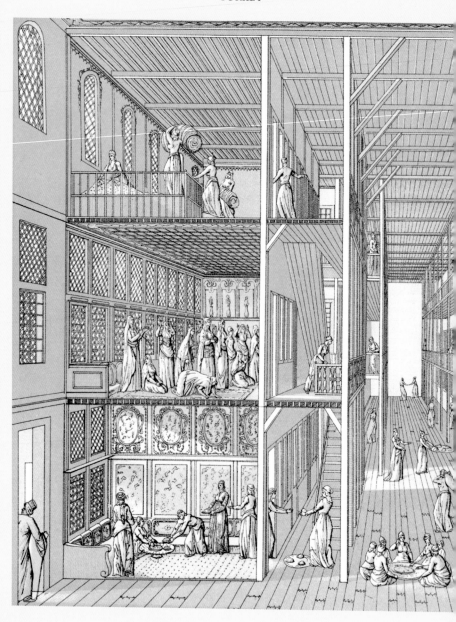

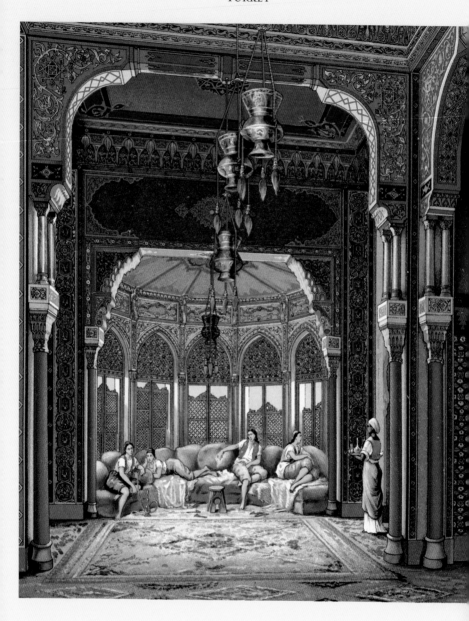

PLATE 175

176 · COSTUMES OF THE VILAYETS OF AYDIN, KONYA, ANKARA.
Bourgeois, peasants, artisans; *shali*-weaver; Muslims, Christians. Kurds. *Hotoz* (see pl. 178); jackets, *mintan*, *tshepken*; overcoat, *kepenek*; waistcoat *à la franka*; handkerchief, *tshevre*, Tunisian belt; stockings, *mest*; shoes, *tsharik* (see pl. 179), *laptshin*, *gandura*. Boots. Ornamental headdress, *tepelik*, *armudie*, *süleymaniye*. Earrings, necklaces, *guerdanlik*, belt-plate, little chains, rings.

177 · ASIATIC POPULATION. Greek, Jewish, Kurdish women, women of Muslim artisans. *Bashi-bazuk*. Turkoman, horseman. Zeibeks; sergeant, *tshavush*, corporal, *onbashi*, their equipment (Vilayets of Konya, Ankara, Hudavendiyya and Aydin). Headgear, cylindrical mitre, *yemeni*, handkerchiefs, *kavez*. Cloaks, *kaput*; waistcoats, *jamadan*. Sequin crowns, *bashlik*, pendants, bells, earrings, necklaces, bracelets. Rifle; *yataghan*; arm-belt, *silahlik*; pistols, ramrods, *harbi*, cartridge-pouch, *palaska*, bag of flintstones. *Shibuk*, tongs, *masha*, tobacco bag; canteen, gourd, *kabak*. *Enam kessest*.

178 · ASIATIC TURKOMANS. Muslims, Christians, Jews (Vilayets of Hudavendiyya, Aydin, Konya). Artisans, peasants, stable boy, *seis* or *sais*; grocer, *bakkal*; doctor, *haham*. *Kalpak*, *fez azizie*, *mandil*, *bonneto*; *oya* crown, veil. Cloak, *binish*. Stockings, garters, half-boots *à la franka*; shoes, belt in precious metalwork; long staff.

179 · MUSLIM POPULATION OF DAMASCUS, BELKIS, LEBANON. FELLAHS, DRUZES. BEDOUINS, BEDEWI. ARMS. *Tantur*; veil, *pushi*, *keffiyeh*, *akal*. The *entari* of *kutnu*, *mashlash*; *bash eurtussu*; *tsharshaf*, *fistan*. Belt, *kemeri*; apron, *eunluk*. Patten, *naleun*. *Tas tepelik*, *tshaprass*, *anilik*; rings, earring pendants, rosettes, fastenings, ornaments of piastres, ecus, thalers; neck-chains, chiselled triangle, bracelets. Scimitar, *pala*; axe, *balta*; knife, *kama*. Rifle, cartridge-belt, cartridge-pouch. Pipes, *tshibuk*, *sebil*, *luley*, tobacco bag.

180 · **URBAN AND INDOOR COSTUME.** Muslim, Christian, Jewish, Kurdish, Armenian, Bedouin and Turkoman ladies (Vilayets of Trabzon, Sivas, Diyarbakır, Al Hijaz, Erzurum, Hudavendiyya, Yemen). Soft-collar pin; veils; *petshe*; *mahramas*; *shemse*; *asaba*; headscarves, *yazma*. Hairpieces. Plastron, *ghiuzluk*; jacket, *fermene*; mitre, *shapo*; apron, *peshtimal*; shoes, *nadass, tshedik. Muhuri Suleiman* (seal of Solomon); hairpins, nasal jewel.

181 · **CIVILIAN AND RELIGIOUS COSTUMES. FURNITURE:** from the 5th to the 11th century. Latin and Greek clergy; patriarchs, bishops, abbeys, ascetics. Greek and Latin blessing. Eastern Emperor and his officers; consul of the Late Roman Empire; patrician. *Sella curulis*, thrones, *bisellium*; seat with back, candlesticks, *phari*. Ribbon-diadem, tiara. *Sceptrum eburneum, mappa, acatia, inmissa* cross. Amice, alb; *sticharium*, tunic; chasuble, *phenolium*; pallium, *homophore*; stole, *epitrachelium*; *superhumerale*, maniple; *hypogonation* (details of the costumes reproduced in the following plate, see also pls. 193 and 194). *Toga trabea, palmata, chlamyda; subarmalis profundum* or *lorum; calcei aurati.*

182 · **SOVEREIGNS, PRINCES; INSIGNIA, IMPERIAL CLOTHING** (13th–15th century). Maronite and Orthodox **PRIESTLY ROBES,** patriarchs, bishops, priests, deacons (19th century). The Abyssinian cross. *Eunapius*; episcopal crowns and mitres (see pl. 193), *kulah* and *kalpak*. Sceptre; hand cross, pectoral; annular; Greek and Latin croziers (see pl. 195). Cope, *jube, entari. Pabuj, kundura.*

183 · **EASTERN EMPERORS AND EMPRESSES: CEREMONIAL, INDOOR ATTIRE.** Effigies of sovereigns. Despots. Diadems, crowns. Sceptres: *nartex* or *ferula; narticophoroi.* Consul's costume (see pl. 181). *palla* and gem-embroidered *stola*, tunic, purple *chlamys; clavus;* shoes, Persian leather.

PLATE 176

PLATE 177

PLATE 178

PLATE 179

281

PLATE 180

PLATE 181

PLATE 183

285

III
EUROPE
400–1800

Middle Ages

We have only the vaguest information concerning the transformation undergone by Roman art during the long centuries of its decadence. Amid invasions, the confusions of barbarity, religious struggles and civil wars, the traditional practices were gradually lost to memory.

The ornaments of the earliest kings of France (pl. 184) were like those of the Roman emperors. As to costume, it was not until 1100 that a radical change took place, especially in male costume; it became long after having been short for more than six hundred years. This was the period when a number of men's bonnets first appeared (pl. 187). Men then wore their hair in Provençal style, that is, with the front cut short and the sides and back thickly furnished. Over the shirt, *la chainse*, a tunic called the *bliaut* was worn; this was a sort of tight-sleeved smock that came down to the knee. Towards the mid-11th century, the skirt of the *bliaut* grew longer. The women's *bliaut* came down to the feet and was a veritable gown. It was made of light, thin material. The textile worn by the upper classes was generally imported from the Orient. Almost all the figures shown combine their tunics with tight *braies*; from these came the first trousers with integral foot. Plate 189 shows several examples of these garments. The *bliaut*, a tunic with no other opening than that for the head, was made of a single piece of cloth, and was tighter at the shoulder than below; the lower part was split to facilitate walking. It was worn over the gown, generally of linen. Men did not revert to the use of a belt in civilian costume till late in the 12th century.

The French house in the 12th century (pl. 190 191) was a large-scale establishment suited to the sedentary life of peacetime. Wars had hitherto excluded such comfort. The 'living' room served all the purposes of life; there one ate, slept, received guests and bestowed hospitality. The dining table was fixed to the floor. The bed was, in general, rather narrow, but otherwise luxurious. Carved wood, with ornaments inlaid or painted, supported a mattress and covers enriched with embroidery and braiding. The walls and ceilings of this room were painted: the principal colours used were yellow-ochre, red-brown, red, blue and green.

The dignity of the bishopric began to be displayed in the form of the mitre (pl. 193). In the second half of the 12th century, the episcopal mitre changed shape: the two horns were now placed one in front of and one behind the head. The bandeau was no longer the solitary ornament. One of the first liturgical vestments was the alb (pl. 194), a full-length linen tunic. When the priestly vestment became luxurious, albs began to be made in coloured cloth. The chasuble (pl. 194) was the sacerdotal cloak chosen by the church when prescribing the nature of the earliest liturgical garments. The thick, cumbersome folds of the chasuble caused it, as early as the 11th century, to be cut back on both sides; thus, from being round, it became oval, finally, in the 13th century, taking on the form of a large cone. Plate 198 shows the various monastic costumes of Poland, Germany and Flanders, while plate 199 offers examples of the costumes of the Doges of Venice from the 9th to the 16th century. Plate 201 shows how, in Castile, as Spain set about the reconquest of its territory, clothing began to evolve. Most nations at this stage, following the French example, were beginning to free themselves of Byzantine influence and adopt a costume related to the new aspirations of that beautiful period, the Middle Ages.

184 · ROYAL CROWNS, SCEPTRES, HANDS OF JUSTICE, SIGNET RING, 420–987.

185 · INTERIOR OF LORDLY DWELLING, 9th, 10th and 11th centuries. Reconstruction. Romano-Byzantine architecture; feudal life; the rooms of the keep; decoration; furniture: bed, cushions, curtain around bed, lamp. *Clotets* (alcoves). Internal service, place setting. Brick paving. *Hypocaustum*.

186 · FURNITURE; from 7th to 14th century. Beds; thrones, including that of Dagobert; episcopal seats, *faudesteuil*, folding chairs, chairs with backs, vases.

187 · CIVILIAN, MILITARY, RELIGIOUS COSTUMES (see pls. 193 and 194); celebrant, 9th century. Helmet, surcoat, coat of mail. Sword, axe, spear, arrows, quiver, club. Hats, bonnets, *esclavine* (see pl. 200).

188 · CIVILIAN COSTUMES, 11th century. Bonnets, tunic, robe, *bliaut*, amice, hood, footed breeches, trunk-hose; cloaks, *pallium, chlamys, poenula*. Women's veil; shoes (see pl. 189). Seats; harness; carriage.

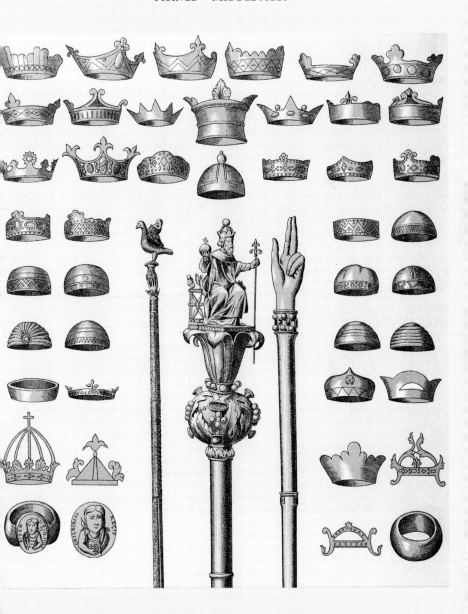

PLATE 184

PLATE 186

PLATE 187

PLATE 188

189 · UPPER CLASSES, CIVILIAN COSTUMES. Mitred **BISHOP, DEA-CONS**, 12th and 13th centuries. Crowns worked with precious metals; non-trailing robes; shirt, bodice, belt, skirt; way in which cloak was worn, chest-plate. Hair loose or plaited; beard.

190/191 · **FRENCH INTERIOR**, 12th century. The hall of the castle. Furniture: the lord's chair, chairs, benches, screen, upholstered form, movable back, stool; dining tables, credenza; chests, holy image; bed, cradle. Fireplace, windows; window-frames glazed or covered in oilcloth; tiling; hangings; decoration of walls and ceilings; beams.

192 · **MUSICAL INSTRUMENTS**, string, bowed, wind, keyboard (from 12th to 16th century). Harp, psaltery, rote, luth, mandora, guitar, cittern, citole. Rebab, *gigue*, vielle or viol. Shawm, flute, horn, oliphant or Saracen horn (see pl. 201), cornets, sackbut or trombone. Clavi-chord, portable organs.

193 · **PRIESTLY VESTMENTS**. Episcopal insignia. Precious mitres, fanons; 14th cen-tury (see pl. 284). *Simplex, auriphrygiata, pretiosa*; crozier (*sambuca*); *sudarium, superhumeral*; ring; gloves, shoes.

194 · **PRIESTLY VESTMENTS**. Bishop, priests, deacons; 14th–16th century (see pl. 284). Hats, tonsure. Under-garment, the cassock. Alba, its ornaments, rochet, amice, dalmatic, chasuble, orfray, cope (pluvial), stole, maniple (*orarium, sudarium*, fanon), liturgical shoes.

195 · **RELIGIOUS OBJECTS**. Archbishop's and bishop's croziers, processional cross, candlestick; 12th–15th century.

196 · **RELIGIOUS PARAPHERNALIA** (see pl. 197). Paschal candlestick, in bronze, silver, with lectern; altar candlestick, censers, *aspersorium*; 13th–15th century.

197 · **CHANDELIERS, ACOLYTE'S CANDLESTICK, COPE ORNAMENTS, QUIGNON DES DAMOISEAUX**, 15th–16th century.

PLATE 189

PLATE 193

PLATE 194

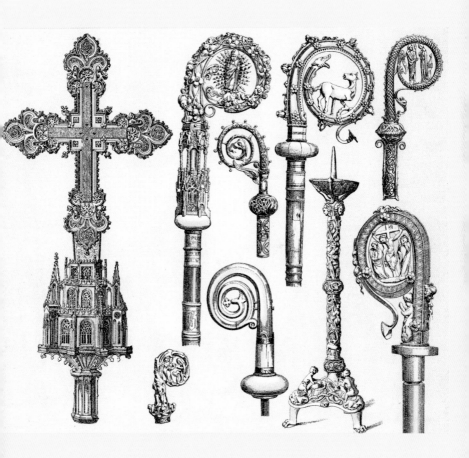

PLATE 195

303

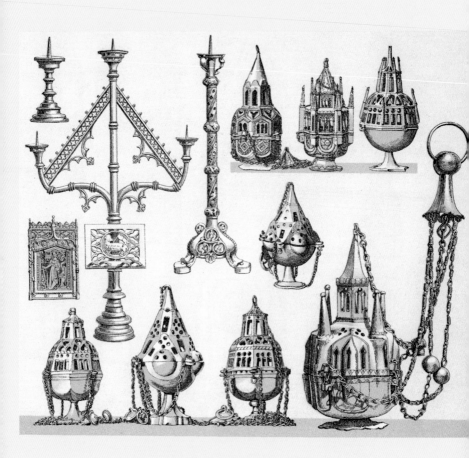

PLATE 196

PLATE 197

198 · **MONASTIC GARMENTS** 15th–18th century. Orders, tertaries, of Saint-Sepulchre, Servites, Lateran, Slavonian, Magdalene, Franciscan ('good fellows'), Poor Clares, Mercedarians, of the Holy Spirit, Carmelites. Canons, monks, friars, nuns, penitents. Hats, bonnets, veils, wimple, cassock, rochet, tunic, cowled robe, scapular, cloak, cope; leather or cord belt; stockings, shoes; staff with crucifix. Head shaven, beard, tonsure.

199 · 9th–16th century. **THE DOGES OF VENICE; MILITARY AND CEREMONIAL COSTUME**. Civilian, military officers, sword-bearer, parasol-bearer, cushion-bearer, trumpets. Example of Jewish merchant. Ducal cap, *corno*, *berretino*, skullcap, headbands. Mail-armour, pieces of steel, brassards, cuissarts, greaves, sollerets. Cloaks, fur collars; sleeves *à la ducale*; *dogalina*; *gavardina*. Brodequins, shoes.

200 · 8th century. **THE KING OF CASTILE; PRELATE, NOBLES, CRUSADERS, BOURGEOIS. WOMENSWEAR, RIDING COSTUME. ALMS PURSE; DOMESTIC OBJECTS**. Royal crown, hat with earpieces, hats; tiara of *cendal*, *barbuquejo*, *alcandora*, *xomordos*. Mail-armour, pieces of plate-armour; brassards, greaves; pike. Cloaks, *paile* (pallium); gimps, *cuerdas*; *esclavine*, *gonella*, fur-lined coat, *quezote*; *loba*, pair of robes, *cyclas*, secular amice, scarf, *faja*; hose, *zaraguellas*; hunting gloves, shoes. Hair hanging loose, *mancebas en cabellos*. Horse harness, *jaez*. Jugs, lamps, candlesticks, snuffer.

PLATE 198

PLATE 200

MIDDLE AGES:
MILITARY AND COURT COSTUME

The complete mail-armour of the time of Louis IX began to change only towards the end of the 13th century. The coat of iron mail had no lining; it was put on like a shirt over a body garment of leather or quilted cloth, front and back being identical. The *grand* or *blanc haubert* (hauberk) is the complete coat of armour that only knights were allowed to wear. It was all of mail: foot armour, a long tunic whose sleeves led directly into a gauntlet (with divided thumb but not fingers), and a hood or *camail* covering the head and surrounding the face. Over this was placed the healm, a large cylindrical helmet with flat timbre and immovable visor. A plate of iron had long been worn on the chest under the mail. After the death of Louis IX (1270), the coat of mail grew shorter. Plates of cuir-bouilli or wrought iron appeared on the legs and at the knee joint. Around 1340, armour changed radically.

During the first part of the 13th century, the sword, *the* arm of the nobility, grew heavier. The middle of the blade was reinforced on either side with a projecting crest and the point was formed by the gradual narrowing of the blade. Thus reinforced and sharpened, the sword could penetrate even a double coat of mail. Around 1346, it became lighter, thinner, narrower and sharper again. The appearance of the armoured knight added to the fear he naturally inspired. The short head of the combat lance, the *arestoel*, was made more for impact than for penetration (pl. 204). Lances were invariably broken at the first impact, and swords were drawn. The combat then consisted in blows with the sword-edge heavy enough to be felt through the mail and break the enemy's arm or shoulder, and more dangerous direct thrusts.

The rather skimpy civilian costume of the 14th century dates, in the north of France, from around 1340. It was worn in all Mediterranean towns from Barcelona to Genoa. The narrow, short camisole known as *jaquet* or *jaquette* replaced the long tunic, under which was worn the *pourpoint* or *gipon*, a sort of padded jerkin, opening at the front and sides. Pointed shoes, having been rejected throughout Europe, found refuge only in Poland; they now returned to the European courts as a novelty. The shortened shirt now became general among the nobility, while squires and pages began wearing parti-coloured hose, with one leg white, yellow or green, and the other black, blue or red. Even shoes might be of different colours. The garments shown in pl. 207 existed simultaneously in Italy, France and England.

The city-dweller's clothing was, as one can see, of very military style. The most characteristic item of clothing worn by women under Jean II and Charles V was the corset with side-opening, which English ladies had brought to France. The commercial and industrial bourgeoisie had its own sartorial conventions (pl. 209). The shepherd and journeyman peasant wore the *gonnel*, a little cloth tunic generally surmounted by a *carapoue* (pl. 209). For as long as workers dressed for their work, they preferred short clothes. Women of the people wore a veil and a gown whose folds when tucked up revealed the cotte. In the 14th century, great nobles (pl. 210) matched the colour of the fabrics they wore to those of their coat of arms. Scarlet mantle and vermilion robe were the mark of kings of old. Among the poor, *tiretaine* or *futaine* replaced expensive woollen clothes. Musicians then wore the same garments as the lower classes.

During the reign of Charles V (1364–1380), costume took on a new and different character (pls. 211–212). Mixed colours and parti-coloured trunk-hose were no longer fashionable. A more austere taste required greater severity in materials, and the result was greater unity. Fur was used in male and female costumes alike. The women of the time, though they were daringly *décolletées*, made sure that their undergarments remained out of sight. From the late 13th century on, soft felt hats were worn, with their rims tucked up to form a point at the front. Men wore their hair short and were mostly clean-shaven, though light moustaches and a fringe of beard beneath the chin were sometimes seen. Women avoided having their hair fall over neck and shoulders, and indeed over the forehead; the desired effect was a broad, high brow.

In the 14th century, luxury was not identified with sartorial splendour (pl. 214). The ideal was to show off a new costume for every new day. The simplicity of the costume in plate 215 is explained by the reforms on which Louis XI had insisted.

The tourney (pl. 219) was a combat between two teams of equal number; jousting involved one-to-one combat. Gunpowder had been discovered in the 13th century and was soon after used in cannons and bombards, which were known as artillery. It was only after the people began to take an active part in war that the use of firearms acquired a certain value (pl. 220).

201 · **MILITARY COSTUMES**. France, 11th–13th century. Warriors from the periods of Charlemagne, Hugues Capet, Philippe I and Louis IX. Leather, ring-mail and mail-armour. Standards, guidon. Helmet convex, ovoid; cylindrical, laced; plume. Norman nasal, chin-strap, rear peak, skullcap, mail hood, surcoat, *cotte à armer*, hauberk, *broigne, gambison*; bodice, tunic, hose, gloves, shields, *umbo*, guige. Cutting and thrusting swords; bronze handle, scabbard, cavalry baldric, belt; dagger, large knife or *miséricorde* (see pl. 213), mace, spear. (See these main items of offensive weaponry in the following plates, 202–210 inclusive.) Cloak, breeches, shoes. Pointed spurs.

202 · **MILITARY COSTUME**, France, 13th–14th century. Plate-armour. Iron and leather (see pl. 217). Arms from the 12th–15th century. Crusaders. Banneret, foot soldier; militia chief. Standards; the red cross, the white cross; harness. *Ouïes, aeillères*, timbre of helmet, baron's coronet, visor, plume, iron or Montauban headpiece, Bavarian, sallet, cervelière, basnet (see pl. 206), gorgerin or *gorgery*, large helmet, large haqueton, habergeon, brigantine, tasset, *cuiries*; paulter; rear-brace and vambrace; couter, cuish, genouillères, greaves, sollerets. (The defensive arms here comprising plate-armour are represented in pls. 203–206 and 217–220.) Emblazoned shields: *écus* with flowers and lions, glazed (see pls. 203 and 208). *Pavas* (pavise), *palevas*, or *talevas*; *paveschieurs* (foot soldiers, see pls. 217 and 220). *Rouelle* or *boce*, little round shield. Buckler, *parma*. Short sword, bow, dart, sling, battle-axe, Danish battle-axe, high spear, sword, guisarm or halberd. Fauchard, *faussard* or *faucil*, Flemish pike or *godendart, godendag*. Rowel spurs (see pls. 206 and 209). Pilgrim's staff, *bourdon*, and bag. Banners, gonfalon, pennons (*bachelier*). Standards. Parti-coloured hood. Ornamental costume. Saddle; cantle, saddle-tree; stirrup (see pls. 204–206).

203 · **ARMOUR OF KNIGHTS. NOBLEWOMEN**, France, 12th–14th century. The great hauberk or white hauberk, double mail *'de Chambly'*, scarf. The large sword, *coustel à plates, alenas, haussart, faussart*. Surcoat or fur-lined mantle. Furniture, the bed (see pls. 213, 223, 227, 231, 232, 241/242).

PLATE 201

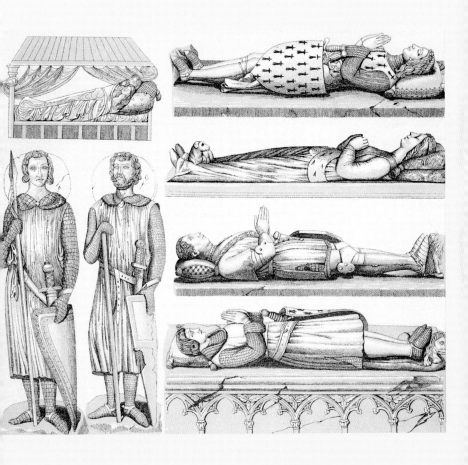

PLATE 203

317

204 · **MILITARY COSTUMES**, 13th century. Horseman charging. Ways of wielding the lance, the sword. Housing of horse (see pl. 205). The conical helmet, fan-shaped plume; *pansière*, back-plate. Combat lance, *arestoel*. Faucre or fewter. Riding dress.

205 · **CIVILIAN AND MILITARY COSTUMES**, 12th–15th century (see pl. 206).

206 · 14th century. **MEMBER OF THE NOBILITY WITH ROBE COURTE** (short robe of the high nobility). *Costume étriqué*. Plates of steel or *harnais blanc*. Litter. Hooded chaperon, hairpiece. *Rondeau* or *cloche* (see pl. 211), conical hat, feather. *Jaquet* or *jacquette*, embroidery, initials, half-sleeves, buttons, button-holes, doublet, *doublet or gipon*; *mouffles* (see pl. 211); belt; *cloche*; parti-coloured hose, *semelées*; cloth used for garments: *scarlet, yraigne*; garters, shoes, sollerets *à la poulaine* (see pls. 207–216). Women's garb: cotehardie (see pls. 211, 213, 214), *cotte pourfilée*, surcoat. Ornaments, necklaces. Hair loose and short; goatee. Crest, lambrequin (see pl. 219); steel brassards, canions. Daggers, *badelaire, bazelaire*.

207/208 · **FRENCH NOBILITY, HISTORICAL FIGURE; CIVILIAN AND MILITARY COSTUMES**, 12th–15th century. Royal attributes, *pallium*. Hennin, wimple-style veils (see pl. 211), circlet, *escoffion* (see pls. 213, 214). *Mantel d'honneur*, emblazoned and parti-coloured cotte. Escarcelle, *escar*.

PLATE 204

319

PLATE 206

PLATE 207

PLATE 208

323

209 · 13th–14th century. **NOBLES; CIVILIAN GARB; KNIGHTLY COSTUMES. HISTORICAL FIGURES. BOURGEOIS. PEASANTS** (see pls. 222 and 331); the player of the Provençal flute or *galoubet*. Labourer, *closier* or harvester, gardener, swineherd. Head ribbons: *chapelet, tressoir; chapel;* woman's veil. Chlamys, men's surcoat, *peliçon, corset-sangle, mahoîtres,* the under-robe, *gonne.* Short sayon, *gonnel;* mail hood, *carapoue; jupel,* trunk-hose, gaiters, *gamaches,* spatterdashes (see these same items of clothing in the following plates up to pl. 316 inclusive). Peasant woman's dress. Shepherd's scrip, short staff, *retorta;* cowherd's horn, club. Hair, beard. Agricultural work, farm labourers: *puotier, rogas, égossier, bassibier, pastour, pastourmajor, bouriagre, botier, trabotier, fournier, prayer, baylets.*

210 · France, 13th–15th century. **ROYAL AND DUCAL COSTUME. COURT, CITY AND WAR COSTUMES.** The sergeant-at-arms. Churchmen; lower classes. Musicians, *menestrandie.* Luth- and *dicorde*-player. Crown (see pls. 211, 212, 214, 216), circlet, chaperon, cornet *à la coquarde* or *en patte* (see pls. 212, 216), *chapel à bec* (see pls. 211, 216), *affiques.* Scarlet cape; silver-gilt (*vermeille*) robe, cloth of gold; mantle, fur, dalmatic, belt, overall, *bombarde* sleeves; ecclesiastical au-musse. Necklace in goldsmith-work, *pantacol* (see pl. 212). Silver mace. Sword, dagger (see pls. 211 and 212).

211 · **FRENCH NOBILITY.** *Armoyés* costumes. Furs. Doctor, 1364–1461 (see pl. 212). Cylindrical *chapels,* bonnet (see pls. 213, 215, 216), chaperon with cornet, veil, *mollequin* (cotton muslin); *surcoat ajusté* (men), with skirt, sleeves, *housse, cotelle;* tight boot, *heuse;* ornamental surcoat (women); *fenêtres d'enfer,* the elbow-pieces of the cotehardie (see pl. 213), plastron, garde-corps, blazoned skirt. Headdresses; braids, coiled hair, fringes, crispine. Belts, necklaces, *arrêts* worked in precious metals. Falconer with chaperon.

PLATE 209

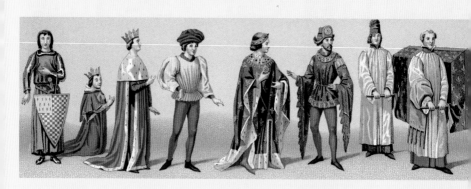

PLATE 211

327

212 · **HAIRSTYLES**: *bourrelet*, conical *chapels*, feathers. Royal mantle; lay aumusse, houppelande (see pl. 215), open sleeves (surcoat). **ORNAMENTATION FOR MEN**: necklaces, chains, little chains, coiled hair, pendants.

213 · France, 14th and 15th centuries (see pl. 214). **CHURCHMAN, ROYAL NOTARY, MINSTREL, MOUNTEBANK, TURNKEY, MESSENGER. FEMALE COSTUME. FURNITURE**. The women's chaperon (see pl. 215). Riding cotte, belt, *bourrelet articulé*, short bodice; foot-hose, hood, *peliçon*. Half-boots *à la poulaine*. The short spear of the infantryman. Chain purse, *escarcelle*.

214 · **SOVEREIGN ASSEMBLY**. Doctor. Women's costumes. Pointed *chapels, barrette, grand escoffion*, turban *escoffion*. Male hairstyles: long, curled hair. Furniture: form or *fourme* (see pl. 216), dais, lectern. Musical instruments.

215 · France, second half of the 15th century. **CIVILIAN COSTUMES. COURT SCENES. JURISTS**. Unrolled chaperon, wimple, *ceinture dorée*. Purse, hanging mirror.

216 · 14th–15th century. **INTERIOR OF A FEUDAL CASTLE**: the *salle de parement*. **FRENCH NOBILITY**. Servants. Furniture. Coach-building (see pl. 310). Riding clothes, jornade (see pl. 217). Dining table, bench with back, step, bench (*banquet*), tablecloth, *linge de haut lice*; serviettes, *touailles; sarrisinois* (Saracen) carpets. Exposed beams, paving. **CARTS OF HONOUR**: *karrâsche*, sweep-harness, *poële* or *mantel, ciel*. *Pilentum, rheda*, sledge or *claie*, roller, *petoritum, benna, capentum, chariot branlant*.

PLATE 212

PLATE 214

PLATE 216

217 · France. **MILITARY COSTUMES**, 1350–1460. Men-at-arms, foot soldiers, *pavescheur* (see pls. 219 and 220). Trappings of war: *cuiries*; plate-armour, partial and complete. Basnet with muzzle or beak; iron *chapels,* haneper, *avantail*; neck-plate; cornet, white cross (see pls. 218–220). *Mézail,* nasal, *bavière,* armet, great helmet, crest, plume, tuft, colletin, mailhood. *Épaulière,* fewter, ailettes, spalier, brassards, cannions, couters, gauntlets. Habergeon in mail, *corselet* or jerkin, *jacque* or *jacquette,* cuirass, tasset, pansière, taces, pleated skirt. Cuisses, cushes, genouillères, greaves, sollerets, *ergot du diable,* spurs. Shield (*écu*), guige. Surcoat, tabard, *manteline, huque, paletot.* Short sword (*perce-mailles*); *chevauchés* cross-guards; sword; dagger or *miséricorde*; sword-chain, baldric, sword-belt; belt worked in precious metal. Mace. High lance, vamplate, *grappe de billette, glaivelot,* partisan, vouge, dart. (For most of these arms, see also the following plates, 218–220 inclusive.)

PLATE 217

335

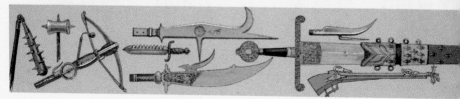

218 · France. **MILITARY COSTUME**, 1439–1450. Complete iron armour. Regulation company, their organisation; *lances fournies*, page, *enfant d'honneur*, valet. *Franksarchers*. Herald-at-arms, trumpet-player, arbalester; arms, standards. Under-gorgerin, brigandine, habergeon, rear-brace, couter, vambrace, leg armour, *harnas*. Connétable's sword. Arrows: *sagettes, quarrel, quarriau, boujon*; bow, quiver, pack. Wind-up crossbow, *à tour* or *à moufle* (see pl. 219), *à cric*. Flail, maul or *plommée*, guisarme or *fauchou*, halberds (see pl. 220). Musket. Haqueton, surcoat.

219 · **WARRIOR, TILTING AND TOURNEY COSTUMES**. France, 15th century. *Adoubement* (equipment) of jouster. High crests. Foot soldier, arbalester, knight. *Cotte de fer*, coat of mail. Joust (*jouste* or *jouxte*) by battles, banners, tourneys or *tupinets, trespignées, combats à la foule*; *recommandation*. Helmet *à tête de crapaud* (toad's-head), armorial bearings, baron's coronet (*tortil*), lambrequin, crest; *chapel de heaume*; basnet or *capeline*, with grid-visor (*treillissée*); cuirass, articulated plate-armour, *faldes* or *fauldes*, fewter; corsage, tasset, cush *en brigandines*; *manche honorable*, half-sleeves; skirt and cape of mail; *clavain*, buckler; pavis or *pavais pavard* (see pl. 220). *Courtesy arms*, blunted sword (*rabattu*). Maul, mace, large dagger, T-shaped cross-guard, *quillons à potences*; lance, three-toothed blade, halberd, *corsèque, roncone. Sabots-étriers*; saddle, *hourd*.

PLATE 220

220 · France, 15th century. **ARTILLERY. VARIOUS ARMS. THE KING'S BODY-GUARD, LARGE AND SMALL** (see pl. 225); lancers, archers, *crenequiniers*, arbalesters; *coustillier, guisarmier* or *satellite*. Large canon, bombard, *veuglaire, crapeaudeau*, couleuvres, culverins, serpentines; round shot, flint, bullets, *plommées* or *plombées*. Carriage; *charpenterie, flasque, tourillon, manteau*; great pavis; hand culverin. *Épées bastardes. Crénequin* or *cranequin*, arbalest *à pié, à moulinet, cry, baudré* or *baudrées; traits, quarreaux, viretons, raillons*, the quiver, *carcas*; crowbar; *empané*, pack. Vouge (*vougier*). *Coustel à plates, coustelière. Hache de Créqui, d'arçon* (double-edged), *couteau de brèche*. Cornets, escutcheons, the golden sun. *Francs-taupins*.

221 · 15th century. **TOURNEYS**, taking of the oath, entering the lists. **CIVILIAN COSTUMES**. Gentlemen; falconer (reign of Charles VIII). *Défendant, appelant*, heralds. Skullcap, *bicoquet* (see pls. 246–251), trailing robes, golden chains. Harness: *housing (housse)*, chamfron, headpiece, bosses.

222 · 15th century. **KNIGHTLY COSTUME. PEASANTS,** *pitaults*. Banneret, *seigneur-chef*, herald-at-arms, page. Labourer, sower, harvester, grave-digger. Golden armour: *hallecret*, flancards, genouillière-guards. Tilting horse, *grand-cheval. Capels*, skullcaps; livery, quartered tabard. Cotte, mantle (*sagulum*), *gonnel* (apron), trunk- and leg-hose, aglets, *heuses à la poulaine*, gaiters or *gamaches*, greaves, shoes.

223 · 15th century. **KNIGHT OF THE TOISON D'OR. CIVILIAN COSTUMES.** Interior. Furniture.

PLATE 221

341

1450-1500.

PLATE 223

343

14TH–16TH CENTURY: JEWELLERY, HEADDRESSES AND FURNITURE

From the 13th century and throughout the 14th century, the luxury of jewellery was added to the splendour of clothing. Enamel was now too affordable to find favour with the nobility. Diamonds soon made an appearance, ornamented silver buttons were used, and pearls stood in for the clasps of the time of Charles VI. Combs (pl. 225) were treated like jewellery, and had their own cases; these were veritable jewel-cases, whose leather trimmings bore stamped and sometimes gilded decorations. The alms purse (*aumônière*), *escarcelle*, *gibecière* or *bourse* contained silver, jewels, remedies and tablets, and formed an indispensable addition to the everyday clothing of both sexes during the Middle Ages. Everyone wore one (pl. 226) from peasants and messengers to pilgrims, whose *gibecière* contained not only utensils but the day's food. *Boursettes* were reduced models of the *escarcelle*. Both were attached to the belt. Some were also made to contain relics. This little bag remained in use throughout the 16th century and even later in bourgeois circles. As time passed, *aumônières* acquired visible hasps made of iron, silver or gold. Care was taken with their decoration, and their materials and workmanship made them valuable.

The *chaire*, *chaise*, *chaière*, *forme* or *fourme* was a seat with back and arms (pl. 227). Until the 13th century, square chairs often lacked a raised back. Around this time, chairs tended to become wider in order to contain the new and more extensive garments worn. Among the objects that decorated the bedroom in the 15th and 16th centuries was an image of the Virgin or the Lord (pl. 228). This image was shut away either in a cupboard or in one of the little cabinets that could be hung on a wall or raised on a wall-mounted plinth. The cupboard-safe (*armoire coffre-fort*, pl. 229) comprised two cupboards, one on top of the other, each with their own ironwork fittings and key, and each with one or two door-leaves. The *crédence* or *credenza* was a little buffet (pl. 230) consisting of a cupboard with lockable doors that sometimes enclosed drawers and other internal arrangements that were not lockable; it was used to hold vases and costly utensils, as well as spices and preserves. Initially a very simple item, the luxury that began to prevail during the reign of Charles V came to include the materials of which the credenza was made.

The interior seen in plate 232 is borrowed from a Flemish painting in the Musée du Louvre. The interior walls are bare. Beams are no longer visible in the ceiling, which has been planked over and battened. The tiling is of enamelled brick. The furniture in this bourgeois room remains very rustic. The bed has a full-length canopy; the *queues* (curtains) and covers hang down to the ground. Bolsters came in only in the 15th century. The three other pieces of furniture are the credenza, the chair placed at the bed-head, and the bench at the hearth.

Starting in the late 13th century, customs had become more refined and feudal over-lords no longer tolerated a life lived in common with their men. Separate bedrooms were created. Most gentlemen, having been to the Orient, returned with a taste for splendour in the home. They wanted better-heated, better-sealed rooms and walls decorated with panelling or tapestries. On the floor were placed woollen rugs or furs, which were often perfumed.

By the 14th century, all these luxuries had taken their place in bourgeois life. The architecture of the room represented in plate 235 dates from the French Renaissance, when straight lines and right angles were restored to supremacy.

PLATE 224

347

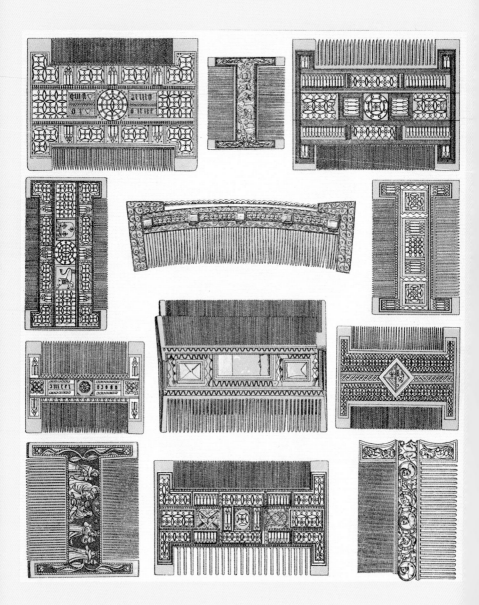

PLATE 226

349

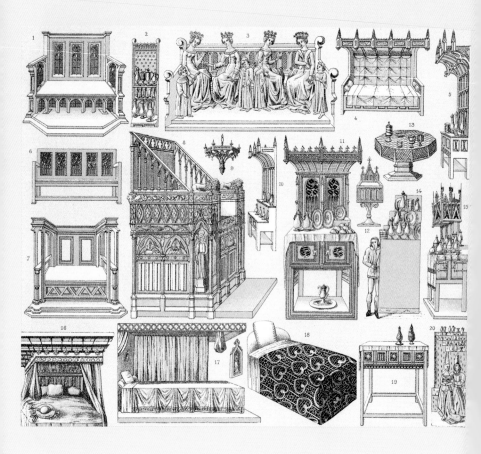

PLATE 228

224 · 14th–15th century. **JEWELLERY, WORKED PRECIOUS METAL D'ACCOUTREMENT**. Belt (precious metals worked *en fenestrage*), fasteners, buckles, clasps, morse for a cape, broaches, pendants, *affiques, enseignes*, reliquary, necklace chains, ring, *escarcelle* mounting.

225 · 6th, 7th, 15th and 16th centuries. **OBJECTS IN GENERAL USE**. Toiletries: combs made of bone, box-wood, ivory, with decorations in silver and precious stones.

226 · 15th–16th century. **ESCARCELLES, PURSE. ITALIAN HAIRSTYLES.** Small purse *à cul de vilain, mystère, demi-ceint, épinglier*, knife, scissors case, pomander; aromatic chaplets.

227 · FURNITURE, 14th and 15th centuries. Royal bed, *poêle à gouttières, couvertoir*; bourgeois beds (see pls. 231, 232). Seats with arms and backs, *chaise*, professor's chair, *chaière, form, fourme*. Seats of honour: episcopal throne; family bench, bench with dais, *confrérie* bench; *banquier, couettes* or *quarreaux* (cushions). Sideboards, tables, chandelier.

228 · HOUSEHOLD OBJECTS, 14th, 15th, 16th centuries. Images with shutters; *ymagiers*; tabernacle, diptych, lectern.

229 · 15th century. **LUXURY FURNITURE**. Cupboards, safes, *sacrarium*, credenzas (see pl. 230).

230 · 15th century. **CREDENZAS** with and without back; chest.

231 · France (Rhine basin) and Flanders, 15th–16th century. **INTERIOR; FURNITURE, HOUSEHOLD FURNITURE, UTENSILS**; bedroom (see pl. 232), bed, valances, bolster, pillow, bedside rug. Dresser, *touaille*, prie-Dieu. Tiling. Pendant clock, its bell, *nolette. Adossé* altar; altar-cloth, *doublier*, candleholders, *mestiers*; reliquary, *custode*. Chest (*arche*): flacons, ewers, pitchers, *platelets*, porringers. Chair without back, throne, throne with dais *seigneurial*; folding chairs in metal and wood; *sièges d'honneur*, armchair, *faudesteuil, fadesteuil, faudestuef, faudestuel*; cradle, *bers*. Chafing dish, medallion, casket, key, hanging mirror, ring-case.

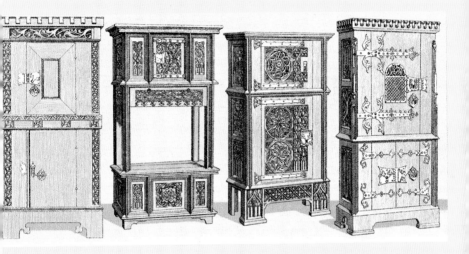

PLATE 229

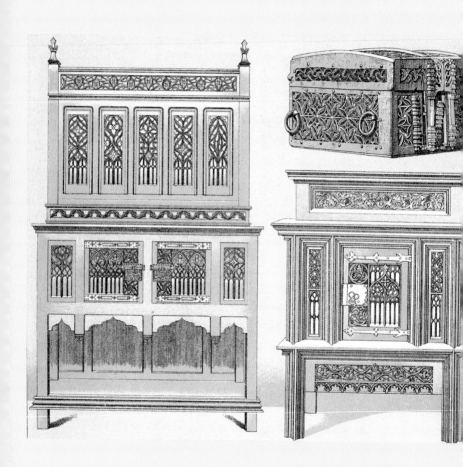

PLATE 23(

PLATE 231

232 · Flemish interior, 15th century. **BEDROOM**: bed on platform, *couchette, pavillons, quete couvertoirs*, canopy, bolster. *Signet* (medallion). Hearth bench, cushions, chair, credenza. *Dinanderie* brass ware: ewer, chandelier. Mantelpiece, hood, iron bracket, screen; windows: mullions, glass internal shutters, recess.

233 · 15th–16th century. **FURNITURE. INTERNAL DOOR**, bolt, door-knocker Choir bench; marriage chest, casket.

234 · **INTERNAL ARCHITECTURE**, 14th, 15th, 16th centuries. The great hall. Exposed beams.

235 · **INTERIOR OF FRENCH HOUSE**, 15th century. Fireplace (see pl. 236): mullions, casement window, shutters; use of glass; wood-panelling, paintings, ceiling, beams, exposed joists, their decoration.

236 · **DECORATION OF FIREPLACES**, 13th, 14th, 16th centuries.

PLATE 232

PLATE 233

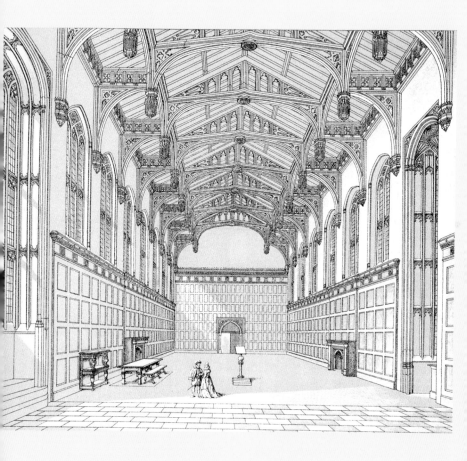

PLATE 234

PLATE 235

PLATE 236

15TH–17TH CENTURY: MALE AND FEMALE COSTUME

The 15th century was the epoch of extreme luxury, which reached a culmination in the patrician class of Venice. Most of the examples presented in plates 238 and 241 242 are contemporary with this magnificence. Philippe de Comines says that at the time of his visit to Venice, the city possessed thirty thousand gondolas. The great epoch of gondola was also that of the galley, so that the poor of the city must almost all have been serving the city as galley-oarsmen or gondoliers. The greatest variety of costume was exhibited by the gondoliers in the service of nobles or the family of the Doge (pl. 239). The others were either *Nicolotti*, who wore sombre colours, or *Castellani*, who wore red. Gondolas in Venice became such *de luxe* objects that a law was passed prohibiting any but the Doge and foreign ambassadors having a vessel constructed to a more elegant or decorative design than the model prescribed. The uniform black paint of gondolas dates from this sumptuary law.

The Italians never adopted the Gothic style, and had always maintained certain traditions of Roman art; with the aid of Vitruvius's recently discovered manuscripts, they returned to these traditions with notable and evident satisfaction. Architecture immediately turned toward the slender, simple forms of pagan antiquity (pl. 240). Life was easier, trust was greater, and houses no longer needed to be defensible in case of attack.

This state of affairs was contemporary with the prosperity of Tuscany, and dates from the late 14th century in particular. The trend was toward a certain simplicity. The greatest citizens could and did walk the streets accompanied by their wives and daughters without compromising their dignity. Meals were sober, clothing simple, modest and always of the same shape and colour; neither colour nor embroidery distinguished it. In this period, women's hair was always blonde, whether by nature or artifice (pl. 243). It was held in place by ribbons of velvet garnished with pearls, by a muslin veil falling on the shoulders, or a by a *fazzuolo*, the bridal veil. Women's gowns of black velvet, of simple, graceful cut, trimmed with vertical bands of fur, and with gold embroidery ornamenting neck and cuffs, were a fashion that survived until the 16th century.

French women looked hard and long at Italian fashions, as we can see from plate 244. In France, for costume as for everything else, the Middle Ages died in the person of Louis XI. Now such vast sums of money flowed through merchants' shops, and such extravagance was shown by the leaders of fashion — the *fringants, freluquets* and *brayards* — that in 1485 the États généraux requested the king to regulate his people's sartorial habits. But fourteen or fifteen years later, when Louis XII came to the throne, such sumptuary laws were forgotten. Displays of jewellery had restarted when Charles VIII took the throne.

Masculine fashions were renewed much more quickly than feminine ones. Replacing tight, thick mannered jackets, methodically slashed and thoroughly inflexible, Italian-style clothes came into fashion; their cut was appreciated, as was the slightly theatrical neglect with which they were worn. This affectation of neglect resulted in the *débraillé* style. Around 1505, all men wore their hair long and topped it with a fashionable hat. Among the beautiful clothes depicted in plates 249–250, we find the surcoat, *the* gown for women with pretensions to elegance.

237 · **POPULAR COSTUMES**, 16th century. Army baggage train: valets, servants, sutlers, pimps and prostitutes.

238 · 14th, 15th, 16th centuries. **CIVILIAN AND MILITARY COSTUMES**; Venetian gentlemen; *bragard; condottiere;* livery officers, pages. Chaperon, hat, chin-strap, coiffe, bonnet, *berretino,* toque, reticulated headdress, hood; silk shirt, *gavardina;* surcoat, *doublet-fringant,* slashings; hoqueton, belt, sword-belt, wallet; mantles, *zimarra, mantellino;* hose, cod-piece; shoes, boots. Bracelets. Hair *tiré,* waved. Sword, sword-knot, pendant, dagger (see pl. 239).

239 · **VENETIAN GONDOLIERS** (see pl. 289). **CASTELLANI, NICOLOTTI**: ordinary wear, ceremonial wear, livery, 15th and 16th centuries. **PAGES, RIDING COSTUMES, DWARVES, COURT JESTERS**, 14th–18th century. Bonnets, pointed chin-straps, slashed doublets, leather cuirass.

PLATE 237

PLATE 238

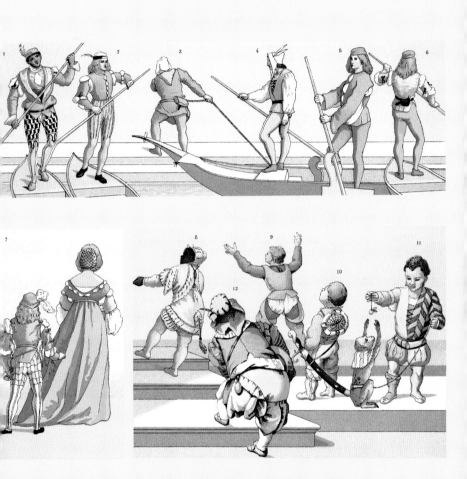

PLATE 239

240 · 14th 15th century. Tuscany. Early Renaissance. **TYPES OF URBAN HOUSE**
Porticos, *loggia, balcone, parapetto*, main building.

241 / 242 · 15th century. **CIVILIAN AND RELIGIOUS COSTUMES**. Lordly wed
ding: gentlemen, ladies, musicians; Dominican. Savonarola's cell. Large bed with dais. Doctors.

243 · 14th, 15th, 16th centuries. **FEMALE COSTUMES**. Noble women, young ladies, their
serving women; Dutch style. Dyed hair, *filo d'oro*. Wimple, veil, married woman's veil, *fazzuolo*, es
coffion, *balzo* (see pls. 244, 252), hood. Chemisette, skirt, robe, *les corps*, mantles, furs, embroidery
Diadems, plaques, head ribbons, *ferronnière*, *tremoli*, broaches, necklaces, belt worked in precious
metals. Hair loose, braided; hairnet.

244 · Early 16th century. **WOMEN'S COSTUMES**. Venetian and Neapolitan women
Noble and rustic. Straw hat, *barreto, capitium, capulatus, tiara-recta (mitra velatus)*; chemise, casaquin
brassards, *manec*, belt (*ventrale*), apron, skirt, mantles, *lacerna, parva casa*, alms purse, pattens. Hair
sheath; necklaces, bracelets.

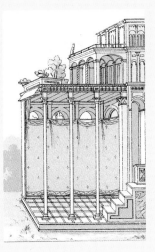

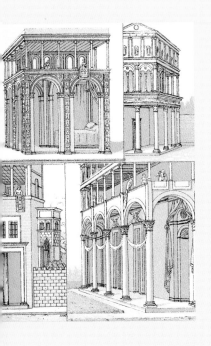

PLATE 240

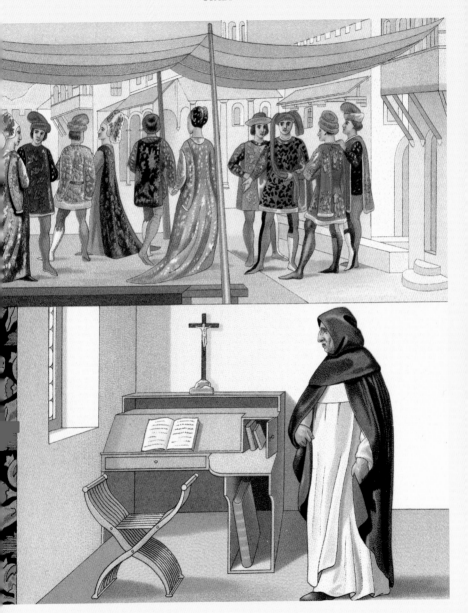

PLATE 243

PLATE 244

373

245 · 15th–16th century. **INTERIOR OF MANOR HOUSE,** great hall. Masters, household servants. Furniture, utensils. **WASHING,** robe without belt.

246 · 15th–16th century. **CIVILIAN COSTUMES,** 1485–1510 (see pls. 247–251). **WOMEN AND MEN'S HEADDRESSES.** Queen, princesses. Torch-bearer. Toque, *bicoquet, mortier, enseigne* or *bague,* coiffe, *templette,* women's chaperon, *escoffion à cornes;* royal crown. Chemise, gorget *de doulx filet,* cotte, surcoat, over-robe; belt worked in precious metals, or *en cordelière, pantenôtres, demi-ceint,* knife, purse, slippers. *Jacquette,* doublet, mantle, descending collar (*dévalant*), pelisse, furs, tabard; trunk- and leg-hose, *pattés* shoes. Necklaces, ring or diamond. Men's hairstyles.

247/248 · Late 15th century. **CIVILIAN COSTUMES.** Hat and bonnet: hat with four *brayettes,* ribbon ties; plumes, jewels; the great *escoffion,* reticulated headdress; nobiliary crowns. Robes of ceremony, nuptial mantle, shoes, *becs de canes.* Woman playing a dulcimer. Oliphant.

PLATE 245

375

PLATE 246

PLATE 247

377

PLATE 248

PLATE 249

PLATE 250

PLATE 251

249 / 250 · 15th–16th century. LORDS, LADIES; FLEMISH HEADDRESSES. ROBES. luxury mantles, sleeves *à la grand'garre.*

251 · 15th–16th century. ITEMS OF WOMEN'S COSTUME: mourning costume; *barbette, couvre-chef.* Men's *tunicelle.* Belts and necklaces with pom-poms.

252 · 16th century. WOMEN'S COSTUME. Marriageable young woman. Headdresses. Golden hairnets, reticulated headdresses, *ferronnière; bourrelet* (see *balzo*, pls. 243 and 244), skullcap, headband, *coquilles* or *cales.* Wimple, corsage, bouffant sleeves, with slashing, long robe, *damasquette* embroidery; Roman-style tunic.

PLATE 252

383

16TH CENTURY: MILITARY COSTUME

Plate 253 shows an infantryman who holds a *trait à poudre* or culverin, an arm then considered unchivalrous. He wears the colours and coat of arms of the city of Beauvais. From this point on, sword pommels grow increasingly long; the grooves in the blade lightened and strengthened it. Till the late 15th century, artillery was used almost exclusively to break down fortress walls. Like his predecessors, François I had an artillery capacity formidable for the time. At the battle of Marignan (1515), it comprised sixty-four pieces, a number then considered prodigious. The various calibres were referred to under the names cannon, double cannon, basilisk, bastard, serpentine, culverin, falcon, *passe-volant*, *spirole*, and so on. To serve these guns, there were ordinary and extraordinary gunners. The company of the *Cent-Suisses de la garde du roi* (pl. 256) was founded by Charles VIII in 1496. Their job was to march before the king, halberds in hand. Only under Henri II did they adopt their black-and-white livery. Louis XII has the merit of first convincing grandees to join the infantry. In 1507, Louis XII formed the *bandes du Piémont*. The earliest companies in the army of François I were made up of this infantry, and reinforced with auxiliary troops such as the Suisses, the *lansquenets* and certain Italian corps. No one had yet had the idea of systematising uniform. In certain cases, the colour of clothing was the only distinctive mark of the various corps. The Suisses were already serving France under the reign of Charles VIII and formed a majority of the infantry. Louis XII had up to sixteen thousand in his army. As regards cavalry (pl. 257), the early years of the wars of religion were marked by certain changes in the equipment of *compagnies d'ordonnance*, such as the widespread adoption of pistols (*pistoyers, pistoliers, pistolets*), the phasing out of leg armour for the rider, and of bards of leather or metal for the horse. The organisation of infantry into regiments dates from the reign of Charles IX. The first French musketeers appeared only in 1572. Muskets differed only in calibre and ammunition. One of the two horsemen who appear in plate 260 is from the early, the other from the late 16th century. The first is Spanish, the Emperor Charles V, the second German, the Elector Christian II. The total weight of the Emperor's armour was 86.94 kilograms. The complete armour of the man on horseback (pl. 261), from his iron *sollerets* to the closed *armet*, was not often seen on the battlefields of the 16th century till around 1570. The helmet was an *armet* surmounted by a continuous crest and equipped with a chin-strap. The *tassets* or tasse were often replaced by a single bell-shaped piece of armour called the *tonnelet*. This was covered with a cloth skirt with thick, round folds. The corselet, whose convexity reached an apex at the centre of the chest, reflected in the point-shaped waist, belongs to this period; it was to become the cuirass of the French gendarmerie under Henri. By the end of the 15th century, it was understood throughout Europe that to be effective, cavalry had to be light. And so, piece by piece, beginning with the armour of his horse, the man-at-arms gradually began to shed the weight of metal that had hampered his movements.

253 · 15th–16th century. MILITARY COSTUME, CEREMONIAL AND EVERY-DAY. War-helmets, tilting helmets. Grooved armour. Knights, culveriner; feudal lord; mounted archer (reigns of Charles VII, Louis XI, Louis XII, François I). *Cabasset,* ear-pieces, armet, colletin, mesail, reinforcing pieces; *haute pièce*; plumes; sallets, tilting sallets, concertina visor, gorgerin, under-gorgerin, chin-strap, hat, headband worked in precious metals. Cuirass, *gambison,* blazons, mail *jacquette,* brigantine *hucque*; plates, paulters, pauldron, small plates, passe-garde, couters, brassards, gloves; sollerets *en bec de cane, en pied d'ours*; shoes in iron mail or leather; rowelled spur. Surcoat, pelerine, skirt. Sword, pommel, hilt-guard, grooved blade, scabbard, dagger, *coustel à plates,* belt, club, mace, *pointe,* halberd, maul. Bow, quiver, feathered arrows. *Trait à poudre* or culverin. Bag, primer (*amorçoir*) (see pls. 254–263).

254 · 15th–16th century. MILITARY COSTUMES. CEREMONIAL WEAR. GEN-TLEMEN, men-at-arms, artillery officer, fuse-bearer; combatants, infantryman, Swiss soldier. Knightly armour. Details of equipment, flag. Armet, burgonet, morion, skullcap, hat, feathers. Cuirass, taces, braconnière, coat of mail, corselet, leather doublet; bellied plastron (*à la poulaine*), frilled ruff. Riding haqueton, doublet, slit sleeves, short sleeves. Trunk-hose, cod-piece. Gauntlets, shoes, boots. Double-handed sword (see pl. 256), *la main gauche, poignard-chargette.* High lance and vamplate. Rondache and guige. Furse-carrier and its branches, *serpentins.* Primer, *flasque.*

PLATE 253

387

PLATE 255

389

PLATE 257

255 · 16th century. **MILITARY COSTUMES**. Reigns of Louis XII, François I, 1507–1520 (see pl. 256). The major and minor bodyguard of the king. *Crénequiniers*, gentlemen with halberds. Scottish archers, their accoutrement. *Estradiots*, artillery (see pl. 257). Gunners, *bastardeurs*, gunner's aids, *boute-feux*. Swiss artillery guards, *gardiens de pièces*. Toque, plumes, hat *à l'albanaise*, sayon, hoqueton, cassock, robe, hose, half-boots. Halberds, lances, arbalest. Calibres, reinforced or double cannons; arquebus *à crochets* (Louis XII), basilisks, *bastardes*, serpentines, culverins, falcons, dummy guns, *spirales* (François I).

256 · 16th century. **KING'S GUARD. THE CENT-SUISSES, THE ÉCOSSAIS**, their livery. **FRENCH INFANTRY, FOREIGN INFANTRY**, *bandes*, Suisses, lansquenets, legionnaires, pikemen, arquebusiers, *morionnés*, halbardiers, swordsmen (see pl. 257), *tambourin*. 1520–1555.

257 · 16th century. Reigns of Henri II, Charles IX, 1559–1572. **PIKEMEN, ARQUEBUSIERS, LANSQUENETS, JOUEUR D'ESPÉE, MUSKETEER, DRUMMER, FIFER, LACKEY, SWISS ARTILLERY MAN**. Headgear, *morion*, armet, regulation cassock; scarves, the white cross; paulter *à preuve*. Arquebus, musket, bandoleer, resting fork, *fourquine*. Calibres of artillery: *canon renforcé*, large culverin, *bâtarde*, *moyenne*, falcon, falconet, hackbut *à croc*.

258 · 16th century. **EQUESTRIAN ARMOUR; ARMS**. Swords: *colada*, handle of espadon. Spur.

PLATE 258

PLATE 259

PLATE 260

259 · 16th century. **HALF-SUITS OF ARMOUR, OR CORSELETS; BURGON-ETS.**

260 · 16th century. **OFFENSIVE AND DEFENSIVE ARMS. HORSEMEN.** Barded horse. Armet, view, nasal; cuirass, pansière, back-plate, tasset, fewter, pauldrons, passe-garde or *garde-collet*, brassards, cannions, couter, gauntlets, cushes, genouillère; greaves, *pédieux* or sollerets, spurs; stirrup, lance-rest. Sword, cross-guards, halberd-pistol, sword, dirk and dagger decorations. Horse harness: headstall, neck- and chest-bards, flancard, ear-pieces, *terminale*.

261 · 16th century. **CHASED ARMOUR** (see pls. 262 and 263). **ORNAMENTA-TION OF WAR-HORSE.** Corselet *en pointe, tonnelet; garde-assielle* or *bas de saie.* Stirrups, *arcade à fenêtres.* Wheel-lock pistol. Headstall or chamfran, forehead band and ornament, tail ornament.

262 · 16th century. **ARMOUR: OFFENSIVE WEAPONS, CUTTING AND THRUSTING WEAPONS AND FIREARMS.** Armet, grid-visor, burgonet, skull-cap, ear-pieces; gorgerin or *gorgery*, corselet, pauldrons. Mace. Sword handles: thrusting, large thrusting and double-sided. Sword with double guard, *pas d'âne.* Dirk, *langue de boeuf, bastardeau.* Wheel-lock pistols.

263 · 16th century. **VARIOUS ARMS.** Morion. Handles of rapier, flamberg, dirk; without dagger, *indague.* Knife; powder-horn; powder-flask; hunting case.

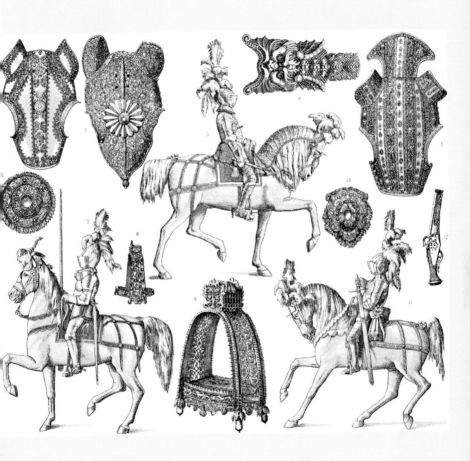

PLATE 261

PLATE 262

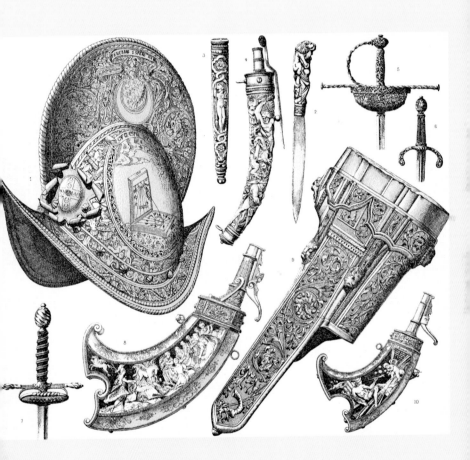

PLATE 263

16ᵀᴴ–17ᵀᴴ Century:
Male and Female Costume, Furniture

The most striking feature of women's clothing for most of the 16th century was the compression of the bust to obtain a slender waist (pl. 264). Clothing thus came to consist in two convexities divided by the belt. The lower part of the gown was at this period a bell shape whose fringe reached the ground. This was not yet the boned corset as worn in the reign of Henri III. In plate 265, we note the reappearance of shoulder-pieces known as épaulettes, which gave a new outline to the dress of the second half of the 16th century. We also see the *collet monté* or Medici collar attributed to Catherine de Médicis, and the increasing resemblance of the bodice to the male doublet. Headdresses were becoming less voluminous under the influence of Italian taste. The Italian women in this plate (265) are all raised to new heights by their platform soles. Since Charles VII, French love of things Italian had 'denationalised' French costume. Only after the arrival of the Florentine Catherine de Médicis did matters change. The future queen showed an independence in the application of Italian fashions that French ladies were quick to imitate. The costume worn by Catherine de Médicis on plate 266 is very different from the Italian. A gown whose bodice and cotte are of the same white fabric is worn under a second gown of redingote form. This was the period when French women earned their sovereignty in European fashion. The costumes of the great ladies (pl. 267), which set the fashions, differed from those of the wealthy only by their splendour. The strange fashion for farthingales (*vertugadins*), borrowed from Spain, took root in France; gowns swelled until they were between eight and ten foot in circumference. Various kinds of court-wear can be seen in plate 268. Luxury in fabrics was now compounded by that of trimmings, which could be so complicated that workmanship could add two- or threefold to the cost of the raw materials. Passementerie was now a naturalised French art, and new effects were discovered. Gold and silver were braided into *guipures* and lace, or woven into *crépés* of incomparable lightness.

No notable changes occurred in costume till around 1470. For men and women, it remained close-fitting on the upper body from chin to waist, and more or less tight for the arms. The upper part of the sleeve was decorated with cut-out épaulettes, stiffened with baleens or brass wire. Plate 270 shows the sartorial taste of the time in Germany, a taste most clearly revealed in the shortening of the upper garment. These over-garments are a clear sign of the proximity of the France of Henri III and of Spanish influence. The cone-shaped bodice with long point (pl. 273) went out of fashion towards the end of the reign of Henri III, while the upper part of the sleeve swelled out to become almost as voluminous as the bodice itself. Gloves, worn night and day, were fringed, slashed (*chiquetés*), cut and invariably perfumed.

Henri II had worn black and white with gold piping. Since his times, Lutherans affected sombre colours. Catholics, unwilling to cede a monopoly of austerity, also took up severe colours (pl. 273). For Henri III, black was the best colour to bring out the pale face so fashionable in France at the time. Make-up at the time was white-lead; the king used a great deal. The royal army, and the infantry in particular, was then in a state of disorder which the decrees of 1574, 1579 and 1584 attempted vainly to redress (pl. 275). These decrees allowed only company leaders to wear cloth of gold and silver or silk on silk. Bright colours were considered legitimate; eight or ten colours might be worn simultaneously.

The display of embroidery counted for a good deal in the development of the tight-fitting female costume of the second half of the 16ᵗʰ century. The collarette, or ruff (it was so called because it resembled a calf's ruffle) grew steadily, as can be seen in plates 276 and 277. Not only did it grow in diameter till it equalled the mill-wheel, but its layers — three, four or five storeys — began to hide the shoulders and flow over the chest, thus distorting the human form. With the ruff stiffening the neck, the *corps piqué* or baleened camisole, the curve of the skirt extending backward, the long robe entirely hiding the foot so as to disguise the use of platform soles, and the skirt supported so as to allow the petticoat to be displayed (noble and bourgeois woman observed this requirement in ceremonial dress), a woman had to learn an entirely new art of deportment. The culmination of these fashion extremes occurred around 1575; at this date ruffs attained their largest dimensions. The ruff was then replaced by the standing fan-shaped collar, which rose from the neck of the gown as though folded up. Cuffs were in the form of small ruffs. Towards the end of the 16ᵗʰ century, western European costume was tending toward unity, as we see in plate 280. The figures in plate 283 represent the procession of La Ligue in Paris in 1590, when Henri IV was battling the Ligue for possession of Paris. Continuous strife and poverty had an effect on costume. Luxury was all but outlawed in Paris. The wealthy gave up sartorial pomp and circumstance. During the 15ᵗʰ century, ecclesiastical vestments took on a more or less definitive form, while modifying the style and cut of certain items (pl. 284). Thus the alb lost its coloured ornaments and was extended down to the feet. The chasuble was now increasingly cut away at the armhole, rounded at the base, and was ornamented with rich orfrays (embroidered bands). Cardinals were dressed from head to foot in red from the moment when Boniface VIII imposed this colour. In Germany (pl. 285), the bourgeoisie for the most part remained faithful to comfortable, wide-fitting and uncomplicated clothes in solid and inconspicuous fabrics. Among the well-dressed, on the other hand, there was an affected tendency to follow exotic fashions.

16TH–17TH Century: Male and Female Costume, Furniture

The bed took on its definitive form in or around the 14th century. In the 15th century, trimmings were increasingly luxurious, and beds began to assume quite considerable proportions. The influence of the Fontainebleau school was strongly felt in the decoration of furniture in France, as we see in plates 290–295. Plate 299 shows an English baronial manor of the 16th century. The ornaments on the ceiling vault are not unlike the curvilinear forms of Celtic art. The walls are decorated in Italian style, which continued in favour during the 16th and early decades of the 17th century; it was dubbed Elizabethan and follows on from the remarkable Tudor style that first appeared around 1509. The main halls of all English castles had minstrel galleries of the kind shown in plate 300. Musicians, women and strangers took their places in the gallery. Plate 304 shows two French examples of the shelved cupboard used for storing crockery and table linen; they were called *buffets*, and belonged in the dining room. The cupboard or *cabinet* was a buffet with several drawers (*layettes*). These two examples, like the pieces in plate 305, show how the taste for carved wooden furniture had remained constant in France during the 16th and early 17th centuries. Plate 315 shows chairs in the Flemish style, which became known as *ameublement français* or 'French furniture'. These are in solid wood. The use of stamped leather and gilded reliefs in the Spanish style is often found in chairs and armchairs. Under Henri II, ebony became the most sought-after wood for furniture, as the furniture and objects of everyday use in plate 316 testify.

PLATE 265

405

PLATE 267

407

264 · LADIES OF THE FRENCH NOBILITY; HISTORICAL FIGURES, 1520–1550. **ITALIAN LADIES**, end of 16th century; young damsel, married woman, merchant's wife, widow (see pl. 265). Collarettes, ruffs, cuffs; widow's veil; basquine, short sleeve or *tippet*; farthingale, *vertugale, vertugade, vertugadin*; cotte, surcoat. Crown, comb, necklaces, chains, belt, *contenances*, chaplet, mirror, *poste*. Feather fan. Hair, hair-dyeing, golden colour (see for these details of costume pls. 265, 266).

265 · 16th century. **WOMENSWEAR; HISTORICAL FIGURES** (France, England, Italy). Chaperon; sleeves *à rebras*, épaulettes.

266 · 16th century. **WOMENSWEAR**. Gala attire, outdoor wear. **HISTORICAL FIGURES**: artisans, pikemen, musketeer, infantry captain. Chaperon *à la française, templettes*, hat *à l'espagnole*, choker, crimped and pleated ruffs; shirt and surcoat sleeves, short, bouffant or slashed; braiding; redingote dress (see pls. 279, 280).

267 · 16th–17th century. **NOBLE FRENCH LADIES; HISTORICAL FIGURES**. Popular costumes. Bourgeois militia, fifers, drummers. Schoolchildren. Cornet waist. Sumptuary laws of Henri II, Charles IX and Henri III.

268 · 16th century. **NOBILITY, MAGISTRACY**: chancellor, counsellor (see pl. 269); historical figures. The *escarcelle* has disappeared, pockets. **COURT HEADDRESS**: toque, hat, *mortier*; ruff, cuffs, turned-down collar, doublet, sleeves *à chiquetade*; magistrate's robe, *épitoge*, belt, scarf, cape (see pls. 269–270); trunk-hose, stockings, aglets, garters; *escarpin à crevés* (slashed); *souliers à pont*. Beards.

269 · 16th century. **CONTEMPORARY FASHIONS** (reigns of Charles IX, Henri III). Official costumes. President of *parlement*, university rector, merchant provost, doctor. Ladies, bourgeois. Women's headdress: hair *en raquette* (see pls. 274, 276, 277, 278). Hats: *à quatre braguettes* (see pl. 274), *chaperon embronché*; mourning suit (see pl. 286); mantle of presidents, parti-coloured robes, *tanné* (grey).

270 · 16th century, part 2. **CIVILIAN COSTUMES**. Germany. Rhine basin (see pl. 271). 'Young Germany'. Lord, page, ladies, merchant, banker, tailor. Brimless cap with feather, woman's manteletta, *harzkappe, puffjacke, schaube*.

271 · 16th century, part 2. **WARRIOR, HUNTING AND DISPLAY COSTUMES** (Germany, Rhine Basin). Prince, hunter, noble child, Swiss knight, reiter or *pistolier*, infantry drummer. Toque, plume, hat, *morion*, panache, skirt, bodice, slashed sleeves, buff doublet, reiter-style mantle. Sword, dirk, high lance, javelin, wheel-lock, *pistole*. Equestrian manoeuvre, caracol or *limaçon*. Harness.

PLATE 269

PLATE 270

PLATE 271

272 · 16th century. **EQUESTRIAN FIGURES**. Count, prince, lady, lords, drummer. Harness, cantle, tufts of feathers, straps, sleeve.

273 · 16th century. Reign of Henri III (see pl. 274). **COSTUMES OF THE HIGH NOBILITY AND BOURGEOISIE**. King. Ladies, young ladies, bourgeois women. Lawyer. Mourning garments. *Grand attifage*. Chaperon, mourning veil, stiffening of lapel with canvas; barb. Fan-shaped and turned-down collars. Bodice: external corset-busk; farthingale *à tambour*; puff sleeves; *rebras*; pierced sleeves; leg of mutton sleeves; closed surcoat, supported skirt, petticoat displayed (see pls. 276, 277, 280, 311); doublet; ladies' breeches; Venetian mules, *pianelles*; pinked gloves. Necklaces, *demi-ceint*, purse, mirror.

274 · 16th century. **NOBLES, GENTLEMEN OF THE ROBE, LIVERYMEN**. Popular types: *demoiselle*, doctor, page, valets, serving-women, chamber-maid. Parisian street-vendors (see pl. 283), peasants. Hat, chaperon, bonnet *à templettes*, mask (see *le touret de nez*, pl. 289); women's collar, binding wire (*fils d'archal*); cape, cope; fur-lined mantle, *mandille*, *jupel, balandrau* or *balandras*, smock; breeches, *grègues*, trunk-hose, shoes, stockings with ties, garters, gamashes.

275 · 16th century. **MILITARY COSTUMES** (reign of Henri III). Infantry. Officers. Standard-bearer; musketeer, drummer. Armour no longer worn. Mix of colours in costumes. Swashbuckling postures. Plumed headdresses; brimless cap, *sombrero*; pleated collar, ruff *à la confusion*; doublet, *panseron à la poulaine*; cuffs; military cloak, scarf; trunk-hose.

PLATE 272

PLATE 273

PLATE 274

417

PLATE 275

PLATE 276

419

PLATE 278

421

276 / 277 · 16th–17th century. **WOMEN'S FASHION. HISTORICAL FIGURES. NOBLE LADIES, BOURGEOIS WOMEN**. Close-fitting bodice, *corps espagnolés*; repression of women's breasts. Prominent lace. Lingerie (see pl. 278). Ruffs, collarettes, now much expanded; mantle-collar; cuffs; lacis (lace), gold or silk lace, *points coupés*, point lace. Choker, corset, *corps piqué*; the three cottes; dyeing of cloth, their names. *Soulier à point, noeud d'amour*. Necklaces, chains, clothing jewellery. Powdered hair, wigs, *arcelets, attifet* (hood, see pl. 278).

278 · 16th century. **PORTRAITS. GENTLEMEN. NOBLE LADIES. MILITARY COSTUMES.** High-ranking officer. Sergeant-major.

279 · 16th–17th century. **WOMENSWEAR**: married women, noble ladies, young women. High-society wedding costumes, bridal and peasant woman's costumes. Crowns, diadems, mob-caps, coiffes, bonnets, head-veils, surcoat dresses, redingote dresses (see pl. 280); tight sleeves, gigot sleeves, hanging sleeves, train, collars, apron, fur muffs. Chains, necklaces. Hair braided or loose.

PLATE 280

PLATE 281

425

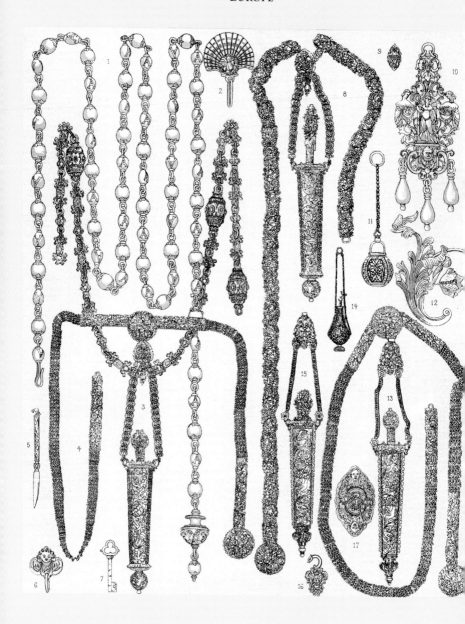

PLATE 282

280 · 16th–17th century. **BELGIAN, FRENCH, FLORENTINE, ENGLISH, MILANESE, PORTUGUESE COSTUMES**. Hats (men), ribbons, torsades, feathers; *cuvette renversée* hats (women); *coiffe du réseau*, draped veil, *rebozillo* (see pls. 280 and 281). Turned-down collar, *col vidé; rabras*. Busked doublet, with épaulettes; basques, corsages, *fausse panse*; cloaks, *simarre*. Trunkhose, breeches, knee-breeches, including *à la sévillane*; stockings, *tassettes. Souliers à pont; oreilles*. Earrings (men). Women's mask (see pl. 283), fan, keys, cases. Hair, gummed powder of various scents, including *chêne pourri*.

281 · 16th–17th century. **OBJECTS IN GENERAL USE**. Watches, *les oeufs de Nuremberg*.

282 · 16th–17th century. **GOLDSMITH WORK, JEWELLERY**. Chains of grace, of honour, belts, knives, keys, perfume bottles, *barillets*, pomanders, fasteners, broaches, pendants, *agréments*, necklace ornaments.

283 · 16th century. **PARISIAN FASHIONS AT THE TIME OF LA LIGUE. RELIGIOUS, MILITARY COSTUMES**: militia men, bourgeois, working class, 1590. Captain, page, *coureur*, priest, Carthusians, Capuchin, wine-vendor, water-carrier, porter. Albanian hat. Black scarf. Polished armour.

PLATE 283

284 · 16th century. **ECCLESIASTICAL COSTUMES**. Pope; cardinal, patriarch, bishop, Benedictine abbé, canons, churchmen, acolyte. Liturgical vestments, colours thereof; *habitus religionis*. Tiara (*tríregnum*), cardinal's hat, mitres, fanons, papal cross, bishop's croziers, *sudarium*.

285 · 16th century. **THE EMPEROR, KING OF ROME**: costume, insignia. **NOBLES, BOURGEOIS**. Composite fashions, decoration of the cod-piece. Tunic, dalmatic, pluvial, sandals, crowns, globe, sceptres, necklace of the Golden Fleece.

286 · 16th century. **FUNERAL OF A CATHOLIC KNIGHT-PRINCE** (see pl. 324–325, funeral cortège). Chaperon *embronché*, mourning mantles with trains; heralds, blazoned tabard. Standards: the imperial crown, the globe; music corps; helmet, shield, combat sword; surcoat; mace-bearers.

PLATE 284

431

PLATE 286

287 · 16th century. **WOMEN'S FASHIONS. NOBLE LADIES**: Italian, Dutch. **HEADDRESSES**: crown *à la ducale*, diadem; *balzo*; lace collarette, wimple; square bodice, slit sleeves, cuffs; *zimarra*. Necklace, chain, broaches, pendant earrings, belt, girdle, fleuron in goldsmith's work. *Contenances*; fan; muff.

288 · **VENETIAN COSTUMES** (second half of the 16th century). *Gentildonne*. Pointed bonnet. Blonde hair. Decoration of head, neck and breast; brocade and silk robes; embroidered lingerie. Men's costumes: black; peltry worn on the back, *dogalines*; toga, stole.

289 · 16th century. **MEANS OF TRANSPORT. CEREMONIAL ROBES**. Gondolas; litters, horses, mules. Turinese, Paduan doctor, penitent, Roman lady, Venetian courtesan. Height, lengthening of women's bust, 'masculine' underwear. Hair in curls, crescent, horns; *touret de nez*; pleated hat (doctors). Riding mantle, bodice, *panseron*; hose; sailors, provençal, and cod-piece breeches; *grègues, braguesques*; stockings with clocks. High pattens; spurs with rowel. Folding fans.

290/291 · 16th century. **GALERIE HENRI II**, *salle des fêtes*, Fontainebleau Palace. Fireplace side; musician's gallery side. Window benches (see pl. 299).

292 · 16th century. **LA BELLE CHEMINÉE**, Fontainebleau Palace. Firedogs, *chiennetz*, *cheminée*, *queminel*; bellows.

293 · 16th century. **INTERIOR DECORATION. STATELY BED, LIT DE PARADE** (see pl. 294); bedroom, *chambre du lit* or *des parements*; *les grands appartements* (royal rooms).

P. VERONÈSE

PLATE 289

437

PLATE 290

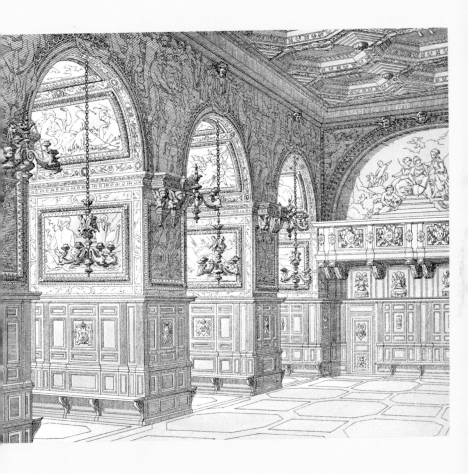

PLATE 291

PLATE 293

294 · 16th century. **FRENCH FURNITURE**. Bed *à ruelle*, buffet, chest, travelling-box, dining table, curial seat, baronial seat, folding chair with back.

295 · 16th century. **FURNITURE**. Chests. Marriage chest. *Huches* (trunks), makers thereof, *huchers* or *huchiers*. Chest-makers, *bahutiers*.

296 · 16th century. **FURNITURE**: Earthenware stove. Wardrobe of various woods.

297 · 16th century. **CUPBOARD. CHAMBER ORGAN**.

298 · 16th century. **THRONES, STOOL, PRIE-DIEU, SMALL CUPBOARDS, KUNSTSCHRANK** (see pl. 316). **CUSHIONS,** *banquiers*.

299 · 16th century. **BARONIAL RESIDENCE**. Reception room. Drawing room (see pl. 300). Elizabethan.

300 · Early 17th century. Baronial residence. **HALL**. Windows, wainscoting, low doors, gallery.

PLATE 294

443

PLATE 295

PLATE 296

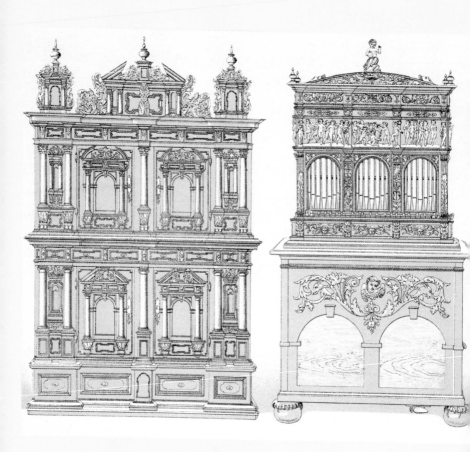

PLATE 297

PLATE 298

PLATE 300

PLATE 301

301 · 16th–17th century. **MILITARY COSTUMES: ARMS, DETAILS OF EQUIP-MENT** (periods of Charles IX, Henri III, Henri IV, Louis XIII). Gentleman, infantry colonel-general, cavalry general, sapper officer, arquebusier, musketeer. Iron helmet, nasal, *cabasset, pot-en-tête, morion,* gorget, cuirass, buffalo-hide jerkin, mail sleeves, tassettes, shield, boots. The colour white: scarf, cross. Sword *en verrouil* (see pl. 311), sword-belt sling; arquebus, *fourquine,* musket, hunting arms, pistols, primer, cartridge-belt.

302/303 · **INTERIOR** (Elizabethan period). Baronial residence. Dining room.

304 · 16th–17th century. **ORNAMENTAL FURNITURE**: buffet, cupboard. Wardrobe (*aumair, amaire, aumoires*), *layettes.* Furniture in carved wood, decoration thereof.

305 · 16th–17th century. **SECULAR FURNITURE**. Table, chairs, armchairs, small cupboard.

306 · 16th–17th century. **EPISCOPAL THRONE** as choir stall; *patience* or misericord. **DOMESTIC OBJECTS**: historiated painting- and mirror-frames.

307 · 16th–17th century. **DOMESTIC OBJECTS** (see pls. 308 and 309). Credenza, *fontaine, brasero,* chair, keys, *clef de maîtrise.*

PLATE 304

PLATE 305

PLATE 306

PLATE 307

308 · 16th–17th century. **HANAPS, PITCHER, CANDLEHOLDERS, GLASSES** (see pl. 309).

309 · 16th–17th century. **ENGRAVED GLASSWORK AND MOUNTED ROCK CRYSTAL**; ewer, comfit box, jug.

310 · 16th–17th century. **MEANS OF TRANSPORT**: *char branlant*, suspended carriage (see pl. 349).

311 · 16th–17th century. **COSTUMES OF THE NOBILITY** (reign of Henri IV). Sombre colours; ceremonial attire. Busked corsage, coloured cotte; *manteau d'étiquette*. Collarettes, cuffs, pearl ornaments, earring pendants, choker, buttons worked in precious metals. *Chapeau français*; ruff, *rabat*, doublet (not busked), *épaulettes à la Henri IV*, cloth of gold, belt, sword-belt sling, sword *en verrouil*, cape or *manteau*; trunk-hose *à bourse*, *grègues* (see pl. 340), small *chiquetade*, loops and bows, garters *longues d'une aune*, *souliers à pont*, spurred boots, *cuir de roussy*, *surpied chiqueté*.

312 · 17th century. **INTERIOR**. Salon.

PLATE 308

PLATE 310

DIRCK HALS — VAN DALEN

PLATE 312

313 · 16th–17th century. **FLEMISH BED**, with cupboard and privy; **ARMCHAIR, CHAIRS WITH AND WITHOUT ARMS** (see also pl. 314).

314: 16th–17th century. **CHAMBER OF HONOUR**. Stately bed, four-poster, inset, with canopy; bed-curtains, *gouttières* (valances), plumes; *bers* or cradle.

315 · 17th century. **FRENCH FURNITURE**. Armchairs, chairs, uprights, *tours tors* (lathe); use of embossed leather.

316 · 17th century. **FURNITURE, DOMESTIC OBJECTS**. Cupboards (*armoires artistiques*), powder-flasks. Ebony furniture, *green, black* and *Portugal* ebony; cabinet-makers, carpenters *de la petite cognée*.

317 · 17th century. **LUXURY OBJECTS: GERMAN GOLDSMITH'S WORK**. Nautilus shells, ostrich eggs, cups, comfit boxes, hanaps, match-holder. Astronomic clock.

PLATE 313

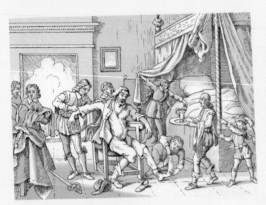

PLATE 314

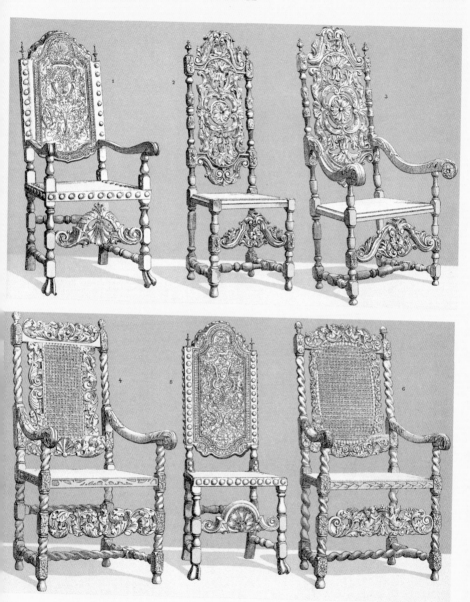

PLATE 315

PLATE 316

PLATE 317

17TH CENTURY: THE NETHERLANDS AND FRANCE

In the Netherlands, in 1630, handsome, stiff, goffered collarettes were still worn. Then, when muslin was no longer starched, the ruff became soft and pleated, and fell forward over the doublet.

In plate 318 319, showing interiors from the early part of the 17th century, we find no trace of the eccentricities and the Chinese taste that reached the Netherlands for the first time at that point. In the matter of furniture, the style is altogether European. Plate 320 shows a rare example of a plant-based labyrinth; it appears with a miniature of a town in the background. The labyrinth is bourgeois in aspect and does not possess that air of grandeur later examples, all hornbeam hedges and marble statues, designedly emanate.

The republic of the Netherlands was for a long time a state apart in Europe, on both geographical and social criteria. Its customs were different. Plate 321 shows three different aspects of female costume: women in town clothes with high, thick, stiff ruffs; two other ladies (nos. 1 and 8) have made greater concessions to fashion and have donned the graceful French costume worn between 1624 and 1635. Figure no. 4 shows a lady walking in an Amsterdam square in the fashion of a previous age that continued in Holland until around 1660.

Plate 322 depicts a bedroom from the time of Louis XIII. In the 17th century, the bedroom was the unique locus of private life. The custom of decorating walls with tapestries, a medieval tradition, was in fact a necessity, since the roughly plastered walls, condemned windows and walled-up doors showed traces of the illogic and inconsistency typical of architects of this period. This interior features a square bed whose canopy, with its fringed valances, rests on vertical columns with the faintest suggestion of Solomonic decoration. One proof of the importance of this item of furniture was the fashion for receiving guests sitting on it: La Bruyère tells us that it was 'a Parish fashion for the newly married wife, during the first three days, to receive guests while seated, magnificently dressed, on a bed'. On the left we see a *cabinet* or *secrétaire*, both of which were then quite widespread. The women in the illustration wear the costume of c. 1630.

Plate 323 presents one of those blonde Dutchwomen whose pale complexions combine so well with white ermine, the freshness of lawn and the sheen of white satins. Plate 324 325 puts before us the funeral of a *Prince-Chevalier* in the Netherlands of the 17th century. It was chosen for its ceremonial aspect, which connect it with customs traceable to the Middle Ages proper. We see that ceremonial and battle arms and horses were preceded in such processions by tilting arms, device and horse, led by a herald-at-arms. This Dutch custom must have had deep roots to survive into the 17th century. The interior scene of plate 326 is French, and dates from around 1635.

We shall return to female costumes, taking more sophisticated examples, and only the men's clothes need detain us here. One gentlemen wears a hunting costume, but this is no clue to his activities. Fantastical costumes, worn simply for the pleasure of ostentation, were then the fashion. Riders or not, the *bon ton* were booted. Sartorial display was combined with the desire to impress the fair sex; the 'hunter' might be in symbolic pursuit of a lady. In 1635, the collars that had once spread like fans behind the head flopped back onto the shoulders; this was called *le col vidé*. Women's necks were finally delivered from ruffs and Medici collars. A decree of 1634 proscribed *galons, cannetilles, pourfilures, franges*, and so on; costumes acquired a tasteful sobriety. Ribbons were replaced by other trimmings. Clothing was made of plain cloth in neutral or dark colours (pl. 328).

The vicissitudes of fashion during the reign of Louis XIII were exacerbated by Richelieu and his sumptuary laws, whose goal was not to forbid splendour in clothing, but to ensure that the money spent on it remained in France. Gold and silk lace were banned in 1620, because they came from Milan, and textile imports from Flanders, Genoa and Venice in 1629. The reform promoted taste and elegance, for the most part, by removing the tendency of clothing to inhibit movement. Women's gait was less constrained, and the movements of the body regained their natural grace. Heavy, stiff cloths were eschewed, as were pleated ruffs, high, heavy boots and mob caps. Beards too disappeared, after Louis XIII had, when excessively bored, succumbed to a whim and himself shaved all his officers. This was the period when the enlightened and the upper classes began to find common cause, resulting in the brilliant society of the *ancien régime*. At this point, a dainty singularity seems to have been the principal goal of the gentlemen of the court. The perfection sought by the ladies of the time required the aid of an accomplice: the hairdresser (*coeffeur*, as it was then spelled). His advent is one of those innovations by which the history of fashion is defined. For the refined lady, he replaced the chamber-maid whose job it had been since the dawn of time to arrange her mistress's hair. Given the pride of these ladies, a considerable vein of impertinence was required to persuade persons of social distinction to agree to intimate manual contact with a man who had nothing to recommend him but his skills.

The cad in question was sieur Champagne, a man of genius, remarkably skilled, and the first to have imagined that a man might make his living from arranging ladies' hair.

Plate 329 shows a marriage contract being drawn up during the reign of Louis XIII. The men are bearded, wear ruffs and low hats, and the large cloak fashionable during Louis' reign. One of the women displays a square turned-down collar (*rabat carré*), the other a round collar reinforced with brass wire; the sleeves of both are extraordinarily puffed out, while their gowns are out of date. In the 16th century, the peasants were very much an object of scorn to the other classes (pl. 331). Gowns were of coarse cloth, serge or fustian, and of a single colour. When the peasant woman raised her skirt, she did so using a little cord that was removed for riding. A white apron was part of working clothes as it was of semi-formal clothing. Diapered or bordered with lace, it was a prestige item. Men still made little use of buttons. Most of them wore a short *saye* or *sayon* (tunic), belted tight at the waist and split at the sides. The cape was now rather shorter. Hats were in straw or felt.

PLATE 320

318/319 · First part of the 17th century. **INTERIORS**; nuptial chamber; dressing a child; costumes, games, customs. Built-in bed, cradle; leaded window; chest, chairs, stool, external mirror, *espion*, warming pan, brush, spinning-wheel. Dance, game of *main chaude*. Example of pump, small gardens.

320 · 17th century. **MEANS OF TRANSPORT; MAZE; GENTLEMEN; BARBER AT WORK.** Carriage, canopy posts, canopy, curtains. **BOURGEOIS INTERIOR**, weight-driven clock.

321 · **NOBILITY AND BOURGEOISIE**, 1630–1660. Womenswear, French fashions. City and indoor wear. Civilian and military costumes. Gentlemen, horsemen; the *raffiné* and the *précieux* (see pls. 326–329).

322 · 17th century. **BEDROOM** (period of Louis XIII). Wardrobe and clothes packed in a trunk. Candleholder with *platine*, snuffers. Tapestries, hangings with animal motifs, door curtains, *huis verts*, curtain-rings, *couchette*, baldachin, valance, cupboard or *secrétaire*, small drawers or boxes, *layettes*. Seats: stool or *placet*. The hierarchy of seats, from bench upwards.

323 · First half of the 17th century. **CIVILIAN AND MILITARY COSTUMES.** The messenger of the confraternity, *knape*. Corporate distinctions. Watch worked in precious metals. Guild of arquebusiers. Corporate meals. Cavalry officer, captain, lieutenant, standard-bearer, sergeant, drummer. Felt hats, corselets, buff jerkins, doublets, doublet *à la Candale*, sword-belt, trunk-hose, cannions, *bas à botter* (see pl. 326); boots, bell-mouthed, *à chaudron*. Guild necklaces, disks, cups, hanaps, *drinkhoorn*. Flag of the confraternity.

324/325 · 17th century. **FUNERAL OF A PROTESTANT KNIGHT-PRINCE.** Mantle, mourning hat, funeral carriage. Guards, domestics, drummers, trumpets, heralds, arms, prince's coat of arms, guidons, pennants, banners, banderoles, pennons, standard, helm, tilting gorgerin, device, helmet, shield, surcoat. War-horse, ceremonial horse. Insignia of knighthood. Sword, crown. Prince, nobles, representatives of the knighthood; ambassadors, deputies, counsellors, magistrates, clergymen, civic guard.

PLATE 321

PLATE 323

479

326 · 17th century. **INTERIOR. CIVILIAN COSTUMES. MUSICAL INSTRU-MENTS**: spinet. **HUNTING COSTUMES**, the colour red, hats, wigs, *moustache* or (later) *cadenette* (see pls. 327 and 328); *bas à botter*, superposed stockings, worsted stockings, garters, boots, spurs. Lace, *point coupé, col vidé*.

327 · 17th century. **NOBILIARY CLASSES; WAYS OF WEARING THE CLOAK.** The *raffinés*, a widow, 1629–1630, a woman rider (historical, 1645). *Castor* (beaver-fur) *à la cordelière*, panache *en queue de renard*, edges *en mauvais garçon*, hair worn *à la comète*, *coins* or sections of wig; rain-proof garments, cloak *à la balagnie*, hooded cloak, *gaban, frisque maintelin*; doublet, doublets with épau-lettes; *rabats*, baldric; breeches *à chiquetade*, aglets, knee-breeches *à fond de cuve*, gloves, shoes; *laitues pommées, bottes mignonnes*, arched spurs, mules, pattens (see pls. 328 and 329). Collar *en rotonde*, hair-net, binding wire, the *modeste*.

328 · 17th century. **COSTUME REFORM: NOBILITY, BOURGEOISIE** (period of Louis XIII). Women dressed for a walk, for town, for *assemblée*; décolleté. Mythological attire, *Diana, Juno*; gentleman of court; *cavaliers, élégants hors de pair*; boules player, *capitaine d'aventures* (captain of irregulars). The King, his train bearer, 1635–1640. The plumed hats of the ladies, *enseigne*; hair *abattus, en garcettes, bouffons*, braided, in torsades, *cadenette, galant, culbute*; hairstyles by le sieur Champagne; *rond* (see pl. 339), *serpenteaux, moustaches*, pendants, *perle, Cadet-la-perle*, beauty-spots, stars, crescents, plasters. Pearl chokers, *esclavage de perles*, pearl wristbands, precious stones, pendants. *Demi-ceint*, chain, keys, scissors, knife, purse, perfume-flasks. Collar *en rotonde*, the fichu-pelerine, *rabat-dentelé, à la guimbarde*. Bodice, *corps de jupe*; guaging; *petite oie*; dress *à la commodité, modeste*, puffed sleeves; underskirt, *jupe, friponne, secrète*; cassock, *hongreline*. Hunting gloves, gloves *à la frangipane*, sleeve. Mob-caps *à l'espagnole*; *point coupé* collars; doublet, *tabit* or *buffle*; large mantle, *petit manteau à la clistérique*. Bouquet *à la royale*. Curling tongs, *brasero*, little cheval glass, comb, comb brush, casket, cosmetics, *le blanc d'Espagne*. *L'espagnol vermillon*, flasks, *eau d'Ange* or *de Chypres*. The mandolin. Persons *de bel air, du beau procédé, de la belle manière*, accomplished person. The *coeffeur*, male hairdresser. Dances.

PLATE 326

483

FRANCE

PLATE 328

485

329 · 17th century. **FASHIONS** (period of Louis XIII). **THE BOURGEOISIE**: interior, the marriage contract, the notary royal. The gallery of the palace, trinkets; linen-draper, collars, bows, farthingales; haberdasher: gloves *à l'occasion, à la nécessité, à la Phyllis, à la Cadenet*, fan. Royal bookseller. The *galants* and their ladies.

330 · 17th century. **ORNAMENTS. WORK IN PRECIOUS METALS AND STONES** (periods of Louis XIII, Louis XIV, see pl. 341). Earring pendants, necklaces, pendants, broaches, fasteners, buckles, rings, cameos, bracelets, trinkets, seals, alms purse. Openwork, enamel, jade, *jayet*, precious stones, jasper, pearls. *Lapidaire-faussetier; haute* and *simple verrerie*.

331 · 17th century. **PEASANTS**: grape harvesters, farmers, farm girls, shepherd, reaper, woman sheaving; tabellion, marriage procession, musicians, the *branle* (dance). Headdresses with hair, hat, straw, felt; bodices, dresses; coarse cloth, serge, fustian; apron, saye or *sayon*, cape, smock, *sorquenie* or *souquenille*; cordons, leg-covers, spatterdashes, *garravaches, calzar, arsoulètes*; shoes. *Houlette en spatule*, spud, hoe, keg, shepherd's scrip. The character of the countryside in the 17th century.

PLATE 329

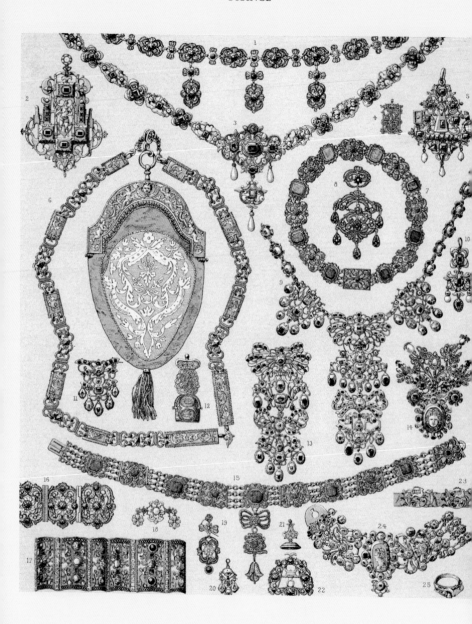

PLATE 330

PLATE 331

17TH CENTURY: RELIGIOUS, CIVILIAN AND MILITARY COSTUME

Plates 332–335 show various examples of religious costumes in Europe. Plates 332–333 show the great diversity of such costumes in Italy. Foundlings and orphan girls had their own uniforms. Plates 334–335 show French religious vestments from the 17th century.

In the 16th century, the Reformation had imprinted a very special mark of veracity on German costume. But with the 17th century came the influence of French fashions, and this severity was somewhat diluted. The lightly worn elegance that replaced Lutheran severity quickly degenerated into crude ostentation. This craze for new fashions affected mainly men; women's tastes were slower to change, and new items only gradually entered their wardrobes. The new style of gown is found here in combination with the fichu of Anne of Austria and the *pelzkappe*, the fur headgear worn in various forms; women gave it up only with the greatest reluctance. In England during the reign of Charles I, high-ranking or merely well-off English ladies followed French fashion so closely that the costumes of the two countries may be considered identical. As a consequence the sumptuary edicts of France reformed English costume as they did that of Flanders. Good taste was forced on the French, and their recourse to simplicity was adopted by their neighbours as if they too were under compulsion. Décolleté gowns were, we know, avoided by noblewomen for anything but solemn occasions. Plates 338–339 present a number of German women from Strasbourg. The most direct evidence of current trends in their costumes is the shortening of the skirt, which thus reveals a relatively high-heeled shoe intended to display the foot. Women at first found it difficult to walk thus shod. By the mid-17th century, however, the innovation of high heels was over fifty years old. The mushroom-shaped ornament visible on certain figures is part of the Dutch *huilke*, which spread throughout northern Germany in the 17th century, finally becoming the preserve of bourgeois women.

Costume no. 6 in plate 340 is a further example of the debraille of which Candale was the principal founder; the shortening of the doublet is exaggerated, and the trunk-hose belt is worn lower in order to display the quantities of inner garments draped around the body.

The regiment of the gardes françaises was founded in 1563; it was abolished in 1573, re-established by Henri II and maintained till 1789. Before Louis XIII, the State supplied neither arms nor clothing. In 1664, the gardes françaises wore uniform (plate 342), though each company had different regulation costumes. In 1670, the king ordered that his troops should be clothed at his own expense. This uniform consisted of a grey-white jerkin braided

PLATE 332

PLATE 333

PLATE 335

495

with silver. The colour of the bunch of ribbons worn on each shoulder (this is the origin of épaulettes) specified the soldier's company. In 1691, the gardes were clothed in uniform blue. After the peace of Ryswik (1697), the uniform was again improved and began to take on what we think of as military form. Soldiers' clothing was blue highlighted with red and jackets were trimmed with metallic buttons. One of the main innovations of the reign of Louis XIV was the institution of grenadiers, soldiers trained to throw grenades. Sieur Martinet, inspector-general of the infantry, was responsible for introducing bayonets or *couteaux bayonnais*. The invention of the cartridge in 1683 meant that large, heavy bandoleers were no longer worn. Only in 1698–1700 was the old musket replaced by the flintlock.

332 · 17th century. **RELIGIOUS COSTUMES**. Orders of San Stefano, San Giorgio, Humiliati, Benedictines, Augustines, Penitents, Dominican Third Order; bearer of the dead. Abbess, ecclesiastical, noble sisters, chaplain, canon; ordinary, choir and ceremonial habits.

333 · 17th century. **RELIGIOUS ORDERS** (Rome). Ursuline, sister of Santa Caterina, orphan girls: *vergine miserabile, zoccoletta*. Students of Salviati, Mattei, Greek, Nazarean, Scottish, German and Hungarian schools. Ordinary, choir and city habits.

334 · 17th century. **RELIGIOUS ORDERS. WOMEN'S COSTUMES**. Carmelite, Sachette, Madelonettes, Penitent sisters, sister of the Hôtel-Dieu of Saint-Jean-Baptiste de Beauvais (see pl. 335), Premonstratensians, novice sister, hospitallers of Sainte-Catherine, noble Benedictine sisters.

335 · **RELIGIOUS ORDERS**. Women's costumes. Lay sister, nuns of the Saint-Sépulcre, Feuillantine hospitaller from Loches, from Saint-Gervais, Trinitarian sister.

336 · 17th century. **COMMON FASHIONS BY CLASS.** Gentleman. German *ruffian*. Protestant minister; women of Augusburg, Basel, Strasbourg, godmother. *Pelzkappe*, arched head-dresses (see pl. 338), hat, bonnets, *cadenettes*. *Kittel*, plastron, bodice, skirt, stuffed headdress, pelisse, tucked-up cloak, muff. Buff jerkin, doublet; trunk-hose, aglets, *galants*, canions; bell-mouthed boots.

337 · **WOMENSWEAR**, 1642–1649. Ladies, bourgeoises, merchants' daughters, the wife of the Lord Mayor of London (see pl. 339). French fashions, their influence, hat, fur-lined winter coat, ruff.

338/339 · England, Brabant, Germany, France, 1640–1650. Noblewomen, bourgeois wom-en, merchants' daughters, marriage costume. **SPRING, SUMMER, AUTUMN, WINTER DRESS. HEADDRESSES.** *Dames houppées. Huiken* or cape. Full-dress costume: bridal, fur (sable) bonnets; béguin, ruffs, piped and pleated collarettes, mask, chin-straps, fichu, corset with épau-lettes, successive layers of skirts; *soulier à pont*. Arrangement of the hair; *anglaises*. Lap dog.

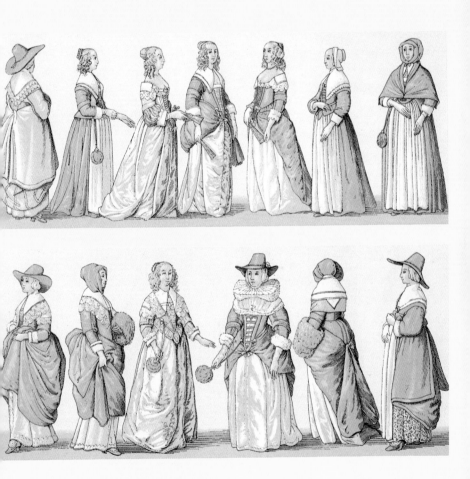

PLATE 337

PLATE 338

Europe

PLATE 339

501

340 · **COSTUMES OF THE NOBILITY**, 1646–1670. Gentlemen, ladies, page. The arbiters of fashion: Montauron, Candale. The *débraillé*. Linen displayed. *Fronde, à la paille, au papier* fashions. Conical, low, plumed hats; rabat; shirt; *jabot*, sleeves, cuffs, laces; *point-coupé*, pourpoint, *brassières, justaucorps à brevet* (see pl. 344/345); belt; Candale-style breeches; *culottes*, petticoat-breeches (see pl. 344/345); ribbons, aglets, canions; baldric, sword; *botte mignonne*, spurs, shoes, bows, red heels. Bodice; lawn, gauze, neckerchiefs; décolleté dress, *la gueuse*; short sleeves; mantle, *galants*, *faveurs*, skirt or *manteau, queue*. Long hair (men), moustache *à coquille, bigotère*. Hair ribbon (women).

341 · 17th century. **ORNAMENTS, ENAMELLED JEWELLERY. EVERYDAY OBJECTS**. Medallion, fastener, belt-hook, necklaces, pendants, seal, ring, watch, cases. Insignia: order of the Garter; Maltese cross.

342 · 17th–18th century. **MILITARY COSTUMES** (reigns of Louis XIII, Louis IX, Louis XV). Gardes-françaises, officers, ensigns, sergeants, soldiers; pikemen, musketeers, drummer, fifer. Royal livery. Creation of the gardes-françaises. *Habits d'ordonnance*. Uniform. The garde outside the Louvre. Helmets, gorget, corselet, cuirass, buff jerkin, tassettes. Pike, *esponton*, halberd, sword, sword-sling, cartridge-pouch sword-belt, baldric, bayonet-sheath, musket, *forquine*, cartridge-belt, cartridges, *cofins* (see pl. 343), powder, bag of bullets. Flag, scarf, cockade. Hats, three-cornered; ribbons, bonnets; *justaucorps, hongreline*, hose, breeches; bell-mouthed boots.

343 · **MILITARY COSTUMES**, 1660–1690. Infantry. *Les vieux corps*: pikemen, grenadiers, musketeers, fusiliers; *couteaux bayonnais* (bayonet); invention of cartridges. Militia-men. General, *officier aux* or *des gardes*; varieties of costume, muff. Sergeants, arms of. Insignia of the commandant, cuirass. Strong boots. Grenade-pouch.

344/345 · 17th century. Interior. **CHAMBRE DE PARADE** (see pl. 347). Ceremonial costume. The effeminate; wigs, *crinière de lion*.

PLATE 340

503

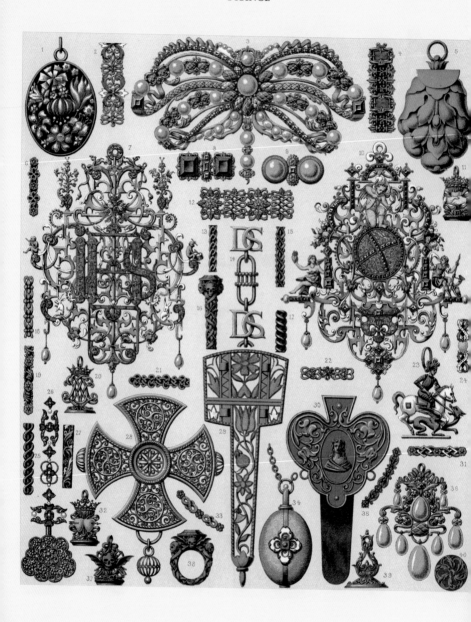

PLATE 341

PLATE 343

505

PLATE 342

17TH Century:
Furniture and means
of transport

The cabinet-making of this part of the reign of Louis XIV is less prized than that of Louis XIII, as it is excessively laden with ornaments of questionable taste. Furniture in precious metals disappeared almost entirely after the king ordered them to be melted down in 1689, giving the example by sacrificing all his large-scale silver pieces. In palaces, from the Renaissance till late in the reign of Louis XV, certain alcoves were veritable monuments, in terms of their composition, luxury of materials and beauty of decoration. The *alcôve royale* or *Italienne* was not simply a recess in a wall, but a second room separated from the first by either columns or partitions. The alcove shown in plate 347 is *royale* in aspect. The panelling, painted white with ornaments picked out in gilt, did not generally cover the entire wall. Plate 348 shows how the houses of the wealthy were all divided by partition walls into small and large rooms as the century progressed — and as architecture under Louis XIV, thanks to Mansart's influence, attained a high point of grandeur and magnificence. The fashion of the times required an *air galant*. The woman wears a dressing-gown, with petticoat and corset. The basqued corset is a *gourgandine*, with laced opening at the front. The little knot of brilliant-cut gemstones, the *boute-en-train* or *tâtez-y*, placed between the breasts to complete the costume, is missing.

Shipbuilding had attained such perfection in the Netherlands that the Dutch became shipbuilders to all Europe (pl. 350). Louis XIV remedied more than one naval disaster by restocking his fleet with vessels from Dutch shipyards.

PLATE 347

PLATE 349

346 · 17th century. **FURNITURE**: cabinet-maker's work, goldsmith's work, buffet, silver cupboard.

347 · 17th century. **ALCOVE** *à la française; à la royale, à l'italienne, à la romaine* alcove. **FURNITURE**: console.

348 · 17th century. **THE MAIN ROOM**. Closets (*réduits*), rooms *entresolées*. Bathroom (see pl. 397). Summer or ordinary bed. Gentlewoman: *deshabillé* costumes, bodice, *gourgandine*. *Précieux, précieuses, illustres, grandes, petites* and *ridicules*. Academies of *préciosité*, beauties, muses, *l'amant du Parnasse*. Honest folk. Furniture, armchairs, 1675–1680.

349 · 17th century. **EQUIPAGE OF THE QUEEN**. State carriage. **KING; OFFICERS** of his and the queen's household; pages, foot valets, driver. Large and small stables. Royal livery: galloons *en bracelet, en quille*.

350 · 17th century. **MEANS OF TRANSPORT**. Navy, merchant navy. Ship-building, rated ship, three-master under repair (*au radoub*), listing (*à la bande*); ornamentation, prow, poop, *tutela*.

PLATE 350

517

17TH–18TH CENTURY:
CIVILIAN COSTUME AND FURNITURE

The way in which the French dressed in the latter part of the 17th century has determined the basis of modern costume (pl. 351). The particularity of costume under Louis XIV was its form: the scale of the hat and its feathered brim, the length of the wig, the cravat, and the near equal length of justaucorps and jacket. Another feature was the broad trimmings of the justaucorps sleeve (*manches à bottes*). There were also the high-heeled shoes (*souliers à la cavalière*), with a *cou[-]de-pied* high enough to make the shoes resemble half-boots. When once the prejudice came to prevail that nothing enhanced male beauty and dignity so much as immensely long hair, curled wigs began to cover almost half the body. In the portraits of the time, everyone, from child to octogenarian, is bewigged. Silk stockings, previously striped or mottled, were now of uniform colour, while gold thread was worked into the fabric of the lower leg. Production of cotton stockings, *bas de Barbarie*, began in 1684.

In plate 352, the king is shown wearing slippers and dressing-gown with a nightcap. The king's example made it fashionable to receive guests during the course of the morning in dressing-gown and short wig or bonnet. Bonnet or wig was indispensable; the head was shaved, and it was not done to appear bare-headed. The costumes in plate 353 belong to the second part of Louis XIV's reign. Despite the severity affected by Mme de Maintenon, women's dress remained sumptuous. The cloak was a descendant of the former outer skirt, and worn with unprecedented ease and freedom. At the time, it was called *le volant*. The overall silhouette of this costume showed vertical lines manipulated to exaggerate the woman's stature. Though the length of the bodice ran counter to this effect, high-heels, the size of the cornet, the effacing of the shoulder-line and the scale of the skirt (which reached right down to the ground), even the length of the train, all was intended to convey a single impression, *un effet de sentiment*.

In Venice (pl. 359), there is no clue in the measured and orderly events of history to show when the austere republic so suddenly transformed its clothing, so completely that in the 17th century, the overall shape of the body is precisely that of a provincial *assemblée* under Louis XIV. In the 17th and 18th centuries, the smaller German courts merely reflected the French court; French fashions had conquered Europe as a whole (pl. 360).

The French workers in plate 362 wear the *sayon* or tunic with an apron whose corners are tucked up into the belt. The two dancers are seen at a private fancy-dress party. In the 17th century, the innate French taste for dance led them to adopt many new steps, some of them of foreign origin. The *menuet, pavane, passacaille, chaconne, courante, sarabande* and *gavotte* were

PLATE 351

PLATE 352

521

the dances of the day. At this point, the chivalric orders had little in common with the former military orders, such as those of the Knight Hospitallers of Malta or the Templars, with their military-religious purposes. Sovereigns used such orders, ancient or modern, as a way of paying for services rendered to the State. The insignia of knighthood took the form of a jewel hung on a ribbon of specific character (pl. 364).

351 · 17th century. **CIVILIAN COSTUMES, NOBILITY.** Wig and sword worn. Riding costume, dressed for the ball, 1670. Hats, *à trois gouttières*, plumed edges; cravate; *la chaconne*; justaucorps; *manches à bottes*; jacket or cassock, buttons, buttonholes; order cordon, scarf, breeches; garters, *bas de Barbarie*, shoe *à la cavalière*; buckles, canes, golden and ivory pommels, sword-tassel (see these items of men's costume in pls. 353, 354, 359, 360, 362, and 364). Wigs: *in-folio, en crinière de lion, à calotte, d'abbé, de bichon, à la moutonne, à l'espagnole, blondes, noires, poudrées; cavalière* or *carrée, financière.* Hair: Moorish grey, agate white, milk white, quarter white, white, yellow undertone, chestnut, pale chestnut, chestnut brown, black, *petit noir*, jet black; *devant à la Fontange, frisures sur rien, à l'angle* (see pl. 361).

352 · 17th–18th century. **DRESSING-GOWNS, BONNETS. GENTLEMEN.** Abbé: wig, soutane, muff, *passe caille* (ribbon from which muff hangs). Women's dress (see following plates): corset, *gourgandine. Grande* and *petite Pandore.* Dressing the king. *Petit lever, première entrée.* Nightcap, camisole, dressing-gown, slippers. The wig of the *lever*, breeches, trunk-hose; stockings, shoes, buckles, garters; shirt, sword, sword-belt, jacket, cordon of the Saint-Esprit, justaucorps, cravat, handkerchief salver, *salve*, watch, relics, *bourserons*, gloves, hat, muff, cane. Master of the wardrobe, cloak-bearer, squire; dis-booting, *débotté*; changes of clothing, of wig. The *grand coucher*, king's, queen's, dauphin's candlesticks. The *petit coucher*, night toilette, dressing-gown, bonnet, camisole.

PLATE 355

525

353 · 17th century. **LADIES' COSTUMES**: prestige attire, décolleté. Bonnet, *fontange* (see pl. 354), *palissade*, *monté-là-haut*, *commode*; curls, *cruches*, hair *en paquet*; pearl necklace: bodice *en pointu*; *tour de manches*, basquines, ribbons, *echelles*; cravat, *steinkerque*; over skirt; *manteau*, *volant*, court cloak, underskirt, furbelows, *prétintailles*. *Langlée*, bustle, *criarde*; gloves, muff, mask.

354 · Late 17th, early 18th century. **AUSTERE COSTUME. GENTLEFOLK, WINTER AND SUMMER GARMENTS**: Abbé, *petit-collet*, short cassock; ornaments *en Amadis*, women's scarf, *cape* (scarf, see pl. 355). Headdress: *fontange*, *duchesse*, *solitaire*, *chou*, *mousquetaire*, *croissant*, *firmament*, *dixième ciel*, *souris*, *effrontée*, *altière fontange*; *culbute*, *cornettes*, *guêpes*, *papillons*; *battant-l'oeil*. Bodices open and closed; half-sleeves, *engageantes*. Make-up, beauty-spots, the tooth-ache sign. Pearl choker (*esclavage*), *boute-en-train*, *tâtez-y*. Perfumed (*ocaigné*) fan.

355 · Late 17th century. **WOMEN'S FASHIONS**: gala, city and indoor clothing. Ceremonial hairstyles, hair in *monte-au-ciel*, *palissades*; palatine, casaquin, basquine, apron, skirt; *freluches*; *cape* (scarf), summer, winter dressing-gowns; muff, women's cane.

356/357 · 17th century. **INTERIOR OF A WEALTHY HOUSEHOLD**: its double character. The two kinds of room: assembly or company rooms; bedroom. Living rooms, *grand cabinet*, *cabinet paré*, *arrière-cabinet*; wainscoting, full-height or *à hauteur d'appui*; panelling, *fausse portes*; fireplace, mirror.

358 · Late 17th, early 18th century. **BOULLE-STYLE FURNITURE**. Plinths or *guênes* (*gaines de termes*). Metal marquetry. Ebony, *bois des Indes*, chased bronze. Domestic objects: snuff grinders, *grivoises*.

359 · Venezia. **FRENCH FASHIONS**. Dogaress, *gentildonne*. Patricians, procurator; winter, summer, mourning attire. Theatrical characters: Donna Angelica, Cassandra. Peddler. *Corno, biretta*, head veil; *dogaline*, cloak *troussé* (tucked up); black, Venetian colour; men's robe; *manches à coude*; stole.

360 · 17th and 18th centuries. **FASHION TRENDS, THE FRENCH INFLUENCE**. Court and city costumes. Winter and summer dress; Berlin and Augsburg fashions. Liverymen, heyduck, messenger, squire. Military costumes: general, drummer. Woman rider (historical). Plumed hat. Headdresses: *à la noblesse, thérèse. Polonaise* or *circassienne* gown (see pl. 389); Spanish-style cuffs; redingote and floating dress.

361 · 17th and 18th centuries. **TRANSFORMATION OF BEARD, HAIR, WIGS**. Churchmen, legal profession, civilian magistrates, teachers, soldiers. Moustache *à la coquille*; beards shaped like fans, artichoke-leaf, swallow-tail, curled; *la royale*. Long hair, crimped hair, hairpieces; skullcap wigs, *in-folio, crinières de lion*, powdered wigs.

PLATE 359

PLATE 361

PLATE 362

PLATE 363

362 · BOURGEOIS, TAPESTRY-MAKER, KING'S WORKERS, 1667–1677. NOBLES; BALL DRESS. DANCERS, MUSICIANS. The different steps: minuet, passacaille, chacony, courante, sarabande, gavotte.

363 · 17th century. LADIES' WEAR. Court dress. Dancers. Child in formal wear. Riding costume. The courtier.

364 · 17th and 18th centuries. CIVILIAN COSTUMES. Wearing the INSIGNIA OF *chevalerie militaire* (reigns of Louis XIV, Louis XV, and Louis XVI). Chevaliers of the orders of Saint-Louis, of les Deux-Épées, of Malte (king's page), of l'hôpital d'Aubrace, of l'Étoile; caballera del Passatiempo del Hacha (Spain); decorated costumes, morning wear.

365 · 17th century. Buffet, dresser. Épergnes; TABLEWARE worked in precious metals.

PLATE 365

18TH CENTURY:
CIVILIAN AND MILITARY COSTUME,
FURNITURE

The variants of the three-cornered hat in plate 366 consist in little more than folding the brim here up, there down, thus presenting greater height or volume. Around 1710 came the fashion for suits with gauged panels. The garment was then shaped to the waist-measurement. It was curved out from the lower back with aid of baleens (pl. 367). So that the sides should swell, five or six folds were arranged hanging from a button at the hips; the folds broadened as they fell, inclining backwards so as to enhance the curve of the back. Starting in 1719, these folds were stiffened with paper or horsehair. Later, these stuffed folds were placed behind the back, and the two edges of the fold stiffened. The bourgeoisie, meanwhile, dressed in coarse cloth, *bouracan* and *ratíne* (rateen). *Camelot* (camlet) and *droguet* (drugget) were used as the season required. Black acquired ceremonial status around 1750. It was now conventional to carry one's hat under the arm or in the hand. This helped to preserve both wig and social countenance.

Plate 367 also shows two women wearing panniers. This was a sort of shaping device composed of circles or hoops of whalebone, rattan or light wood, tied together with ribbons to form something like a chicken cage. Such 'hoop petticoats' spread to every echelon of society. It was awkward in salons, spectacles, promenades and particularly in carriages, since it made it impossible to sit down, go up or downstairs or even walk in company. However, the fear of indiscretion was not so grave as to warrant underwear, which was then considered a sign of immorality. The open corset was still as stiff as the *gourgandine*. The *tour de gorge* (necklet) too remained the same. This was yet another sign of the forthcoming 'reign of the coquettes'.

Plate 368 shows several *mantilles*, little scarves with pointed ends. In the first part of the 18th century, clothing was now supple and loose, now stiff and tight-fitting. In 1729, the sides and back of the suit were puffed up 'to create a pannier effect'. Jackets (or waistcoats) were worn almost entirely open, to display the linen shirt and cravat. Grandeur was no longer the fashion, and the notion of beauty was altered to match. The main thing at this point was 'physiognomy', and true beauty was not admired. A certain irregularity of traits afforded greater possibilities for the creation of a 'sweet little face' and an *air chiffonné* such as met the prevailing taste. The costumes presented in plate 371 belong to different periods of the century, from around 1720 to 1789.

Plate 374 shows two examples of the sedan chair, which was invented by the English. It was the only vehicle suitable to Paris, given the foul streams into which household and other waste water (along with the blood of butchered animals) was ejected. The buffets of plate 375 belong in the dining room. With little or no decoration, their ornaments merely draw the eye to the part they adorn. The candlestick (seen in pl. 376) was an object of great luxury, not least because it played an important role in etiquette.

French taste had originally been the preserve of courtiers, but had, over time, spread to the bourgeoisie. Towards the end of the century, the contrary occurred. The English freed themselves from the yoke of continental fashion, and contrived to impart a particular originality to costume. Plates 377–378 shows how the English way of doing things was soon to cause Anglomania in France. Indeed, France suffered a veritable invasion of new fashions. The English interiors seen in plate 378 are alive with the objects then typical of a nation that had set up many profitable trading-stations overseas. Plate 380 is abundantly furnished with French ornaments and jewellery, allowing certain common features to emerge. The use of coloured stones in expensive jewellery was not common before 1758. A fashionable lady could not do without a ring in which a very large diamond was set in the middle of a paste 'stone'.

The military costumes in plate 381 prove that horsemen were now armed not only with the sword but with the blunderbuss or cavalry carbine and pistols. Until 1772, cavalry musicians (pl. 381) did not wear the regular costume. The 1772 decrees prescribed that the army as a whole should wear the royal livery with the blue suit of the king, *à la Polonaise*, that is, turned up and ornamented with white braid. From the time of Louis XIV, blue and red were the distinguishing colours of the king's household regiments. Until 1757, the long jerkin, the tall three-cornered hat, long boots and cloak were, as we see in plate 383, the insignia of the cavalry. In 1725, the two companies of musketeers were divided into grey and black musketeers, according to the colour of the horses of each of their companies (pl. 384). During the first part of Louis XV's reign, there was little variation in army clothing (pl. 385). Tight breeches, broad jerkin, and a tall three-cornered hat were the rule. Only the colour of the garment and its lining distinguished one regiment from another.

During the reign of Louis XVI, French fashion went through three very distinct phases. The first was marked by excessive luxury, frivolity and extravagance, as if it were the final outbreak of the carnival begun by the Regency. This was the time of lofty headdresses, panniers of unexampled circumference (four or five metres) and volumes of hair never before seen (pl. 388). The second phase was the return to simplicity. Women appeared in chemise dresses, in *déshabillées* known as *pierrots, colinette* camisoles, and with their hair done in childish fashion, their powder matching their hair. The Jeanne d'Arc-style costume consisted in a garment *à l'austrasienne,* and a *péruvienne* jacket. In this costume, the breast was all but bare and the legs were unimpeded in their movement. The third period is that of American and English fashions, in which women began wearing redingotes, waist-coats and men's hats, and adopted a very masculine style, reinforced by the *badine* or switch in their hands. Plate 390 offers several examples of the many fashions for headdresses, hats and bonnets that prevailed at the time. Their names were often borrowed from the events of the day: 'Union of France and England', 'Tartar', 'King Theodore in Venice'. Plate 391–392 reproduces a page of *Cabinet des Modes Nouvelles*, which appeared in Paris in 1785. The founding of a journal combining images with description was an important event in the history of costume. Changing tastes in dress were there recorded as and when they took place. The empire of fashion now required its own official monitor rendering sartorial decrees binding on all Europe: the laws of the furbelow were freshly transmitted from their birthplace.

The impression left by Louis XVI furniture is of simplicity and prettiness (pls. 393–395). At this time, the art of cabinet-making was in the throes of development: on the one hand, people were tired of the exaggerated complications of the previous style, and on the other taste was awakening under the influence of the excavations at Pompeii, whose discovery was one of the major events of the century. The wood carvings of this time are painted in grey, grey and gilt or willow-green.

Plate 397 shows some examples of women's wigs of the *chignon* type. Beginning in 1750, women wore hairpieces whose artificiality was far from evident. Plate 399 presents three place-settings with the three utensils, the knife, spoon, and fork. Several centuries separate the invention of these three objects: the most recent was the fork, which only became an integral part of cutlery in the 17th century.

In the period 1792–1793, the army's clothing was much the same as it had been under Louis XVI.

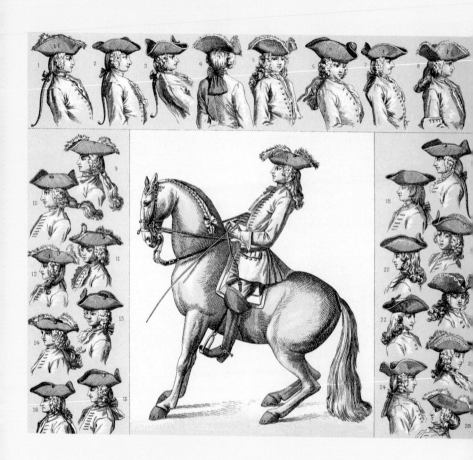

PLATE 366

PLATE 367

545

PLATE 369

547

366 · 18th century. **MEN'S HEADDRESSES**; hats, wigs. Horse for riding and driving. Three-cornered hat, its variants, braid, galloon, feathers, braid. Wigs: knotted, *à bourse, à la brigadière; derrière de bourses, touffes, cadenettes, queue, bout-de-rat*; wigs *à la régence*. Powder *à la graine d'épinard* (spinach-seed); *toupet en vergette*.

367 · 18th century. **SUITS. WOMEN'S FASHIONS**. Hoop petticoats, panniers. Pastoral dress. The reign of the *coquettes*. Suit with ruffled insets (see pls. 368–370). Luxury clothing. *Habit complet européen*: justaucorps, jacket, breeches. Travelling clothes, gaiters, stockings, shirt, cravat; wigs, *ailes*, high wigs, *le fer à cheval*. Bourgeois cloth: coarse cloth, ratteen, *bouracan*, camlet, drugget. Straw hats; mob-caps; curled hair, *le tour de gorge; le parfait contentement* (see pl. 389); the palatine; *volant en queue*; styles of pannier, *à guéridon, à la coupole, à coudes; traquenard*; half-pannier; *les jansénistes*; French, English, Spanish, Italian-style panniers, *les considérations*; the caraco, or *pet-en-l'air*; apron, shoes.

368 · First half of the 18th century. **EXAMPLES OF FASHION**: *mantille, bagnolette,* panniers (see pl. 369). Ordinary suits, pagoda sleeves.

369 · 18th century. **COSTUMES OF THE NOBILITY, OF THE BOURGEOISIE, OF THE PEOPLE** (reign of Louis XV). *Casaquin*; Polish-style clothes. Chignon; *la physionomie, les crochets, les dragonnes*; headdress *en marli; dormeuse* (see pl. 371). *Devant-de-gorge*; fan-shaped sleeves, *engageantes; robe volante*.

370 · **DRESSING ROOM**, 1760. Deportment, men of court. '*Philosophes*'. Women of the Louis XV period. 'Physiognomy', piquancy, face 'more than pretty', convent complexion, *rengorgements d'ostentation*. Hair *à la grecque*; shirt, bodice, *l'oranger en caisse*; stockings with clocks, shoes, heels. Gallant; soubrette.

371 · **WOMEN'S CLOTHING**, 1720–1789. Light colours; ladies, young girls, nobility, bourgeois women. Cornets, *papillons*; powered hair, *tapé*, sidewhiskers. Watteau gowns, ribbons and tresses, furbelows, *échelles de rubans*, *fausses-robes*, *fourreau*, *corps*, *engageantes*, fan-shaped sleeves. English and American fashions.

372 · **THE WORLD OF FASHION. YOUNG WOMEN OF THE PEOPLE**, 1735–1755. Ladies, gentlemen, with crutch-handled walking stick (*bec de corbin*); examples of abbés; seamstress, lacemaker, *grisette*. Half-dressed state, *en négligé*, *en polisson*. The three-cornered hat, cockade, *mouche assassine*, *cadenettes*; neckerchief, *venez-y-voir*, bib-style apron; men's muff.

373 · **MIDDLE CLASSES**. Petit bourgeois women, their children; the bedroom. *En négligé*, 1739–1749. *Coqueluchon*, *fanchon*.

374 · Second half of the 18th century. **LIVING-ROOM FURNITURE**: sofa, armchair, chair. **SEDAN CHAIR** (see pl. 369). The origin of the glazed sedan-chair. Gilded sedan chairs.

375 · 18th century. **BOURGEOIS FURNITURE**. Cupboard, buffet.

376 · 17th and 18th centuries. **DOMESTIC OBJECTS, GOLDSMITH'S WORK**. Candleholders, torches, snuffers. Ceremonial of candleholder. Gilded bronze.

377 · 18th century. **BOURGEOIS INTERIOR** (see pls. 378, 379).

378 · 18th century. **INDOOR SCENES**. Fashion trends. Customs of the nobility. The *Mariage à la mode*. The Joys of Marriage. Dressing for the Ball.

379 · 17th–18th century. **PURITANS, SAINTS, ROUNDHEADS; THE BOURGEOIS HOME**.

PLATE 371

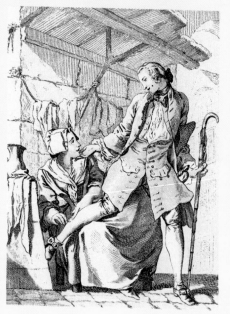

PLATE 372

PLATE 373

553

PLATE 375

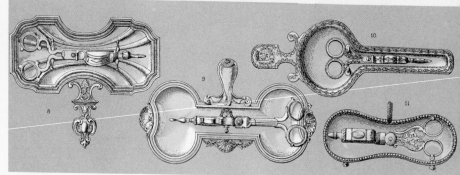

PLATE 376

PLATE 377

PLATE 378

PLATE 379

559

380 · 18th century. **ORNAMENTAL OBJECTS, JEWELLERY,** *menuerie.* Parade
swords. Box with portrait, *croix branlantes,* sword-handle, shell, toilet cases, pin-boxes, depilatory
tweezers, scraper, *escurètes,* pin-heads, *guêpes, papillons,* pendant jewels, watch charms, *apanages, fafioles,*
seals, tassels, broaches, rings, belt jewel, *châtelaine,* watches. Gold, gilded silver, steel; *bijoux rustiques*
(in steel), *pierres de couleur, similor.* Paste jewellery, imitation-jewellers, three *ors de couleur* (enamel);
jewellery for full mourning, for *les grandes pleureuses,* bronzed jewels, half-mourning.

381 · **MILITARY COSTUMES** (see pls. 381–387); cavalry, infantry (reign of Louis XV,
1724–1745). Maréchal de France. King's household; light cavalry (see pl. 383), black musketeer (see
pls. 382 and 383), gendarmerie, officer (see pls. 382 and 383). *Colonel-général* of regiment, sergeant
(see pl. 382); *Royal-carabinier, colonel-général;* dragoon (see pl. 382 and 383); garde de la *connétablie;*
mounted constabulary (*maréchaussée*); provost general. Grenadier, sergeant, *fourche à croc;* foreign
infantry, Linck regiment; drum-major. Halberds, swords, muskets, carbines, pistols, cartridge-
belts, guns, bayonets, axes, picks, spades. Hats, fur bonnets, over-jackets, crosses, leather breeches,
strong boots, gaiters, braid, embroideries, ornaments, colonel's livery. Colour of horses (see pl.
382). White cornet; *compagnie colonelle.*

382 · 18th century. **CAVALRY MUSIC.** Tympanists, drummers, oboe, trumpets. Musketeers, gardes du corps, gendarmes; king's companies, princes' companies; dragoons du Dauphin,
d'Orléans, de Bauffremont; regiments Colonel-général, Villeroy, Royal-Pologne. Royal livery; the
royal blue suit, termed *à la Pologne.*

383 · 18th century, first half. **THE KING, HIS MILITARY HOUSEHOLD,** cavalry;
the body guard, *Gardes du dedans du Louvre,* the Scottish company, *gardes du dehors du Louvre,* light horse,
gendarme. Foreign volunteers: hussards (*Cravates, Polaques*), Ratzky Hussars, hussards de Berchény,
noble volunteers, uhlans, *pacolets, poulcoménics.* Regiments of the maréchal de Saxe, de Clermont-
Prince. Lance, mace, sword-belt, cartridge-belt, cartridge-pouch, cartridge; curved and straight
sabres, sabretache (*paneretesche*). Bonnet, plume, helmet, cockade; blue suit; *red squadrons;* épaulette,
guenille à la Choiseul (see pls. 385–386); jacket, *veste-habit,* cloak; *à la tartare* clothing; trousers, soft boots,
half-boots, spurs. Saddles, stirrups.

PLATE 380

561

PLATE 381

PLATE 382

PLATE 383

PLATE 384

PLATE 385

FRANCE

PLATE 386

567

384 · **THE DAUPHIN. MILITARY HOUSEHOLD OF THE KING**, 1757. Grey and black musketeers; mounted grenadier, garde de la porte (constable of the capitaine de la porte, porter of the garde du roi), 1745. **ROYAL ARTILLERY**: campaign cannons, limber with galoper carriage, trunk, harness; *hussards de Leuchères*. Bearskins, *pokalem*, smock, cloaks, knee-breeches, stockings, half-boots, braids *en onde*, embroideries, checks. Leather equipment, baldrics, guns, bayonets, muskets, pistols, spontoon (see following plate).

385 · **GARDES FRANÇAISES AND GARDES SUISSES**: ceremonial and ordinary uniforms, 1724–1786. Maréchal de France, colonel of gardes françaises; officers, coporal, grenadier, soldier, drummers, cymbal player, invalid officer. Busbies, horned hats, ribbon cockade, gorget; *à la française* suit, lappets; gaiters, stockings, shoes, buckles. *Sabre-briquet* (short sword) or *coupe-chou*. Argenson and Saint-Germain reforms; breaches, pack, decoration thereof, use of wigs. Trumpeter schools.

386 · **ROYAL, LATER REPUBLICAN NAVY**, 1786–1792. Body of officers: admiral, vice-admiral, Western and Eastern vice-admirals; ship's officers, surgeon, guard of the admiral's colours, marine guards (candidates), sailors. Naval infantry, coastguards, officers, soldiers. Hat edged *à la mousquetaire*, cockade; suit, jacket, edging *à la bourgogne*, lapels, ornaments, gilded buttons; knee-breeches, stockings, aglets; *habit-veste*, sailor-style waistcoat, striped trousers; national colours. Hair cadogan-style.

387 · **MILITARY COSTUMES** (Seven Years War, 1756–1763). Prussia. Austria. Historical figures: sovereigns, princes, generals, dragoon. Uniforms of the royal Prussian guard, of officers of the cavalry, of the Austrian infantry, of the Hungarian hussars. Insignia of the order of Mérite militaire; cordons of the Black Eagle, the order of Maria-Theresa, of the Golden Fleece.

PLATE 387

PLATE 388

PLATE 389

571

388 · WOMEN'S COSTUMES. The grand gown *à la française* or decorated gown. Fashionable ladies. Generic types, 1774–1785. Bonnet or *pouf à la Victoire* (see pl. 389), *charmes de la Liberté* headdress; English-style hat. *à la physionomie* curling. bows, buckles, *confident*, collarette or *médicis*, gown ornaments, guaging, furbelows, ribbons, cuffs; manteletta. Ornament, necklace.

389 · 18th century. WOMEN'S FASHION. Formal court dress, hoop petticoat, reign of Louis XVI, first period (see pls. 390, 391 392); tall headdresses. Bonnet *à la laitière*; scarf tied over the hair; *thérèse, calèche, Belle-Poule; fichu en marmotte*; headdress *en baigneuse* (see pl. 391 392), *à l'enfance*; hat *à la Jâquet*; gala headdress, *'le loge d'opéra'*, variants thereof; *toque accompagnée de deux attentions prodigieuses*, bonnet *à la Gertrude*, *à la Henri IV*, *aux navets, aux cerises, à la fanfare*; bonnet *attristé, des sentiments repliés, de l'esclavage brisé*. *Poufs* (Léonard). *pouf au sentiment*, headdress *à la grand'mère* (Beaulard). *Contentement*; caraco; English, Circassian gowns; gowns *en lévite; Amadis* cuffs; trimmings *à la Chartres, au glorieux d'Estaing, aux plaintes indiscrètes, au désir marqué, préférence, vapeurs, agitation, regrets, doux sourire, composition honnête*; belt, *polonaise* gown, with ailes and queue; garment *à l'Austrasienne*, sleeves *à l'Isabelle*, jacket *à la péruvienne*; manteletta, pelisse; embroidered shoes, *venez-y-voir*, high-heels. Fan *du combat naval*. Canes for women.

390 · 18th century. Reign of Louis XVI, second period. The revolution of simplicity. **HEADDRESSES** with hair, bonnet and hat. *Les déshabillés* or *Pierrots* (see pl. 391 392). Dress for ball and for walking. 'Woman by day'. Curling *à la Chartres*, the *hérisson, Gabrielle de Vergy, Montgolfière*; loose hair, steel *coulant*, chignon; gala headdresses, *candeur, zodiacale, au Colisée, de printemps, d'un nouveau goût, le pouf*, curls *à la chancelière*. Mob-cap *à l'espagnole*; hats *à la duchesse, à la Théodore, à la Tarare, au héron, au Palais-Royal, d'un nouveau goût;* Bonnet *à l'anglomane, à la fusée*. Négligé *à l'espagnole*, caraco, sleeves *à soufflets, à la Pierrot*, waistcoat, redingote, petticoat, apron; shoes, toes *en sabot chinois* (see pl. 391 392). Muff, marten tails.

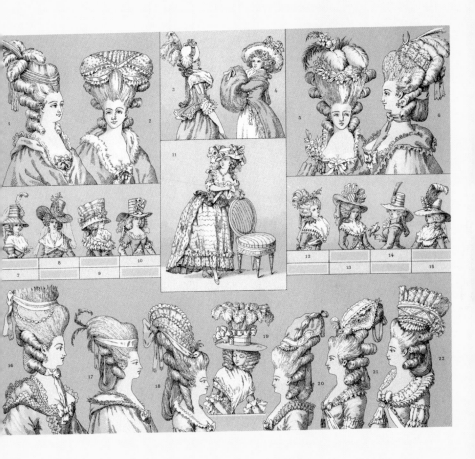

PLATE 390

573

FRANCE

391/392 · Reign of Louis XVI, second and third period. **THE BEAU MONDE**, 1785–1786. Masculine look for women. Ceremonial dress. Court mourning, half-mourning. Riding costume. Children's costumes.

LADIES: *À l'ingénue, le hérisson à crochets, le demi-hérisson,* hair down, *en tapet, à la conseillère, le toupet à temperament;* chignons: *plat, en dessus;* powdering of curls, *pouf en rocher;* white, blonde, russet powder; *à la Cagliostro* pins. Bonnets: *à la turque, à la Jeanette, à la Captif, à la paresseuse, à la Figaro, à la laitière.* Ribbons *au diadème,* velvet *barrières, papillons;* round bonnet, *grande baigneuse,* toque, *pouf,* mob-cap *à la Virginie;* gauze, straw, rush and *à la Malborough* hats; English- and Maltese-style hats, hats *à carcasses, chapeau-feutre, chapeau-bonnette;* helmets *à la romaine, à la Bellone; héron* of feathers, *follettes,* aigrettes. Fichus: *à la Henri IV, à collarette; à l'arc-en-ciel ribbons;* camisole *en colinette;* cuffs *en sabot;* bodice, stomacher; caraco *à l'innocence reconnue* or *à la Cauchoise;* Ball dress *à la paysanne;* chemise gowns, sheath-dress *à la lévite, à l'anglaise, à la turque, à la janséniste, à la circassienne;* redingote with collar; sleeves *à la marinière;* apron, skirt, manteletta, pelisse, marten tails; court wear; truncated pannier, *le cul postiche, les petits coudes;* shoes *à la Jeanette,* with flat heels; gloves, muff, angora. Earring pendants *en mirza, large anneaux branlants, anneaux unis, à perles, à pois, en plaquettes,* watches, trinkets. Canes, switches, hunting-crop (see pl. 398).

MEN: Hats: *en jockey, à l'anglaise, à l'androsmane.* Hair in pigtail, knotted, *catagan, bourse;* hairstyles: *grecque carrée,* braided *à la Panurge;* toupets: square, *en petits crochets, en vergette, en hérisson;* fastening with two or three buckles, or *en marron;* wigs *sans tissu, à jour, crêpé naturel.* Collar *à l'anglaise:* jabot, lace cuffs; *broché* waistcoat; suit, frac, *surtout;* sleeves *à la marinière;* enamelled buttons; knee-breeches, garters, stockings, shoes, red heels, square buckles, boots, spurs; canes; parade swords.

CHILDREN: Headband, felt hat; shirt *en collerette,* corset, petticoat; jacket, redingote, belt, knee-breeches *à la marinière.* Fashionable colours. The importance of the fashion-leaders. The masters of trimmings. *Figures à sentiment* (faces expressive of sentiment). The influence of morality on fashions. *Le grand simple,* etc. The *Cabinet des modes ou des modes nouvelles,* the first fashion periodical.

393 · 18th century. Fontainebleau Palace. Interior decoration, the **BOUDOIR OF MARIE-ANTOINETTE**.

PLATE 393

PLATE 395

579

PLATE 396

394 · 18th century. Louis XVI period. **FURNITURE**: commode, clock, chairs. Chased and gilded bronze (see pls. 395 and 396).

395 · 18th century. **HOUSEHOLD OBJECTS. FURNITURE**. Mantelpiece, clock, candelabras, *girandoles*; armchair, screen.

396 · 18th century. **SEDAN CHAIRS**. Independence **CANDELABRA. TABLE**, gilded wood. **ORNAMENTS** in chased bronze.

397 · 18th century. **DOMESTIC BATH**, bathtub *à la Dauphine*. **WOMEN'S AND CHILDREN'S WIGS**. Bath at home: the antechamber, the bedroom, the bathroom, the garderobe, the dressing room, the steam room. Women's wigs: *chignon, chignon plein, à la paresseuse, croissant, favoris de boucles, boudins, physionomie*. Hair powder. Glover-perfumers.

398 · **WOMEN'S FASHIONS** (reign of Louis XVI, 1787–1792). The *seconde toilette, le grand lever*. Caracos. Hats *à la couronne, au transparent*; Flemish hat, *bourdalou*; *bonnets à cylindre*, chignons *en poire*; chemise *à la grecque, la gorge anglaise, fichu menteur, demi-fichu*, fichu *en chemise*, with jabot, cravat; sheath-dress *en col de canard*; caracos: *le juste, à l'Amadis, à l'Arlaise, à la Suédoise, à la Bostonienne*; sleeves *à l'enfant*; dresses: *négligente, demi-négligente, coupée, en redingote* (see pl. 405). Decoration: *la Cléopatre*, drugget *à l'enfantement, à firmament, en pierres de Cayenne*. Objects in steel: cane pommels, cases, bracelets, earring pendants, chignon-bands. Fan *à la Montmédy. Le joujou de Normandie* or *cran* (yo-yo). *Le rouge de Serkis*.

PLATE 397

PLATE 398

583

399 · **UTENSILS, PERSONAL OBJECTS, TRINKETS**, from the 15th to the 19th century. Place-setting, spoon, fork, *furcheste, forchète, fourchète*; its use in the Middle Ages; forks with two and three prongs. Knives, *gros coustel, parepain* (bread-knife), *serpette, tranche-tige*, chopper. *Forces*, scissors. Cases, cylinders. Engraver's point. Primer, lighter, almoner's purse-clasp, wheel-lock pistol, watches, keys, hairpins.

400 · **MILITARY COSTUMES. REGULAR TROOPS**, 1792–1793. Artillery, hussards de la liberté, line infantry, sappers. The tricolore. Commandant, officers, sergeants, soldiers, drum-major, drummer. Horned hat, cockade, panache, busby, helmet *à chenille*. Hair curled, in tresses, braided, horsetail; powdering *à frimas*. Frac, caraco; knee-breeches *à l'écuyère*, striped trousers; gaiters, half-boots. *Sabre-briquet*, pistol. Harness, shabracks.

401 · **PROVINCIAL INTERIOR**, 1794.

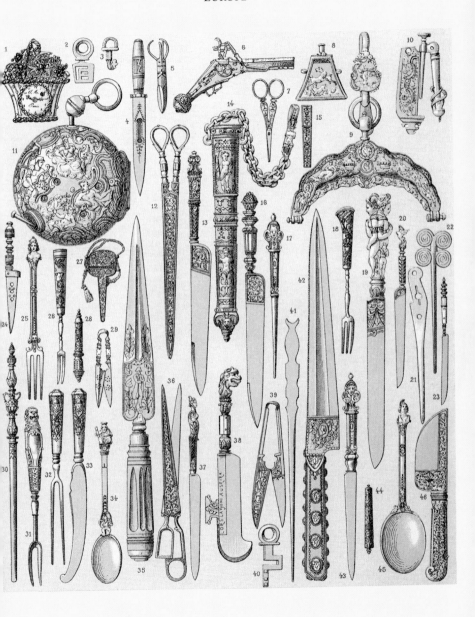

PLATE 399

PLATE 401

18ᵀᴴ–19ᵀᴴ Century: Male and Female costume, Headgear

The illustrations in plate 402 come from journals of the period and tabulate the gradual modification of the length and trimming of bodices. The progress toward the First Empire and reminiscences of Ancient Greece is already clear. Before 1794, the only modification in women's clothes was in the fabrics, which were often striped. The use of silk was avoided, replaced by *toiles de Jouy* (cretonne print). In 1796, women's clothes were suddenly emancipated from the baleened and elongated bodice and tight-fitting gown. The *postiche* was worn with the vast linen *fichu menteur*; tender colours were preferred, with white predominant. This was a comfortable outfit, with the belt at the waist, but it was soon replaced by a tight-fitting gown belted just below the breast, worn with hairstyles borrowed from Greek statuary. To resemble the victims prepared for the guillotine, hair was worn cut short on the back of the neck, *à la sacrifiée*. But this was a passing fashion (pl. 403). As the taste for things Greek and Roman intensified, short, curled hair *à la Titus* was adopted. From this time on, wigs were not openly worn. Hair was dyed. The tight gown in light cloth, with a slender belt beneath the breast, was worn over a simple batiste shirt, and was very revealing. A woman's attractions were barely veiled. The Directory loved dance to the point of folly, and the dance it loved was the waltz, which was of German origin. The women in their all but transparent gauze 'span like tops'. The costume of the dancer grew increasingly scanty; arms were bare to the shoulder, and foot and leg were soon after bared in their turn. On the leg, the slender laces of the classical sandal were not the only feature visible: long, tight pants of pink silk, hugging the body, were at first worn under a chemise dress of pale lawn that did little to impede scrutiny. The pocket was eliminated from women's costume. The fan was slipped into the belt, and the purse worn in the breast. The gentleman's costume (pl. 404) was a square-cut coat-jacket with the *écrouelique* cravat. Breeches were tight and long, and beribboned at the base of the leg. The light shoe was very open and pointed. (The man's waistcoat has risen in the dance to reveal the batiste of the shirt.) Elegant women did not affect ugly or *négligé* effects as the men did. Their outfits combine Anglomania and an intoxication with things classical. 1797 marks the point when military costume began to invade civilian life. The main features of French costume are to be found in the special German fashion journals of the turn of the century (pl. 405).

After the fall of Robespierre, luxury returned. The regents of fashion had been the noble *émigrées*, whose taste had been infected with English opulence during their exile in London. Headdresses became lower. The head was no longer powdered. The German women of plate 405 belong to the period of the Consulate and wear gowns of silk, muslin, percale or gauze. Trousers were increasingly in the ascendant, as the nascent trade in braces testifies. We note, too, that many young people of this period adopted the hunting or postilion's jacket for riding. The bearing of all men savoured of the battlefield and the militaristic tastes of the time. The form of jackets varied extremely; some were tailored in two hours and worn for barely twelve. French fashions, which English fashion had so strongly influenced during the latter years of Louis XVI, underpin the costumes of the figures in plate 405. The publication of these examples by the German fashion journals is clear proof that the infatuation with French fashions had not faded during the Revolution. The adoption of Greek and Roman costume dates from the Directory. Roman costume suited the larger woman whose opulent forms were closer to those of the Roman *matrona*. Greek costume rather suited the younger woman of elegant figure who had nothing to fear from its indiscretion. These *merveilleuses* took care to model themselves on ancient statues and were spoilt for choice with gowns *à la Diane*, *à la Flore*, Vestal-style veils, and so on. The seamstresses who created these archaeological garments were assisted by painters and sculptors. Most of the light cloths used in them, almost exclusively white, were of English origin. Satin, taffeta, velvet and the richer silk stuffs were eschewed. By means of these archaeological restorations, nudity was gradually attained. The gown gradually moved down from the throat. The *merveilleuses* suddenly decreed that chemises were superfluous, and gave them up. In the later Directory, the tunic-shaped dress with short sleeves was still common. Long sleeves were highlighted with a border of coloured silk. Women wrapped themselves in enormous shawls that reached their feet.

During the Consulate, the incessant revolutions of fashion were tempered by the freedom every woman arrogated to herself of dressing just as she wished. The Consulate bestowed aristocracy on talented men and beautiful women. Modern man dresses, but no longer adorns himself. Alongside men buttoned to the neck and constrained by the tightness of their clothing, women in light dresses, devoid of petticoats, were adorned by their bare neck and breast, and the revelation of much else besides. Plate 408 409 bears witness to the peculiar spectacle afforded by year X and its excessively severe winter, which demonstrated how fatal thoughtless fashions could be. The doctors of the time inscribed the names of these literal fashion-victims on the lists of the dead: Mme de Noailles, dead at nineteen, leaving a ball, Mlle de Juigné at eighteen, Mlle de Chaptal at sixteen, and Princess Tufaikin, who died at seventeen in St. Petersburg of the epidemic of French fashions. It was no deterrent. The more ornate women's fashions of the Consulate were more moderate in kind, but during the Directory, nudity was close to becoming women's favourite fashion, and a costume *à la sauvage* was afforded serious consideration. A gown with bodice, narrow épaulettes, and a long, trailing skirt was undoubtedly less audacious than a gauze tunic, or a lawn skirt open to the hip and offering a view of pink silk tights. The classical costumes of the Directory and Consulate made a stir abroad and were seen throughout Europe. In 1801, all the young men were wearing the short woollen frock-coat in grey-blue, grey-green or dark brown cloth, shorts and white stockings, or wide trousers with *à la russe* boots. Men's collars were extraordinarily tight. Not only scarlet but even white waistcoats had their lower part tailored in the style of the Prussian jacket.

1798   1796   1797   1797   1798   1796   1798   1799   1797   1800

1794   1794   1796   1799   1798   1799   1799   1796

PLATE 403

PLATE 404

402 · WOMEN'S COSTUMES. 1794–1800 (see pls. 403 and 405).

403 · WOMEN'S FASHIONS. DECORATION OF HEAD AND BODICE. 1794–1800. Bonnets, *à la lucarne* hats, capotes, low coiffures, curls, pendant chignon; hair *à la sacrifiée*, dyeing of hair. *Fichu menteur.* Pleated, close-fitting dresses, skirt; *postiches*; ribbon belts; copper and steel buckles. Lawn, striped cloths, *toiles de Jouy.*

404 · DIRECTORY. EXAMPLES OF FASHION. *Sabots tournants, croyables, incroyables, merveilleuses, impossibles,* speculators, ruffians. The mania for classical antiquity. Anglomania. 1795–1797. Ladies. Jockey-style hat, bonnets, wigs; lawn shirt; *ailes de papillon* costume; dress *à l'hypocrite, à la Diane, à la Flore, à l'Omphale*; silk knee-breeches; scarf, mantilla; clocked stockings; sandals, shoes; half-length gloves. Men. Hair *à la Titus, à la Brutus,* powdered wig; *écrouelique* cravat, cravat *à la Laignadier, habit carré,* waistcoat *à revers,* knee-breeches, pendant ribbons; corkscrew stockings, dancing-shoes, half-boots (see pls. 405 and 408–409).

PLATE 405

PLATE 406

405 · Military and civilian costumes. **FRENCH FASHIONS IN GERMANY**, 1783–1803. Ladies of Frankfurt and Augsburg, *incroyables, merveilleuses*. Hats *à la Suisse*, round, *bourdalou*, opera hat, two-cornered hat *à la russe, à la Vintimille* (see pls. 408 and 409). Suit with basques, redingote *demi-carrée*, swallow-tail frac, lapels, long frock-coat (*lévite*); knee-breeches, trousers; gaiters, shoes, top boots; cudgel. (For women's fashions, see pls. 398 and 402–404.)

406 · Late 18th century. **WOMEN'S FASHIONS OF THE DIRECTORY AND CONSULATE**. Mania for things Greek, **GRÉCOMANIE**. *Une héroïne d'aujourd'hui. Modes et manières du jour*. Dressing *à la Vestale* (see pl. 408–409). The *volubilis*. Indoor, evening, ball and city wear. Wigs (see pl. 408–409). The phaethon. The crown of corymbs, *frisons d'ébène*. Head veil, hairnet, capote (*sphendoné, cecryphale*), bonnet, aigrette, *esprit, chapeau-bonnet, bonnet-calotte (vesica)*. Tunics (*hemidiploïdion, chloene*). *Tunique coupée*, skirt with train, with half-train, belt (*zona*); shawl (see pl. 407), fichu-shawl, scarf; *coulants* in precious metals, broaches, clasps, bracelets, rings, necklaces, hairpins, earrings. Toe-rings, *carlins*. Pointed shoes, narrow straps. Gloves, *le ridicule*.

407 · **FEMALE COSTUMES. THE SHAWL**, 1802–1814. Cashmere, cloth, woollen, silk, cotton, percale, muslin, lace shawls, ornamental, Turkish shawls. *Pas du schall*.

PLATE 407

408/409 · The Consulate years in year 10 (1802). **FASHIONS. THE PROMENADE DE LONGCHAMP.** Men dress, but are no longer ornamented: *ci-devant, charmant, godiche,* speculator, *riz-pain-sel.* Carriages, box-coat, *jockey.* Men wear boots. Ladies. Hair *à la Titus, moutonnés;* blonde and brown wigs, *tour de cheveux, cache-folie,* veil, coiffure *à serpenteaux,* percale, straw or esparto hat, English-style hat, Hungarian-style capote, *bonnet de négligé, en battant l'oeil,* turban, aigrette, *chefs d'argent.* Square fichu; peignoir *à la Galathée;* bodice *à pièces, à l'Étrurie;* sleeves *à l'espagnole, à la grecque, à l'athénienne;* dresses *à la Philomèle, à la Glaonice, à la romaine, à la Pomone, à la Psyché, à la Rusina,* apron *à la créole;* redingote *à la Naxos;* surtout *à la grecque;* spencer; long, square, cashmere shawls. Blue pearls in lapis lazuli, *serpents,* bracelets, necklaces. Fan, handkerchief. Men. Hair *à la Titus, à la Caracalla.* Formal and semi-formal wear; *chapeaux français;* short frac; waistcoat, Prussian-style jacket; *juponné* or short knee-breech; stockings, boots *à la Souvarow,* iron-tipped heels. Fashionable colours.

410 · **CIVILIAN COSTUMES. MEN FOLLOWING FASHION,** 1801–1805. Dressing according to profession. Rich man, fashionable man, poor devils; poet, painter, musician, architect; bootmaker, tailor, *ci-devant,* petitioning women. The hairdresser as artist. The *costumier intime.* Ornamental, dress and morning costumes. Redingote *à l'écuyère,* waistcoat in swan-down, capote, box-coat, trousers.

PLATE 410

603

IV
TRADITIONAL COSTUME
TILL THE LATE 19ᵀᴴ CENTURY

Sweden, Norway, Iceland and Lapland

The Lapps (pl. 411) occupy an infertile country that is snowbound for nine months of the year. Nomads by necessity, they live in tents and are the last case in Europe of a population living more or less the life of the savage. Lapps preserve themselves from the cold by a system of hermetic closure, wrapping themselves in two or three layers in which fur and wool combine to exclude the outside air. If we except certain headgear, men and women wear the same. No one knows why the men's *kapte* is called *vuolpo* when worn by women. Both sexes wear the boot-trouser, which comes half-way up the thigh and is worn over the shoe. Both wear the same sock and the same pelisse. Women cut and sew these garments, and make shoes and gloves. They also make the harness, collar, saddle and traces for the reindeer. Their preferred material for fur is the skin of the reindeer kid, killed when the first bloom has just moulted and is replaced by thick, silky and tractable hair.

In Iceland (pl. 412), men once had a national costume; they have gradually altered it, and now their jacket (*vadmal*) and their long woollen waistcoat might almost be cut from the same model as those of the Alsatian peasant. The diversity of parish costume that is so striking a feature of Sweden no doubt results from the time when the country was divided between innumerable tribes, and the territory of each group was a kingdom asserting complete independence. The rejuvenation of male ornament and costume are a direct consequence of the traditional character of Swedish men. Whereas women dress in time-honoured outfits, men's clothing antedating the earliest stage of the emancipation of the peasants is entirely lacking. It would seem that one of the laws of Scandinavian costume is that exotic elements should be introduced. In Norway, the tradition that women make clothes for themselves and their families went into abeyance towards the end of the 12th century. Men's clothes then became Germano-Frankish in cut. Swedish women favoured green, blue, and a light and vibrant red. All voyagers speak of their beauty, their slim, graceful figures, the natural elegance of their manner, their blooming complexions and their beautiful hair.

Pine timber is the material best suited to the Norwegian and Swedish climate. Villages do not at all resemble the clusters of houses found in France; a single village often occupies an area of several leagues. The most complete form of rustic timber dwelling is found in the group of buildings constituting the Norwegian *gaard*, whose untranslatable name seems essentially to designate an enceinte. The *gaard* is not a single building, but is made up of independent cabins. The main construction is the family sleeping quarters, and is often in chalet form. Often the complement of a single *gaard* constitutes the entire population of a village. The Norwegian *saeter* is a little farm, uninhabited in winter; in summer it is occupied by a young girl who manages the grazing of sheep and cows all by herself. The houses represented normally comprise only two rooms: a sort of hallway, and a common room in which the woman spins and the man has his workbench. There they cook and there they sleep.

PLATE 412

611

411 · LAPPS. WINTER AND SUMMER COSTUMES; OBJECTS USED. DWELLING. MEANS OF TRANSPORT: winter sled, *pulke* (see pl. 412). Women of Swedish Lapland. Bonnet, *seite*; varieties of *seitares: kalla passe ware, kalla dem passe, saivo-aimo, saino-olmak, haltia, varalde-olmail, varalde-leib* or *tjatse-olmak, biagga-gallas*, square bonnets, bonnets with crest (women), cowl, *kladd*, cravat; jacket, collar; *silfverkrage* (see pls. 412 and 414). Women's belt, *gvinno-balte; kapte, vuolpo*; boot-trouser; summer boots, *sommar-skor*; winter boots, *winter-skor*; Chinese-style shoes; gloves. Braided hair. Rings. Spoons in reindeer ligament, *skedars*; wooden spoons, *kokse af bjork; knif*; sleeve, case; ear-pick, *orslef*; pipes, *lerpipa, tobaksdosa*; purse, *peiningpungar*. Skate, *suksi* (see pl. 413), skate-stick, crook, *klakka* (see pl. 412). Larder in the wilderness, *njalla*. Carry-keg, *mjolk-kagge*. Tent, *kata*, and frame; furnace and ladder; place of husband and wife, *baschio-hiaeshie*, of children, *kask loido*. Covered sleighs, goods-sleigh; *lakkek; kerres*; sleigh-driver's staff, *kor-kapp*. Reindeer, its harness. Coastal and mountain Lapps (see pl. 412), nomads; *Graanlaper*, Lapp of pine-forests; their physiognomies. Tribes, chiefs, home; *laume-gatte*. Work of women: making clothes, shoes, gloves, harness, embroidery. Superstitions, witchcraft; the runic drum; the magus or sorcerer, *tietaja*; demi-god, *puojumala*; the fortune-teller, *noaaid*.

412 · COSTUMES. POPULAR CUSTOMS. Lapp of Kaitum, groom (*brud*), bride (*brugdom*) from Karajosk. Mountain Lapp, *Fjall-lapp*. Carrying the child: cradle, *katkem* (see pl. 411). Winter and summer costumes; the snow-boat, *akkja*; harness (Lappmark, Swedish Lapland; Finnmark, Norwegian Lapland). Young girl from Reykjavik, ceremonial costume. Embroidered collar, medallions, button, headdress with crest (see pl. 413). Peddler. Rustic classes, the free peasant, *danneman*; women, children; marriage costume, fiancé; everyday and Sunday wear. Summer clothes (Sudermania, Dalecarlia, Bleking, Scania). Women. Coiffure, fringed wool, bonnet; married woman's, that of the young woman, *kallarma*; children's bonnet; Shirt; sleeves, bodice, braces; fichu, apron, *shalong*; skirt; overcoat; leather bag, gloves, handkerchief or book-wrap, *baklappen*. Arrangement of hair. Necklaces. Head-needles. Men. Hat, *bourdalou*, cravat, collar, waistcoat, redingote, épaulettes, embroidery, knee-breeches, stockings, garters, shoes, the fiancé's whip (see pl. 415).

413 · COSTUMES. ORNAMENTS. CUSTOMS. OBJECTS OF DAILY LIFE.

Lap skates, *suksi*; metal pipe. Family from Hnappavellir: shirt, breeches, *vadmal*; braces, stockings, shoes, straps, bonnet, tassel, skirt, braids, embroideries, gloves, loose hair. Fishing costume: seal-skin, bonnet or hat, jacket, hood, trousers; woman's saddle; planchette; snuff-box; belt ornaments; buttons; bells. Churching and mourning clothes. Winter costume, bonnets, hood, coiffures, that of the *sjelfvan* or married woman, *sharlakana-mossa*; that of the bride, *crown of tin*; fichu, bodice, its fasteners; apron, cape, pelisse; jewellery worked in precious metals, use of canes; the knights of the wedding, *rudiman*. Candlestick, tripods, candlebra. Rustic manor, the house of Ornas. *Essay on the philosophy of costume*. The German in Tacitus. The Indo-German race. The Swedish and Norwegian peasant. Parish costumes; their local unity. The former tribe. Men's dress rejuvenated by women, who, for themselves, persist with immemorial custom.

414 · LAPPS, NORWEGIANS, SWEDES. LAPP HUSBANDS, WOMEN, CHILDREN: summer costume (Nordlanden, Finnmark). Bride, bridesmaid; diocese of Bergen. Boy, girl; marriage dress; peasant below the age of majority. Whites and blacks (Scania, Dalecarlia). Riding costume; minor's apron, *forskinn*; dagger-knife, *dolkknif*; pelisse, sheepskin. Crown-like headdresses (see pls. 415 and 417), cravat, bodice, épaulette, plastron, layers of petticoat, apron, the fiancée's handkerchief.

PLATE 413

PLATE 414

615

415 · **PEASANTS** (Scania, Dalecarlia, Sudermania, dioceses of Bergen and Trondheim). Woman harvester, farmer, Sunday best, boy, girls, marriage and ceremonial costumes; women, children. Shining crown, the high bonnet of the fiancée; fichu, pelerine, autumn shirt, *hoste sarken*, apron; seasonal colours, yellow, the colour of mourning; *chalong, vadmal*; muff; shoes with straps, with central heel. Hat, beaver hat, bonnets, fur, frac, suit, waistcoat with basques, long frac, *walmar*, hide knee-breeches, stockings, boots. Gifts of fiancé and fiancée: riding gloves, belt-cord, *pengtrossen, the suitor's box.*

416 · **PEASANTS, CLOCK-MAKERS, BRIDE, BRIDESMAID, SUNDAY BEST. MARRIAGE AND CEREMONIAL WEAR** (Dalecarlia, Scania, diocese of Bergen).

PLATE 415

617

PLATE 417

619

417 · GOLDSMITH'S WORK IN SWEDISH AND NORWEGIAN PEASANT ORNAMENTS. Marriage crowns, earrings, necklaces, plates, pendants, medallions, hearts, crosses, broaches, fasteners, roundel. Ornament in plain copper, popular jewellery of great antiquity. Scythian jewellery set with gems reflected in the tawdry rustic ornaments. Lapp stones set by Swedish lapidaries. Sumptuary laws, among the Germans, authorising for girls and young ladies what they forbade married women, widows, Beguines, etc.

418 · WOODEN HOUSE. Interior, house with raftered ceiling, *ryggastuga*; rustic life; domestic articles and utensils. The caravan, *seiter* or (Norwegian) *gaard*. Isolation of settlements. Rooms of the house: vestibule, common room; walls and paintings thereon; stove, fireplace; bed, trunk, desk, table, clock box, benches, spinning-wheel, butter-pot, candleholder, tripod, snuff-box, tobacco-pouch; child's clogs; plates of earthenware and wood; wooden objects: coffee-pot, jugs, pancheon, butter-box. Double and triple cups and spoons 'for amusement'. The soup spoon and marriage spoon.

PLATE 418

621

The Netherlands

In the Netherlands, as elsewhere, peasants and those who live off the sea are naturally backward. Among the Saxons who occupy Zeeland, children are dressed like their parents as soon as they can walk. For his wedding, the peasant receives from his parents a doublet, a waistcoat, a pair of short black breeches and the *kappe*, the full-length redingote. Jacket, waistcoat, cravat, short, tight breeches and buckled shoes are products of more or less recent times. The replacement of the three-cornered by the straight hat is an indication of the existence of certain trends. A further index of this relative modernity is that the *huiken*, an ancient pluvial surmounted by a hat, which is the Dutch cloak *par excellence*, is no longer worn. Tobacco is used as a sort of local homeopathy. Some physiologists have claimed that tobacco smoke wreathes the mind in fog. The Dutch are a living refutation of this; they live in a cloud of tobacco smoke and their minds are more positive and precise in details than any other people's. In 1807, Maaskamp noted that every town in the Netherlands had its own costume and even in Amsterdam, costume varied in almost every area of the town. Plates 421–422 show how the costumes of Dutch women are a composite of clothes of modern cut and the national headdress. The masculine costume of the island of Urk comprises a fur bonnet, a short jacket, a double-breasted waistcoat, baggy pleated shorts that resemble short skirts, black stockings and broad mules with a large silver buckle.

The *aanspreker* is a kind of beadle dressed all in black, who announces the death of inhabitants in lugubrious tones and prays at their funerals.

The national costume of Frisian women is complicated. It is affected by the age and condition of the woman, whether marriageable, married or widowed. The furniture of the bourgeois interior in Hindeloopen has a very oriental savour to it (pl. 424). If there is an overall style, it is a somewhat cumbersome version of Louis XIV pieces. There is also a striking contradiction between the garish colours of the furniture and the severe timber construction of the alcove with its two beds.

PLATE 420

419/420 · **POPULAR COSTUMES,** early 19th century. **TRADITIONAL CLOTHES.**
Fishermen, labourers. Island-peasants, boatman, *schipper-oom*, lady, serving-woman, dairymaid,
fishwife; festive, formal (visiting) and work wear (Rotterdam, Scheveningen; Walcheren, Marken,
Ens, Zuid-Beveland, Nord-Holland; Friesland). Men: three-cornered hat, upright hat, skullcap,
cravat, waistcoat, doublet, jerkin, redingotes, *kappe*, waistcoat, jacket, belt, buttons worked in precious metals, trunk hose, knee-breeches, shoes, buckles; knife and sheath (see pls. 422 and 423).
Women: straw hat, marked hats, hoods, coiffe, lace, embroidery, bonnet strings, ribbons. *Casque,*
forehead plates, forehead irons, *hoofdnald* (see pls. 421–423). Jewelled capbands, neck-chains, ear
pendants, pendants, disks, necklaces, fasteners, rings. Chemisette, sleeves, choker, neckerchief,
bodice, camisoles, pectoral, apron, frieze, layers of petticoats (see pl. 422), pockets, manteletta;
shoes, buckles, flat shoes, clogs. Hair-washing using lye.

421 · 14th century. **WOMEN'S COSTUMES. COIFFURES; HEAD ORNAMENTS.**
Frisian woman; village women from Zaardam, Krommenie; young women from the islands of
Ameland, Groningen, Zuid-Beveland; women from Beyerland, Dordrecht. Coral necklaces, *bloed-
koraal*, golden and silver fasteners. (See also pl. 422.)

PLATE 421

627

PLATE 423

629

422 · **COSTUMES** from the early 19th century; **MODERNS**. Married women, village women, fishermen's wives, orphan girl, ladies, fishermen, funeral prayer-speaker (*aanspreker*); headdresses; working and festive costumes. The right of passage. *heule*; the Frisian sled, *steeksledje* (Merken, Urck, Marken, Schowen, Walcheren islands, Zandvoort, Volendam, Ziericksee, Scheveningen, Nord-Holland, Friesland). Women. Golden pins, *krullenne bellekens*; bodice, *manteltge*; plastron, *buck en kleuren*; flower-pattern dresses, apron; little chains, scissors, needles, rings, jewelled rings; perfume, pastille and coin boxes. Men. Round hats, stovepipe hats, fur bonnets, earrings; shirt, trimmings, buttons, medals; sleeved waistcoat, *borstrokken*; hooded jacket, knee-breeches, baggy or with large flaps, buckles in precious metals; boots, shoes with laces or buckles; umbrella. The skate, the true shoe of the Frisian woman.

423 · **PEASANT JEWELLERY. OBJECTS IN GENERAL USE.** Ornamental objects in precious metals. Iron plaques for women. Forehead ornaments, *hoofdnaald*, brow pins, pendants, *krullene bellekens*, spirals, forehead plate, buckles, earring pendants, necklaces, *bloed koraal*, clasps, broaches, fasteners. Chain, trimmings of shirt- and jacket-buttons, belt-plate, watch-chain. Knife, sleeve, sheath, pipe-carrier. Varieties of plaque varying with province: Groningen, Over-Yssel, Zeeland, Zuyderzee, Nord-Holland. Women of Volendam and Kruiningen; plaques for formal and less formal wear; slender headbands, *voor hoofden*, flat headbands, *hoofdyzer*; the Frisian woman's gold circle, the double 'spike' ornament, little flags. Peasant's knife, weapon of combat.

424 · **OLD FRISIAN DWELLING. BOURGEOIS HOUSE: INTERIOR, TWO ASPECTS.** Alcove, doors with openwork sections; built-in bed, cradle, prie-dieu, glazed cupboard, folding tables, stool, chairs, cuckoo-clock, brazier, warming-pan; Delft dishes, plates, cups; faience tiles. Fireplace, heating, *veenen*. Colours of furniture. The ancestral chest.

PLATE 424

631

SCOTLAND AND ENGLAND

Until 1745, Razunah [Rannoch] moor, a wasteland of some twenty thousand miles in Perthshire, Scotland, remained impenetrable to any but the natives who guarded its narrow passes. Before the 18th century, there was little or no communication between the Highlands and Lowlands. Only in 1811 could a carriage first travel between them. The characteristic of Celtic organisation that has remained the preserve of the Highlanders is the well-known division into clans. The clan chief is called the *laird*, and all the members of the clan have the same name, with the prefix *mac* (son). Among the Britons, the production of *tartans* goes back to the earliest times; the same is true of the plaid. The overall design and colour-scheme, the *breacan*, varied for each clan, becoming a badge of community. It too was regulated by rank, as the *Ilbreachta* law prescribed: peasants and soldiers had clothes of a single colour, officers wore two colours and the clan chief three. The higher class of nobles, *Beatachs* or *Bruighnibs* wore four, the greatest aristocrats wore five, the *Ollamhs* or philosophers six, and the royal family seven. The *arisaid* is a plaid no longer in use today; it was long enough to wrap a man from head to foot.

By bringing together the popular costumes of England (pls. 428–430), some of which are more than a century distant one from another, we have sought to demonstrate, in spite of transformations, a certain permanence in national customs. In England, neither man nor woman ventures out without a hat.

PLATE 425

PLATE 426

635

425/426 · NATIONAL COSTUMES, FROM PAGAN TO MODERN TIMES.

Irish bards, *awenydd, ollamh.* Pictish warrior. Ancient Gaels. Lairds, chieftains; gentlemen, *druine usual;* Highlanders; archer, *cearnaich;* piper. *Breacan,* plant insignia of the clan; the *Ilbreachta* law; colours and forms of clothing, dark red colour, *ruadh;* Stuart tartan, *breacan deary na Stiubartich;* coats of arms, symbols. Clans: Mac Dugal of Lorn, Ferguson, Mac Inne, Mac Cruimin, Mac Coll, Mac Donald of the Isles, Mac Qaaries, Sken, Graennes, Robertson, Mac Ivor, Grants of Glenmoriston, Mac Intoshes, Mac Lead, Forbes, Mac Donnel of Glengarry, Frasers, Chisholms, Campbells of Breadalbane, Menzies, Ogilvies, Davidsons, Stuarts, Buchanans, Kennedys, Mac Machtans, Mac Intires, Murrays, Mac Donald of the Ranald clan, Mac Aulays, Mac Leans. Helmet, *clogaid;* hauberk, *lurich;* buckler, *targaid;* its boss, *capan;* handle, double internal handle. Handspear, *aseth, triniframma; aropstara;* one- and two-handed claymores: basket-hilt, *cliabh;* sword, *claidheamb;* dagger, *bidag;* sabre, baldric, bow, arrows, quiver. Hood, *barrad,* cloak, *cochal,* of the Ollamhs. Bonnets, *bonaid-gorm, glengarry;* shirt, *Lein-Croich;* surcoat, jacket, doublet, skirt, *fheile beag, kilt;* plaid, *breacan fheile;* breeches, *trews;* stockings, *moggans;* brodequins, *cuarans;* purse, *sporran;* tobacco horn, *snaoisin* (see pl. 427). Long hair, low chignon.

PLATE 427

637

PLATE 428

427 · HIGHLANDERS. Women's costumes, dairymaid, *banarach*; horseman, his mount, Shetland pony. Offensive and defensive weapons. Sinclair, Cloqhons, Mac Nicols, Farquharsons, Urqharts, Mathesons, Mac Niels, Mac Ivor, Chisholm, Mac Lean, Frasers, Guns, Mac Lachlaim. Scarf, tartan, plaid, *tonag* or *guailleachan, arisaid*; broaches, shoes, brodequins. Braided hair, ribbons. The large pike, *tuagh-cath*; *targaids* in which the boss is replaced by a steel blade, claymores. Horse harness, garrot, hazel-switches, bridle, horsehair cords, saddle, goatskin.

428 · 18th–19th century. OUTDOOR WEAR. Examples from the lower classes. Historical figures. The *bliaut*. Women almanach-, pudding-sellers, fishwife; fortune-teller, milk-girl; peddlers of nostrums, onions. Draymen. Watermen of public carriages; sailor with paralysed legs; drover; postman; sailor; shoeblack; fireman; market-gardener, cauldron-maker, tinker (see pl. 429).

429 · 19th century, first part. **LOWER CLASSES.** History of the street cries of London. Concert of vendors' voices. Top hat. Milkmaid; match-girl; barrow woman; woman shrimper; Billingsgate fishwife; postman; fireman (pickaxe); newsman; watchman; (linkboys, linkmen); baker; Welsh washerwoman, with wooden paddle. Gypsy.

430 · First part of the 19th century. **HIERARCHICAL AND PROFESSIONAL COSTUMES.** Dignitaries: judge, bishop, the Speaker, the Lord Mayor of London, alderman, invalids of army and navy; Chelsea and Greenwich pensioners. Women's costume: lady, summer wear, 1814. Working class: dustman, Hastings fisherman, beadle, schoolboy of Christchurch Hospital or 'blue-jacket boy'.

431 · Early 19th century. **INLAND TRANSPORT.** Gates on roads, the toll-gatherer. Coaches: wicker governess's cart, caravan, stage-coach, post-chaise, rustic tilbury, market-gardener's cart. Toll-money, payment which the king himself is not excused.

PLATE 429

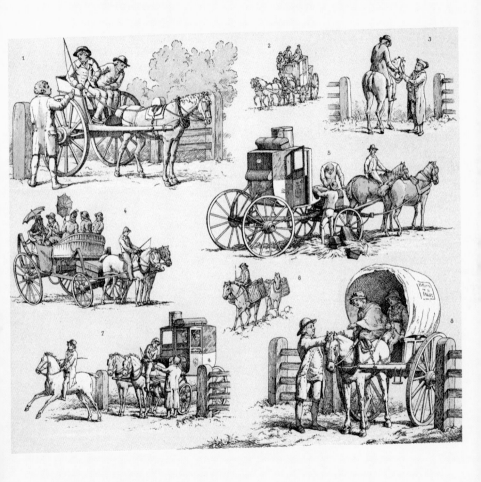

PLATE 431

643

GERMANY AND SWITZERLAND

In the regions of Bavaria where religion divides the population, Catholics and Protestants are marked out by their costumes. In general, Catholics prefer light colours, while the Protestant chooses dark ones. The Catholic's hat is adorned with yellow and green ribbons, the Protestant's with black ones. Over their shirts, whose sleeves never go beyond the elbow, Bavarian women wear corsets either very open at the breast or closed to the collar. These are accompanied by fichus of cotton, normally with flower patterns printed on a bright red background. The thickly pleated gown is mid-length and is generally in very striking colours: bright red, carmine, green, blue, and so on. The apron is generally in the same range of colours. On festive days, it is in shaped silk, trimmed with lace and embroidered ribbons. The wide hats worn by the men are of soft felt, and consequently of highly unpredictable shape. The peasant is normally clothed in a simple jacket without waist. But for Sundays, he puts on a redingote in dark-blue wool decorated with metal buttons; these last are made of coins, from the six kreutzer piece to the thaler. When a man has been on a spree, he takes his knife to the buttons of his jacket or waistcoat, and the coins re-enter circulation. The plates that follow (433–437) show examples of the costumes of the Tyrol and of Switzerland. In Bohemia, Germans have all but abandoned their national costume. In Saxony, the women's costume is a silk skirt trimmed with embroidery, a woollen fichu embroidered with silk flowers and an apron covered with embroidery. Everywhere in Switzerland, brilliant, joyous colours are worn. The inhabitants like to wear light-coloured fabrics, and there is something strikingly fulfilled about their entire demeanour. The tranquil position adopted by one of the countrywomen in plate 434 brings out the coquetry of her costume admirably. Even today, in the countryside one may find traces of the Berne costume, including the coiffes comprising a halo of black lace. But in the canton of Berne itself, as in many other regions of Europe, the native costume is only ever worn by peasant- and serving-women.

PLATE 432

647

PLATE 433

649

432 · **POPULAR COSTUMES** (Bavaria, Saxe-Altenburg). Upper and Middle Franconia. Aschaffenburg. Lower Bavaria. Upper Palatinate. Swabia. Altenburg bride (see pl. 433). *Pelzkappe*, headband; frontlet, bonnets, coiffes, embroidery, lace, bonnet-ribbons, 'wings', ribbons, braided hair; bridal crown, *hormbt*; corset, fichu, jacket, stuffed and bouffant sleeves; gowns, apron, necklace, pearls, garnets, goldsmith's work; clocked stockings, shoes; fringes. Round, conical, cylindrical, broad- and narrow-rimmed hats; waistcoat, jacket, redingote, silver buttons, knee-breeches, trousers. Catholics and Protestants distinguished by the colours they wear.

433 · **POPULAR COSTUMES**. Womenswear: bonnets with crests, coiffure with long ribbons. Altenburg women. Austria. Tyroleans: mountain people, peasants, women of Zillerthal, Pusterthal, Sarnthal, Ötzthal, the valleys of the Inn and Passeyer; Bohemians from Auherzen and Klattau. Germany, Württemberg, Silesia. Women of the Black Forest; peasant of the Monts-Géants. Saxony, woman of Tennstedt, young Wendian Woman. Woman fruitseller from Hamburg; woman of Coburg. Student of Heidelberg from Romantic period. Headband, *stirntüchel*, diadem, *nadel*; hat, coiffe, bonnet, ribbons, metallic embroideries, collar, lace, tucker, fichu, bodice, braces, clasps, jacket, *miederleibel*; linen cuffs; *kurass*, embroidered initials, belt, skirt, horsehair bustle, apron, shoes, rosettes; braided hair, chains, crosses. Felt hat, tassels, aigrettes, cravats; waistcoat, *brustfleck*, jacket, *joppe*, belt; metal buckles, belt-plate; redingote for festivities (*der gottestischrock*); knee-breeches, stocking, laced shoes, broad-headed nails, *stossnagel*.

434 · First part of the 19th century. **POPULAR COSTUMES**. Lucerne, Fribourg, Zug, Berne, Schwyz, Schaffhausen, Valais cantons (see pls. 435 and 436). Peasants, peasant women, dairymaid from Oberhassli. Formal and work wear; light colours. Long and shortened clothes. Straw hats, flowers, ribbons, toque, forage cap, loose hair, with horsehair hairpieces; ruffle, chemise; initial letters; bodices, embroidery, braces, apron, tunic, skirt, belt; stockings, garters, necklaces; *Agnus Dei* (see pl. 435). Doublet, jacket, bouffant hose, knee-breeches, leather belt.

PLATE 434

651

PLATE 435

PLATE 436

PLATE 437

435 · **WOMEN'S COSTUMES.** Berne, Appenzell, Fribourg, Uri, Lucerne, Schwyz, Unterwalden. Bridal wear. Ancestral costume. Coiffures, gauze crest, tall bonnet, head decoration, silver spoon; flounced bonnet, choker in precious metals, gold chain with locket, pendants. Bracelets, plastron, caraco; shoes, buckles, metal heels.

436 · **UNTERWALDEN, SAINT-GALL, BERNE, VALAIS, ZURICH, ZUG, LUCERNE, BASEL.** Bodices cut Italian-style, little chains, half-sleeves, *gigot* sleeves, long and short skirts. The influence of habits and the physical and moral environment on the appearance of the costume, its gayness or dullness. For active women, length of skirts dependent on whether the town or countryside is hilly.

437 · **PIPES ANCIENT AND MODERN**: pipe-cases, smoker's accessories, tinderbox, tobacco-bag. Norway, France, Italy, Belgium, the Tyrol, Hungary; Bohemia, Greece and Germany.

RUSSIA

No other empire in the world presents so great a diversity of race as Russia. This diversity is naturally reflected in costume. Alas, lack of documentation makes it impossible to determine the nature of those of the most distant past. The Normano-Varangian incursion to which the political foundation of the future (9th century) empire is attributed must have left some mark on costume. Russia took from Byzantium not just its religion, but its entire civilisation. Byzantine costume first penetrated the court, then spread to the upper classes as a whole. The relatively short man's garment, open from the belt up, was succeeded by the long Byzantine robe without opening, which was bordered by strips of coloured fabric. The women followed this trend even more enthusiastically than the men; it was, however, interrupted by the Mongol invasion of the mid-13th century. The upper classes then quickly adopted their conquerors' costume; at first blended with Byzatine fashions, they eventually eliminated them altogether, the costume of the sovereign once excepted. The closed Byzantine robe gave way to the Mongol robe, which opened full-length at the front but was buttoned on the chest. The sleeveless coat was replaced by an overcoat often possessed of a very broad collar that was sometimes folded down over the shoulders but often worn upright, or extended to form a hood. The new costume lasted longer than Mongol oppression, which continued into the 16th century. This costume is still worn in certain regions. In the 16th century, menswear began to include a broad, short shirt with a small collar between the shoulders of which was sewn a triangular piece of embroidered red silk. The rich now adopted a tight garment called the caftan, which came down only as far as the knees and had very long sleeves, which were allowed to hang down in company far enough to hide the hands. The cloths used for this garment were silk, velvet, taffeta, wool or cotton. The boots used by Russians since the 10th century were normally in coloured morocco leather with pointed toes. Women's costume was very largely the same, though somewhat broader and looser; it did not generally include the caftan. Popular costume in Russia is very various. The Byzantine influence never affected it. According to region, it is of Slavic or Tartar origin. The primitive originality of popular costume has survived principally among women. The most important part of this costume is the headgear called the *tshepatz*, in all it many varieties (pl. 441). Women of the people continue to use very crude cosmetic effects, covering the face in layers of white and rouge. This custom formerly prevailed among the upper classes too. Plate 443 shows the main room of the *izba*, the Russian peasant dwelling. This room, the *svetlitza*, though it is on the first floor, is reached from outside.

PLATE 439

PLATE 440

RUSSIA

The *izba* shown is of the Moscovite type, and typical of the northern part of Russia. Plate 444 gives an insight into Russian dance, which is a sort of pantomime of courtship. Young Russians are very agile and light-footed. They sometimes spin round on one foot, almost sitting down, then spring up and take up a grotesque attitude, which they vary continuously as they spin. Plat 446 shows a *kibitka*, the tent of the Kalmucks, who live on the shores of the Caspian sea or at the foot of the Altai mountains.

438/439 · 16th–19th century. **HISTORICAL FIGURES:** tsars, princes, boyars, boyar's daughter, Cossack chieftain, *ataman*. Camp, ceremonial and morning clothing. Popular costumes: women, young women of Tver, Torjok (see pl. 440) and Riazan. Festive costumes. Byzantine, Mongol and Polish fashions: bonnets, fur, velvet, embroidered shirts, collars, triangular piece, *caftan, half-caftan, ferez*, smock, *zipoune; kozir* collar; pelisse, long sleeve; frogs, Brandenburgs, cordons, tassels, hand-towel; trousers, belt and cord, Tartar-style boots. Beards worn. Women's costumes. Diadem-bonnet, canvas bonnet, *volosnik*, coiffure rising to a point, *kokoshnik*, hood, *kitshka*, piece of cloth, *povoynik*, veil, *nadzatylnik*, collarette; long robe, *sarafan*, manteletta-casaquin, *dushegreyka*; over-garment, *ponka*, half-mitten.

440 · **SLAVO-RUSSIANS.** Mordvin, Kalmuck, Tartar. Artisan's wives, labouring women, farmer, inhabitant of the steppes. Bonnets: *tshepatz*, headbands, headband as bonnet string, headscarves; white linen sleeves. Mosquito-net veil, long and short sleeves, overall, belt, boots, strong shoes.

441 · **POPULAR COIFFURES; HEAD ORNAMENTS** (see pl. 442). Inhabitant of Tikhvin. Women of the governments of Novgorod, Kursk, Kaluga. *Tshepatz, kokoshnik*, bonnets, hairbands, toques, turbans, hoods, crowns, diadems, veils, flounces, embroideries, cloth of gold, spangles, pearls, precious stones. Necklaces, earrings.

442 · **POPULAR COIFFURES OF SLAVO-RUSSIAN WOMEN**, in the governments of Novgorod, Kaluga, Tver and Kursk. Use of cosmetics.

Russia

PLATE 442

443 · IZBA, DWELLING OF THE MUZHIK. First-floor room, *svetlitza*. Stove, bed; benches, table; images of the Virgin, of a saint (icon); portraits of the tsar and tsarina; pine walls. Additional rooms, dressing room, *seny*; tool and utensil room.

444 · SLAVIC MARRIAGE. RUSSIAN DANCE. The priest, priestly habits, the icon of the house, candles, the bride and groom, silver crowns, *drugeki*; blessing of the rings, entertainments. Ancient customs: asking for bride's hand in marriage, celebration of betrothal, presents (*dari*) of the bride, marriage procession, church wedding, the kiss of love, *kitra*, return to the house; women's coiffe, *svakha* or *pronuba*. Balalaika, guitar

445 · POPULAR COSTUMES. Little Russian, Russian: Cheremiss, Bulgars (governments of Orel, Kherson, Nizhni Novgorod, Simbirsk). Women. Coiffures: *tshepatz, kakolshnik*, bonnet, hood, veil, necklaces, earring pendants, belt, clasps, scarf, tucker, embroidery, plastron, coins, disks; tunic, dress, apron, manteletta; boots, shoes, laces. Men. Bonnet, *kalpak*; waistcoat, *beshmet*; *tulup, caftan*, pelisse; trousers, *chirivari*; strong boots, *laptis*.

PLATE 443

PLATE 444

PLATE 445

446 · **KALMUCK TENT, KIBITKA.** Nomad customs. Temporary village, *ulus*; building of *kibitka*; wattle, felt blankets, wood-framed door. Tripod, bed, trunks, shelves, seats, samovar, utensils; images of gods, prayer-wheel. Kalmucks, a people of horse-riders. Costume, diet.

447 · **OSTYAKS. TUNGUS. INDIANS OF RUSSIAN AMERICA (ALASKA). KOLOSH OR HINKITE. CRIMEAN HEADGEAR.** Bonnet, hood, robe, overall, wool, cloth, fur, earring pendants, pearls, *perlines*. Hide garments; light, waterproof shirt made from the guts of sea animals; waterproof shoe, made from seal throat-skin.

448 · **POPULAR COSTUMES.** Russians: Cossack shepherd; Romanian peasants. Crimean Tartars. Tartar class: children and schoolmaster. Muslims, speaking Osmanli. Podolia, Orel, Romania, Crimea. Hats, ball-shaped bonnet, *kalpak, caciola*; shirt, waistcoat, jacket, *kyssa-hurk*, smock, belt, trouser, *shalwar*; felt leggings, shoe, laces, sandals, *opinci*. The 'Golden Horde'. Women's nails stained red, a reminder of their Asiatic origin. The great antiquity of the Romanian stock.

PLATE 447

PLATE 448

671

POLAND, HUNGARY, CROATIA AND THE UKRAINE

The unity of the Slav race is indisputable, and can still be confirmed today, despite secondary differences, in the generic character of its popular costumes. The Slavs are nowadays divided into three main groups: East Slavonic (White Russians and Ruthenians), West Slavonic (Poles, Czechs, Serbs and Slovaks) and South Slavonic (Bulgarians, Croatians and Slovenes). From the 2nd to the 10th century, Slav costume must have been a uniform of great simplicity. The reasons for this were several: racial unity and the relative uniformity of central Europe's temperate climate were contributing factors, but the main one was the social unity of these peoples, who governed themselves according to perfectly democratic rules, took up arms only against aggressors and had no privileged classes. The rare documents of this period show us men wearing trousers of greater or lesser width, a long belted robe that came down below the knees, and a bonnet of conical section, either truncated or pointed. The outside garment was a sleeveless cloak of coarse wool, generally fastened on the left shoulder and thus covering the left-hand side of the body. The women wore a double robe. The under-robe was long, the upper robe came down to the knee and had short sleeves. This outer garment was borrowed from the Roman women of antiquity. A similar overcoat is still worn in Poland today by the peasant women of certain provinces; it has long sleeves and is known as an *amie*. The sleeved robe of the Dacian is still the standard garment of the Polish peasant.

The history of Poland itself does not really begin till after the introduction of Christianity in the 10th century. With it arrived the feudal influences of the West. Thereafter costume became one of the distinctive signs of the nobility. Placed on the border of two different civilisations, the Christian West and the Arab world of Asia, Poland was necessarily influenced by both sides. In the 14th century, the traditional component of the costume was still a long tight-fitting tunic with an upright collar measuring some three centimetres in height. This tunic is the Slavic *zupan*, whose form remained unaltered. It was still worn in Poland at the beginning of the 19th century. From the 14th century on, the fashions of western Europe exercised a strong influence over Polish costume. The various figures in plates 449–453 show how royal and princely costume grew increasingly remote from that of everyday life. The clothes worn over the *zupan* by nobles and the bourgeoisie in the 16th century show great variety. The sabre was an indispensable part of the gentleman's costume. The populace wore a short tunic, tight-fitting trousers, a long overcoat or pelisse of sheepskin, boots or shoes woven from bark, a conical hat with a small brim, and finally a belt of wool and leather that might be broad or narrow. The women wore a chemise, a petticoat, often a bodice and a long overcoat. Towards the end of the 18th and at the beginning of the 19th century, the costumes of the various regions of Poland took on more precise form, such that today we find in them an anthology of all the old forms of the national dress. They present too great a variety to be described in detail, but our figures show the principal types.

449 · 13th and 14th centuries. **KINGS, NOBILITY, CLERGY, RELIGIOUS OR-DERS, BOURGEOISIE.** The origins of the Slavs. Their division into Oriental, Western and Southern. The costumes in general. Bonnet, fichu, robe (*amicula barbarica*), the amict or *przyaciolka*; mantle, trousers; scale and leather armour. Middle Ages. Nobility. Influence of oriental costume; fashions of western Europe; *zupan* (see pls. 450–454). Hood, the colour *karmazyn*; belts in leather- and goldsmith-work; robe, trunk-hose; shoes, straps, boots. Shaven head, beard. Helmets, nasal; mail, plate- and scale-armour; sword, cutlass, spear, crossbow. Coiffe of married woman, *podwika*. Crowns, bonnets, dresses, sable, belts; hair loose or braided. Costumes of the bourgeoisie; influence of German and Italian fashions.

450 · 14th–15th century. **TYPICAL AND HISTORICAL FIGURES. ROYAL AND PRINCELY COSTUMES.** The Teutonic Order; the white mantle of its knights. Gentlemen, bourgeois, peasants, working clothes. The under-garment, *kontusz*.

451 · 14th–15th century. **MILITARY AND CIVILIAN COSTUMES; ORDI-NARY AND CEREMONIAL CLOTHING.** Princes, feudal lords, bourgeois, arbalaster, judge, executioner. Cloaks, *szuba*; garments of Turkish origin, *ferezya, delia* (see pls. 452 and 453). *Deliutka* or *deliura*. Pointed shoes.

PLATE 449

PLATE 450

PLATE 451

PLATE 452

PLATE 453

PLATE 454

452 · 16th century. **THE KING, THE GREAT HETMAN** (see pl. 453). **BRIGA-DIER, LADY OF THE NOBILITY, GENTLEMEN; PEASANTS OF KALISZ AND LITHUANIA.** Garment of Hungarian origin, *bekiesza*. Trousers, boots, heels shod with horse-shoes; national dance, the *mazur*. Distinctive mark of the nobility, the curved sabre, *karabela*; war and parade sabres; *obuk*.

453 · 18th-19th century. **COSTUMES OF THE NOBILITY AND THE PEOPLE.** Hetman, aristocratic lady, peasant women, peasants from Lublin, Cracow, and Lithuania; mountain-dweller from the Carpathians. Bonnets: *konfederatka, krakuska, kolpak*. Garment of Tartar origin, *oponjecka*. Turban, aigrette; *kontuszik*.

454 · 17th-18th century. **THE ASIAN INFLUENCE.** Polish General; royal guard; captain of musketeers; *billicpassi; januszars*, lieutenant, *otapasz porutsznik*, standard-bearer, *wartapsi-conski*, ensign-bearer, *beuraktar-gurugi*, corporal, *jeszmek*. Turban, bonnet, *kulah*, panache, *uskiuf*, aigrettes; dolman, *dolama; chalwar*. Sabres, halberd, gun, battle-axe. The Polish-Lithuanian army, its organisation; the 'army of the watch', *woysko-kwarciane; husarz, pancerns, petyhorces*; infantrymen, dragoons, light cavalry; rear-guard, *pospolite*. The military household of the kings of Poland; a living record of their victories over the Turks. Swiss Guards, the Hungarian heyducks.

455 · 17th– 18th century. **WAR-HORSE IN HOUSING**: harness, saddle, housing or shabrack. Knightly ornament: jewellery, plaques, fasteners, pendants, chest necklaces, quiver. The standard of chief, the *butszuk*. The splendours of 'the horseback nation'. Horses shoed in silver. The Scythian character of Slavic jewellery.

456 · 19th century. **POPULAR COSTUMES** (see pl. 457). Examples of Jews; the coachman, peasant women. Peasants from Lithuania and Samogitia. Lawyer, poultry and onion merchants, sawyers. Milkmaid.

457 · 19th century. Farm servant and serving-woman; **PEASANTS** from the Cracow area, from Samogitia and Lithuania; Ukrainian Cossacks.

458 · **HUNGARIAN NOBLES: MAGNATES. POPULAR COSTUMES.**
Magyar; example of mountain-dwellers, *goral*. Northern Slavs; Galician Poles; *Wasserpolaken*; *Mazures, Gorales*. Ruthenians: *Podolians, Boyïks, Huzuls*. Slovaks (*feher-nep*, white people). Southern Slavs, or *Yugoslavs*: Croatians. Saxonian fiancée: Hungary. Wallachian women. Study on the *Huzuls* or *Hutsuls*, a branch from which the Ruthenians derive. **MEN**. Headdress: *kucsma*, hats, bonnets, the image of the patron saint, aigrettes, ribbons, flowers; cravat, shirts, embroideries, camisole, jacket, dolman, belt, *pass*, redingote, *attila*, cloaks, *mente, gunia, sziir*, houppelande, pelisse, *ziezak*, knee-breeches, fly-ornaments, lace handkerchief, brandenburgs, trousers, *gatyen*; sandals, *skirpze*, boots, tassels, Sarmatian-style spurs. Buckles, chains, belts worked in precious metal. Sabres, hatchet, pistol, powder-flask. Knife, pipe, tinder-box, bag. Canes. **WOMEN**. Toque, mob-cap, bonnets, *krakuska*, headbands, head-cloths, crown. Shirt, *camasia*, wide and bouffante sleeves, little chains; bodice, plastron, jacket, embroidery, épaulettes, belt, *cingatoria*, straps, dress, skirts, apron, *catrintia*, lace, mantles, embroidery, frogs; boots, sandals, leather shoes, *cisme* or *ciobote*. Diadem, frontal, necklaces, glass beads, medals, coins, earring pendants, belts, jewelled rings. (See also pl. 499)

459 · **RUTHENIAN EMBROIDERY**. Their traditions deriving from Asian traditions.

460 · **HUNGARIAN JEWELLERY**: men's decoration, women's jewels. Bonnet, cloak-fasteners, sabre attachment, flowers, openwork background; *Transylvanian enamel*.

PLATE 455

683

PLATE 457

PLATE 458

687

PLATE 459

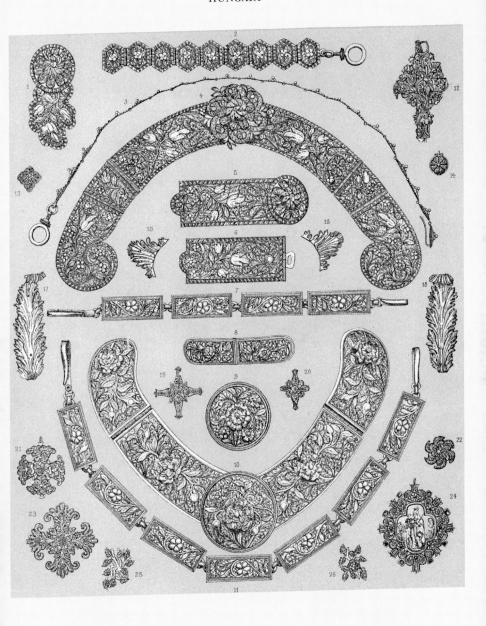

PLATE 460

689

European Turkey

The examples in plate 462 come from what was ancient upper Moesia and upper Albania. It is a peculiarity of history that the barrier of the Danube formed a barrier not only to the armies but to the civilisation of Greece and Rome. This is all the more remarkable for the fact that, despite the proximity of Turkey and the propagation of Islam, the South Slavonic peoples have remained themselves. Tapestried and embroidered Slavonic clothing was much admired at the recent Paris World Exhibition. Their frank and felicitous harmonies and the refined nature of these productions, ancient and modern, are thought to have their roots in ancient Asian arts. Clothing is made in fine but very durable cloth, which is enlivened with coloured designs in tapestry and chain stitch. These garments are made of one of the finest forms of linen known to man. As to tapestried garments, those of the peasant woman of Malissor (pl. 462) speak for themselves. Her costume comprises twenty-nine items, each with its own precise function: the *gueushluk* or tight bodice, the *dublitm*, a stiff skirt without pleat, the apron and the *terba* or sewing bag are the main ones. Using regular and clearly spaced designs, often comprising stripes and unrestrained colours, the South Slavs obtain their effects by ornamenting almost every item of their clothing. The two Christian women in this plate wear harem pants, like the Muslim women. The main industry of the Epirots or Albanians (pl. 464) is costume. The tailor-embroiderers of Ynia [Ioannina], the capital of Epirus, supply the whole of Greece with splendid garments whose fabric is all but invisible under the layer of embroidery. On average, a man's costume of this kind is sold for 1,600 francs (8,000 piastres) and that of a woman for 1,800 francs.

PLATE 461

461 · POPULAR COSTUMES: GREEK AND BULGAR PEASANTS. Fur and cloth bonnets, *fez*, toque, veils, fichus, headscarf, *bashlik*, tow cords, sequins, glass beads; shirt, apron, knee-breeches, harem pants, redingote, pelisse, appliqué work; hose, stockings, gaiters, sandals, leather shoes. Silver belts, fasteners.

462 · EVERYDAY COSTUMES (SCUTARI OF ALBANIA). *Hodja*; peasant woman, lady, Christian priest, Muslim lady. Town, indoor wear. Shepherd, peasants. Southern Slavs: popular arts, original sources; customs of inhabitants, communal life; women's work, lined clothes, Slavonian ornamentation, embroideries, appliqué work, jewellery and goldsmith's work (see pl. 463). *Bashlik*, serviettes, helmet, *tepelik*, little chains, sequins, metallic plates, earring pendants, necklaces; shirt, *beurundjuk*, breast ornament, moulded bodice, *gueushluk*, belt, handkerchief, serviette, buckles, fasteners, *chapras*; cloaks, *ustrugha*, *entari*, *jubbe*, *feredje*, apron; *shalwar*; stockings, *pabudj*; work-bag, *terba*. Fez, *puskul*, *sarik*, *mintan*, *dolama*, *binish*, shoes, *pabudj*, *mest*, *charyk*, *yemeni*; hide garments. Shepherd's flute, *duduk*.

463 · ORNAMENTS OF ASIAN KIND WORN IN TURKESTAN, EGYPT AND BULGARIA. Frontal, *tepelik*, earrings, necklaces, *guerdanlik, orge, eckd, tock*, necklace hangings, *hegab* cases or amulets, bracelets, jewelled rings, *dibleh, khatims*, leg-rings. Women's headdress: helmet-bonnet.

464 · ARNAOUT: RICH AND POOR: *hodja, the hamam-bashi*; peasant, bourgeois, Muslim lady; vilayets of Yania and Selanik (Epirus, or Lower Albania, Thessalia, Macedonia). *Fez, puskul, takke, kaveze*; waistcoats, *djamadan, yelek*; jacket, *chepken*; belt, *silahlik; fistan*, overcoat, *akluha kebeci; calchun, potur*; gaiters, *dizlik, charik, laptshin, gundura*. Women's *entari*, skirt *à la franka, mintan jubbe* and ornaments; trimming, braid, embroidery, *finition. Yashmak*.

PLATE 462

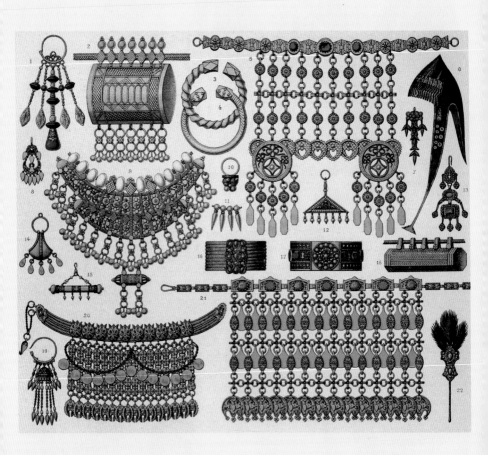

PLATE 464

697

Italy, Spain and Portugal

In the hinterland of Rome, the picturesque clothing of the *contadini* has all but vanished. Today, the men and women of the Roman *campagna* have adopted modern fashions and dress, in the form of second-hand bourgeois clothes. In the surrounding provinces, national costume makes an appearance only on feast days and rare occasions. Thus one sometimes sees in Rome, aside from 'costume wearers' who belong to the numerous dynasties of models, whole families of country folk wearing the traditional costume of their region. The piece of cloth that constitutes the coiffe of most such peasant women is worn in some cases as a veil, in the manner of the Sibyls and vestals of Ancient Rome, in others folded several times to cover the top of the head and fall over the shoulders. The poorest women nevertheless love tawdry stuff, and cannot do without golden chains or necklaces. All still wear a hairpin as in classical times, along with the long earrings called *navicelle*. The *devantiers* or bodices worn by Roman women are of various forms, but generally consist of a simple corset, worn under the arms, laced at the back and held in place by thin straps. This item foregrounds the shirt, whose neck is cut wide and deep. In most places, the cut of the skirt or open gown changes only rarely. The elegance of the Roman woman lies in the way she brings out the colours she wears. The women of Monte Cassino (pl. 468) wear a typical flat headdress known as *amadille*. The linen *camisa* is a tunic with long sleeves, which are often very wide and float around the arm; this garment originated in Ionia and was worn by women in Ancient Rome. The *palissade corset*, often used by peasant women, is unexampled in antiquity. This form of bodice they call simply *corset* when it is reinforced with wicker rather than baleens. The belt is the *scinda*; the gown, that is, the skirt, is called *veste*, and cloth is *panna*.

The *fiestas de toros* have long been the prevailing popular entertainment in Spain (pl. 470). It was not until late in the 18th century that *picadores, banderillos, chulos* and *espada* appeared in regular *cuadrilla*. The *espada* kills the bull on foot with no other arm than a flexible sword and a small piece of red cloth called *muleta* or *engaño*. We give some examples of the combat outfit of the founders of this sport. The comparison shows that in the contemporary *cuadrilla*, consistently tighter costumes have been adopted. The very open jacket, which has épaulettes but no lapels, no longer hangs at all loose, and the breeches are as tight as possible. The belt is both tighter and thinner. The long hairnet has been replaced by a fixed chignon, as one can see in plates 470–471. These plates also show examples of costumes commonly worn by the populace, such as the *gitano* from the province of Grenada, the village women from the province of Toledo with a skirt in painted cotton, and the man wearing the costume of the Andalusian *majo*, notably the *calesera*, a jacket draped over the arm but never worn. All the costumes in plate 472 are still current. The festive costume of the women of Segovia (Santa María de Nueva) includes a black *montera*, adorned with a silver button and made in silk velvet. The skirt is bordered in passementerie of regular design, and the shoe has a rosette. The waistcoat of the peasant of this province is in painted cotton bordered in plain cotton. The two peasant women from the Avila province wear black straw hats with ribbons of goffered velvet. The skirt is in very brightly coloured and rather thick woollen cloth. The bourgeois woman from Asturias displays a gown in merino and a velvet fichu with silver passementerie. A *rebozillo* of white linen is thrown over the shoulders and casually knotted. The Maragatos (pl. 473) occupy the mountains of Astorga, in the province of Léon. This is an ancient tribe that has maintained character, costume and customs different from those of its neighbours. For the most part they wear a jacket held tight to the body by a belt, and wide shorts attached at the knee, where the garter is invariably red. The four Galicians in the same plate are all from the province of Lugo. One of them wears a waistcoat of red wool with ornaments attached to the back. Another is a young peasant, not yet married, as the arrangement of his *montera* (cap) shows; its pom-poms face right, whereas those of married men face left. The peasant from the Valladolid area wears one of those costumes whose appearance can be attributed to military traditions. The *montera* is like a helmet; the cloak, in coarse wool, is like the cassock of a 17th-century man-at-arms. The Catalans do not consider themselves Spanish. Their language is close to old Provençal. It is said that Catalonia, blessed with all of nature's products, could manage quite well without Spain or indeed the rest of the universe. The costume of the Aragonese has been less modernised than that of the Catalans, a fact consistent with the proverbial obstinacy of the people of Zaragoza. This has engendered many anecdotes. Thus, when an Aragonese is born, its mother hits it over the head with a plate, and if the plate breaks, the head is hard and the child will be a good Aragonese. If the head breaks, he will not. The extreme climate and poor soils of Old Castile have always prevented extensive population growth. The inhabitants of this region are the true representatives of Spanish character: dignified and majestic. The costumes in plate 480 belong to the Balearic and Ebusi islands, and to the province of Valencia. In the costume of the Mallorquin man, there is much of Moorish origin: the wide belt and ample breeches, and so on.

The ethnic components of the Portuguese population are more or less those of the contiguous Spanish provinces. Strabo tells us that the ancient inhabitants of these regions wrapped themselves in black cloaks because their sheep were black. The *lenço* which now covers the head of peasant women is a woollen handkerchief placed flat on the head, as these women frequently carry heavy loads on their heads. The 'jacket' is independent of the skirt, and made of red wool; it should be perceived as a bodice with épaulettes. It is closed on one side by concealed buttons. The striped part of the skirt is in merino wool, the lower part, a sort of wide border, in ordinary wool. The apron is in woollen tapestry. It has long been observed that Portuguese women show particular coquetry in the matter of footwear.

PLATE 465

PLATE 466

465 · 19th century, first part. **POPULAR COSTUMES** (see pls. 466–468). Transteverine, Roman, Milanese, Venetian women, women from the Kingdom of Naples; *ciucciardas* of Mola and Fondi.

466 · 19th century, first part. **TRANSTEVERINE MEN, FROM ROME.** *Sgherri romaneschi, capo popoli.* Hats, bonnet, hair in chignon, hairnet, cravat, Neapolitan-style waistcoat, carmagnole, belt, *fascia*, trunk-hose, knee-piece, knee-breeches, rosettes, shoes, buckles. Women's headdress. *Il meo Patacca*, the burlesque hero.

467 · 19th century. **PROVINCE OF ROME. CONTADINI, COCIARE OR MOUNTAIN PEOPLE; PROVINCE OF ANCONA, INHABITANT OF LORE-TO, BARRETTINO.** Headdresses, piece of cloth, veil, headband, *planchette*, shirt, arm-band, fichu, bodices, *devantiers*, jacket, skirt, apron. Chains, necklaces, hairpins, earrings, *navicelle*. The mountain-dweller's shoe, *cocie*.

468 · 19th century. **RURAL COSTUMES.** Peasants from the *Terra di Lavoro*; *pifferari.* Items of women's dress. The flat headdress, *amadille*; fichu, *fascelete*; tunic, *camisa*, armband, *manec*; corset, *corsaletto*; skirt, *casacca*; belt, *scinda*; dress, *veste*; cloth, *panne*; decorated aprons, *scenalis*; woven, embroidered and appliqué ornaments; shawl, *fascelettone*; shoes, *giugieri, scarpe*; necklace, *cannac* or *canac*; earrings, *rocchine*. Instruments of the *pifferari*: flute, bagpipe, Basque drum, triangle.

469 · Late 18th century. **SCENES OF UPPER-CLASS LIFE AND POPULAR EN-TERTAINMENT.** The game of the spoon; stilts race; *clarines, espadas.*

470/471 · **BULLFIGHTING.** *Las fiestas de toros.* Famous *toreros.* The contemporary *cuadrilla* (bullfighting team). Combat dress, old and modern costumes; popular types. The procession of the *cuadrilla*; the *alguaciles*, colours of the *ganaderías, vara de justicia,* key of the bull-pen (*toril*). Those on foot (*peones*); *espadas, banderilleros, chulos* or *capeadores. Picador. Monterilla*, pompons, braided hair (*coleta*), silk chignon, *mona*, hairnet; jacket with epaulettes; waistcoat (*chaleco*); belt (*faja*); tight knee-breeches, leather trousers, greaves; *capa.* Harness, Arabian saddle, wooden stirrups. *Banderillas, palillos, zarcillos, rehiletes. Muleta* or *engaño.* Gypsy, *gitano*; village women (Toledo province); *majo* or Andalusian man, his jacket, *calesera.*

PLATE 467

PLATE 468

PLATE 469

PLATE 471

PLATE 472

472 · POPULAR COSTUMES: Old Castile, León. Village mayor, bourgeois woman, peasant, farmer's wife, *charra*, woman in festive costume (Provinces of Léon, Segovia, Burgos, Avila, and Asturias). Straw hats, *montera* (see pls. 473–476), madras, pins, ribbons, pigtail; shawl, fichu, *rebozillo*, bodice, plastron, apron, embroidery, skirt, appliqué decoration; shoes, rosettes; necklaces, filigree jewellery, buckles, earrings, jewels, *joyas*, cross, medals. Headscarf, jacket, waistcoat, belt, knife, knee-breeches, *alpargatas* or *espardeñas* (see pls. 473–476).

473 · MARAGOTOS, León province. Galicians, with their cudgels (*garrote*), the women's apron (*manteo*, see pl. 476). Asturian women, their fichu (*dengue*). Aragon. *Pregonero*, town crier. Peasant of Old Castile; his *montera*, headdress, etc. Peasants calling each other 'Don ...'.

474 · CATALANS, ARAGONESE (*zaragozanos***).** Mountain people, rich peasants, *pagesas*, young woman, *muchacha* and her *novio*; farmers, small-holders, bede of the confraternity. The wearing of the jacket (see pl. 475). Bonnet, *gorro*; overcoat, *gambeto*; jacket, *marsilla*; *capa de muestra*; espadrilles. Woman's hood, cuffs, and spencer (*corpiño*). The Catalans do not consider themselves Spanish.

475 · OLD CASTILE. Aragon. Murcia. Basque or *vascongadas* provinces. Reapers, *segadores*, peasant women, peasants, children, bride and groom's costume, working clothes. Village priest. *Sombrero*, beret; *faja*; *navajas, cuchillos, puñales*, cloak with collar, trousers, pieces of velvet. Headscarves, braided hair, mantilla.

476 · COSTUMES OF GALICIA. *Gallegos. Baila de la muyneira*, bagpipe-player, *gaitero gallego, músico tamborillero*; dancers; *castañuelas*, Basque drum, *pandero*. Emigration, professions: costume, waistcoat, *manta*, gaiters, *polainas, abarcas, alpargatas*; umbrella; hair in 'dog's ears'. Women's dress: *dengue, mateo*. Feast days, *magosto*. The national dance, *gallegada*.

477/478 · ANDALUSIAN DWELLING. Bourgeois house: exterior, reception room, patio. Popular costumes. *Casas de pupillos* or *de huespedes*: interior, tiling, exposed beams, walls, alcove, bed, furniture, *brasero. Aguador*, peasant, horse-dealer, carter, *arriero*, muleteer, small-holder, *gitana* (Provinces of Toledo, la Mancha, Valencia, and Burgos). *El tricornio*, canvas knee-breeches, *zaraguellas de lienzo*. Castilian and La Mancha mules.

PLATE 473

PLATE 474

713

PLATE 475

PLATE 476

479 · PORCELAIN ROOM (Buen-Retiro, Royal Palace of Madrid). Tiling *à la Trianon*.

480 · POPULAR COSTUMES. Province of Valencia. Balearic Islands, ancient Pytius or Ebusus: Majorca, Menorca, Ibiza. Herdsman, boatman, villagers, ladies, bourgeois. Women's headdress, *rebozillo*. Men's hair: tonsure (see pl. 481).

481 · BALEARIC ISLANDS. *Pageses* (peasants) from Majorca and Mahón (Minorca), 18th and 19th centuries; shepherd, farm-hand, farmers, small-holders. Hats, *moxine*, headscarf-turban, *rabat*, waistcoat, *guardapits*, jacket, *sayo*, bouffant knee-breeches, cape. *Rebozillo en amount, en volant*; hair *en estoffade*; collarette, *floque*, mantilla, *mantele*; fan.

482 · POPULAR AND RELIGIOUS COSTUMES. Mountain dwellers, province of Minho; woman of the civil wars. Peasants, *rusticos*, peasant women, *tricanas*; festive and working costumes. Carrying of loads, shepherd, straw clothing, cowherd, fish- and mussel-merchants, *aveiros*, shrimp-merchants; fishermen, *pescadores*. Ordinary priest, parish priest, monastic orders, Antonian, Dominican, Carmelite, Benedictine orders. Headscarf, *lenço*; cloak, *capa*; parasol, *chapéu-de-sol*, shoes, wooden soles (see pl. 483). Cloak, *houra de miranda*, *alpargatas*. Biretta, cassock, *batina e capa*.

483 · POPULAR JEWELLERY. Golden and silver jewels; Viana peasant women in ornamental costume; her shoe. Earring pendants, necklaces, broaches, pendants, medallions, hearts, crosses, one of them *astrale*. Peasant woman's costume, apron, bag. Portuguese industries: lace, Honiton-style; *rendeiros*; cloth: ordinary cloth, *serguilha*, and *saragoça* cloth. Rural population: soil, 'blessed land', cultivation of vine and pastoral farming.

PLATE 481

721

PLATE 483

723

FRANCE

The population of Upper and Lower Auvergne is, without exception, strong and industrious (pl. 484). The highlanders, unlike the valley-dwellers, are perfectly unchanged in their customs. They take as much care to maintain these customs as others would to slough them off. Some years ago, one might still see Auvergnats in Upper Auvergne wearing the traditional costume generally made of *raze*, a coarse woollen cloth. This costume included a long jacket with large pockets called the *poulacre*. The *coubertie* (ancient *sagum*) is still worn; this is a striped cloak called *argo peillous* when it is old and patched. But the rest of the costume has changed completely. Today, it consists in a cassock of blue or grey velvet. On Sundays, the *gougou*, a long woollen cloak, is put on. Among women who have not yet succumbed to modern fashions, the costume is generally a homespun gown whose bodice is covered by a foulard of printed calico.

Plate 485 shows various examples of the Bordelais costume. Nothing could be more dainty than the Bordeaux shop-girl of around 1820: the silk gown is just short enough to show her little feet finely shod in flat soles. She also wears a *fripon*, a jolly velvet apron, while her knotted headscarf leaves two bandeaux visible. This was a time when rank could still be perceived by dress.

The Landais, strictly speaking, live close to the ocean. The shepherds of the Landes (the *Lanusquets*) are shown in plate 486 on decorated *escasse* or *tchanques* (stilts). The woman on stilts wears a brassière and a skirt, beneath which can be seen the *camauo* or ewe-skin protecting her feet. Women are the heads of the household.

In the Pyrenees, the population is undoubtedly of Spanish origin, and throughout the mountain range, men's costume is composed of the same elements: jacket, double-breasted waistcoat, shorts and high gaiters, in short, traditional highlander's dress. The cocked hat has nowadays completely disappeared. In the Basses-Pyrénées, Basque and Bearnais costumes predominate. The Basque woman wears a headscarf, whereas the Béarnaise wears the hood usual in the other Pyrenean *départements*. Otherwise, the broad linen shirt attached at the neck, and drawn tight at the hips by the ties of a simple and very short black skirt of fustian, is almost universal. Between Bayonne and Saint-Jean de Luz one meets troops of young women walking at great speed and carrying baskets on their heads; these are the *cascarottes*, the intrepid sardine couriers who deliver the night catch.

The individual way of life of the former comté of Nice (pl. 487) still survives. In Saône-et-Loire, the inhabitants have conserved some of the distinctive qualities of their old customs. Women's costume, for example, remains unchanged. All still wear the old *chaperon* or *cape*, which affords a striking analogy with the *huiken* of the Rhine women of the 17th century. This headdress is sometimes decorated at the top by a 'flower' of lace and a tuft of feathers. Sometimes it is adorned only by an immense veil hung from the flat rim of the hat. Some years before the annexation of Alsace (1648), a rigorous social hierarchy existed there. As in the Middle Ages, highly detailed regulations prescribed the display of luxury, determining the quality of silk, velvet, ribbons, fur, and the expense of jewellery. The first of the six categories comprised the wealthy Alsatian nobility, the senators, the *Amtmeister* and the *Stadtmeister* (county and municipal magistrates). This class could dress according to its own conventions. When Strasbourg was restored to France, men followed French fashions, but the women retained their affection for traditional costume (pl. 488). This state of affairs continued until the Revolution. The dressof Alsatian country people is very simple, and has survived and perfected itself over generations, while yet experiencing the influence of the dominant taste of each epoch. But in recent years it has begun to disappear.

Plate 489 offers some examples of the popular costumes found on the shores of the Channel, particularly among the fisherman of Dieppe. There are currently few differences between the fishermen of Le Pollet and those of the rest of the coast. Almost all wear a long jacket over a double-breasted waistcoat and the same skirt-like garment with a strong belt at the waist. In Normandy, the women's costume affords a certain variety, in which the traits peculiar to each little region are blended. The true ancestor of the Norman bonnet is the horn-shaped *hennin* long worn in England. The Caen *calipette* is a headband whose side has been raised to form a sort of halo around the head, using a broad piece of flounced lace.

The Breton costumes reproduced in plates 491–496 testify to the rich diversity of clothing worn in that region. The *bigouden* is the coiffe of lawn or cotton with which the peasant women of Pont-l'Abbé cover their embroidered silk headband. There is a form for the young single woman and another for the married woman, and within these categories several further variations occur. Time has made the agreeable name *bigouden* synonymous with those who wear it, and such women, whose coquetry is proverbial in Lower Brittany, are called the Bigoudins of Pont-l'Abbé. The population of Les Sables-d'Olonne is among the most robust in all France. The men are expert sardine-fishermen, and wives assist their husbands. Their costume has an overall character that is varied by several kinds of headgear, the most elegant of which is illustrated in plate 496 (figure 16): the *coiffe frisée* or *cabriole*. Even today, the inhabitants of former Armorica still conserve much of their originality. Clans are distinguished by the colour of their clothes. Quimper is the region of the *glazeiz*, or blue; Pleyben that of the *ardaaeded*, the brown. Pontivy is the region of the whites, *guenedouriens*, Plougastel of the reds, and Kerlouan that of the blue bonnets. The men for the most part wear a round felt hat, which is almost universally adorned with broad ribbons of black velvet that hang down, and are kept on the crown of the hat by one or more silver or tin buckles. Over the velvet they place chenille of various colours. The women's headdresses vary from town to town. They generally wear three sorts of petticoat. The top petticoat is called *bros-uhelen*, the middle one, *lostenn-greiz*, and the nethermost the *bros-gueleden*. All three are bordered with braiding. On Pardon days, the women add the *tavanger*, which is made of the finest old watered silk, dove-coloured shot silk, pompadour cloth, or other such. The Breton house (pl. 499 500) comprises a single ground-floor room, over which is an attic. Breton furniture is never older than about 1600, and is never cabinet-maker's work, but that of a *malvunuzein*, a country carpenter. They include the *gwilé*, or bed, which forms part of the woman's dowry; in Finistère, these beds are enclosed.

484 · 19th century. **PEOPLE OF AUVERGNE, FROM LIMAGNIE AND VEL-LAVIE. PODOTES** (inhabitants of Le Puy). **BOURBONNICHONNES** (inhabitants of the Bourbonnais: see pl. 487). **WOMEN OF MOULINS. POPULAR COSTUMES: WORKING CLOTHES, SUNDAY BEST.** Hats, cape, hood, capette, bonnet, coiffes, head-bands, tin circlets, serre-malice, shawls, fichus, bodice, armbands, apron, pièce, tucked-up dress, cape; golden chains, Saint-Esprit, pendants. Round hats with broad brims, two- or three-cornered; biaude (former bliaut); casaque, surtout, paulacre, sword-belt, breeches, gaiters, cloaks, pubertie, argo peilloux; sabots, recolle. Fabrics, raze, homespun. Knife, gougou, tailladou, coutelière; iron-tipped staves.

485 · First part of the 19th century. **INHABITANTS OF BORDEAUX. WOMEN'S COSTUMES, POPULAR CLASSES.** coiffes. Grisettes (working girl). Women of the people, portanière; women poultry-, fish- and baked-apple-sellers; dairymaid, fille de peine, village wom-en; little girls from Laroque, Cauderan and Blaye. Béarn handkerchief, madras, head-protector, capedur, collars, collarettes, fichus, brassières, apron, fripon, pockets, clavier, capes, shawls; buskin-style flat shoe; watches, hair-chains, cross à la Jeannette. Inhabitants of Chartre. Bordelais francs (pure) or métis, les filleules de Bourdeaux (surrounding towns).

486 · 19th century, first part. **LANDES. WESTERN PYRENEES. POPULAR COS-TUMES.** Inhabitants of the Landes; winter and summer garb; mountain-dwellers; maritime pop-ulation (Haut-Garonne, Hautes-Pyrénées, Basse-Pyrénées). Hood: capulet. Escasse, tchanques, stilts; hood, tuft of feathers, barrette, dolman, camauo, pelisse, capot, manteau de Charlemagne. Saucepan a cruchades. Cascarottes (women sardine-porters).

PLATE 484

729

PLATE 486

PLATE 488

FRANCE

487 · 19th century. **MORVANDELLES (MORVAN) PEASANT WOMEN, FROM THE COMTÉS OF NICE AND THE DAUPHINÉ;** Savoy mountain-dweller (see pl. 496). Bourbonnichonne. women from Mâcon, Bresse, hat *de grande parure, cape.* Straw hats, *capellina,* hairnet, *scuffia; poulan* dress, collarettes, jackets, armbands, neckscarfs, fichu, *kaireu,* apron, cape, mittens; shoe, clogs, slippers. Earring pendants, necklaces, neck-chains, ornaments hung on gold chains.

488 · **ALSACE. VARIOUS HEADDRESSES,** *bendel,* 17th century. **POPULAR COSTUMES,** 19th century. Woman gardener, peasant women, simple bonnets, with broad ribbons, modern style. Former Alsatian society, classes of the population: magistrates, *Amtmeister,* mayors *Stadtmeister,* bourgeois, country people; sumptuary laws; French fashions.

489 · 18th and 19th centuries. **CHANNEL SHORES. MARITIME POPULATION:** fishermen from Dieppe. *Polletais* (Pollet, Dieppe suburb), festive and working costume; peasant women, pedlar. Coiffes, barbs, collar, fichu, bodice, shortened skirt, armbands; mittens, flat shoes. Bonnets, mob-caps, aigrette, wig, earring, cravat, jacket, cassock, knee-breeches, petticoat, clocked stockings, mules. Fishing tackle.

490 · 19th century, first part. **NORMANDY. WOMEN'S COSTUMES. BONNETS.** Women of Rouen, Le Havre, le Pays de Caux, Bayeux, Caen, Pont-l'Evêque, Varangeville. Cauchois bonnet, back brim, front brim, pointed; *calipette,* veil; *bavolet,* ribbons, cotton bonnet. Hair in chignon, hairpieces, pins. The *juste-au-corps* or caraco, aprons with bib. Women riders, *planchette,* side-saddle stirrup.

491 · 19th century. **BRETON COSTUMES.** Finistère département, Quimperlé, Châteaulin, Lorien arrondissements. Bride's costume. Young woman from Île-de-Batz (see pls. 482 and 486).

492 · **BRITTANY.** Costumes from Morbihan and Finistère départements. Pontivy, Quimper, Châteaulin, Quimperlé, Morlaix arrondissements. Woman from Île-de-Batz.

493 · **FINISTÈRE DÉPARTEMENT. FORMAL AND WORKING COSTUMES:** men from Brest, Quimper, Châteaulin arrondissements.

PLATE 491

737

PLATE 492

PLATE 493

PLATE 494

PLATE 495

PLATE 496

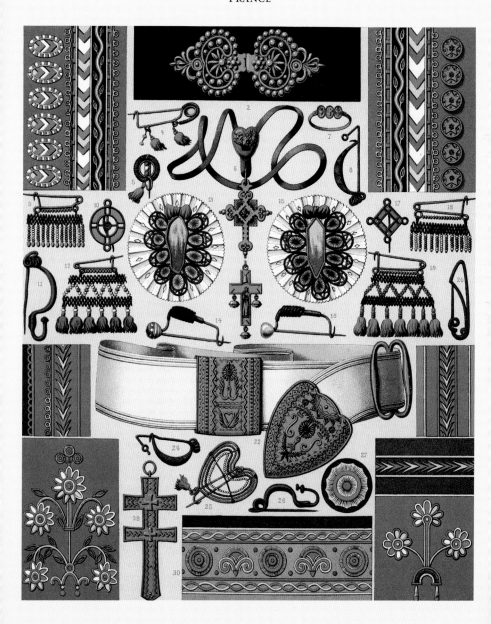

PLATE 497

743

494 · BRITTANY, FINISTÈRE DÉPARTEMENT. MEN'S AND WOMEN'S
COSTUMES: bride and groom from Kerfeunteun. Hat, *toc*, waistcoat, *roqueden maoues, rokedennou*,
belt, *gouriz*, jacket, *corquen*, knee-breeches, *bragou-braz*, leggings. Coiffes; shirt, *hirviz*, bodice, *justin*,
pardon (pilgrimage) apron, *tavanger*.

495 · BRITTANY, FINISTÈRE DÉPARTEMENT. MEN'S COSTUMES.
Roscovites (from Roscoff), the 'whites' or *guenedouriens* from Quimperlé. Shoes, *btou-lezr*, clogs, *botou-
coad*; sticks, *pen-bas*.

496 · BRITTANY. WOMEN FROM LES-SABLES-D'OLONNE: fishwife, wom-
en market-gardener. Women from Île-de-Batz, salting workers; bride and groom from Saillé.
Churching cloak, *ventel*. Savoy woman's costume, like that of Breton women. Headdresses, *bigoudens*,
coiffe frisée or *cabriole, cabellous*; bonnets of boy, of children. Mantle, *pièce (devantier)*; stockings, *viroles*,
clocked stockings *à fourchette* (clocks); clogs, *patines*. Three-peaked hat, *chemisette*.

497 · 19th century. BRITTANY. EMBROIDERIES; ORNAMENTS. Pilgrimage
rosettes, hearts, crosses, fasteners, buckles, little pins, jewelled rings. Old fibulae. *Chupen, corquen,
rokedennou, justin*, belt, *gouriz*, slipper-edge embroidery. Different regions of the blues, *glazeiz*, browns,
ardaaeded, whites, *guenedouriens*; and of the blue bonnets and red bonnets. Women's costume: over-
skirt, *bros-uhelen*, intermediate skirt, *lostenn-greiz*, underskirt, *brosgueleden*.

498 · BRITTANY. RURAL FURNITURE. *Arche*, bridal chest; Celtic character of
sculptures.

499/500 · BRITTANY, THE 'DWELLING' (DEMEURANCE) HOUSE;
INTERIOR. POPULAR COSTUMES (Finistère, Loire-Inférieure). Breton house, *ti* or
Kear; assié de hu; full door, *hu;* half-door, *contre-hu;* fireplace, *place*, hearth, *chipots, le g'llaumé*. Furni-
ture (*malvununzein*): beds, *gwilé cloz, gwiléou steng*, chests, *arch'iou, grinoliou*, dresser, cupboards: *armel,
presse;* dining table, *taol*, spoon-stand, *cliquet*, chair, *kador*, stool with three *quilles. Moques, briques, touques.*
Bread-board, *râté*. Preparations for a wedding. Bride's dress; crêpe-making; Batz salting-worker;
Breton bagpipe(*biniou*)-player, *kerniad*.

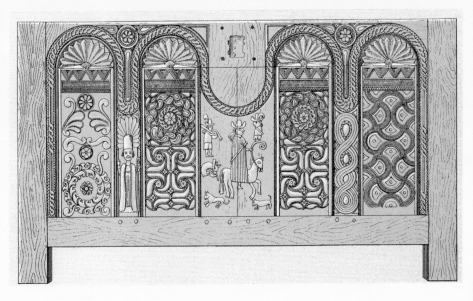

PLATE 498

BIBLIOGRAPHY

ABOUT RACINET Archives nationales, dossier de légion d'honneur, n 20 691, 5 August 1878. G. VAPEREAU, *Dictionnaire universel des contemporains*, 6th ed. (enlarged), Paris, 1893. R. COLAS, *Bibliographie générale du Costume et de la Mode*, Paris, 1933.

BY RACINET Contribution to P. LACROIX et F. SÉRÉ, *Le Moyen-Âge et la Renaissance, histoire et description des moeurs et usages, du commerce et de l'industrie, des sciences, des arts, des littératures et des beaux-arts en Europe*, Paris, Rivaud, 1848–1851. Contribution to Ch. LOUANDRE et HANGARD-MAUGÉ, *Les Arts somptuaires. Histoire du costume et de l'ameublement et des arts et industries qui s'y rattachent*, Paris, Hangard-Maugé, 1857–1858. *L'Ornement polychrome, 2000 motifs. Recueil historique et pratique*, Paris, Firmin-Didot, 1869. English and German eds. 1873, 2nd (French) ed. 1875, 3rd éd. 1885–1887. *Le Costume historique. Types principaux du vêtement et de la parure rapprochés de ceux de l'intérieur de l'habitation dans tous les temps et chez tous les peuples avec de nombreux détails sur le mobilier, les armes, les objets usuels, les moyens de transport, etc...* Paris, Firmin-Didot, 1876–1888. Art editor of the *Collection archéologique du prince Saltykoff*, Paris, Firmin-Didot, 1878. Art editor of *La Céramique japonaise*, in English and German, Firmin-Didot, 1878, reprinted 1881.

CHRONOLOGY OF THE MOST IMPORTANT WORKS ON COSTUME HISTORY IN THE 19th CENTURY C. BONNARD et P. MERCURI, *Costumes ecclésiastiques, civils et militaires des XIIIe, XIVe, XVe siècles*, Rome, published by the author, 1827–1828; Paris, Treuttel, 1829–1830, reprinted Goupil, 1845. Id., *Costumes historiques des XIIe, XIIIe, XIVe et XVe siècles tirés des monuments les plus authentiques de peinture et sculpture*. Revised ed. by Charles Blanc (former Director of the École des Beaux-arts), Paris, Lévy, 1860–1861. Supplemented by E. LECHEVALLIER-CHEVIGNARD et G. DUPLESSIS, *Costumes historiques des XVIe, XVIIe et XVIIIe siècles*, Paris, Lévy, 1867–1873. J. H. von HEFNER-ALTENECK, *Costumes du moyen-âge chrétien d'après les monuments contemporains*, Mannheim, Hoff, German and French editions, 1840–1854, further German ed., Darmstadt, Beyerle, 1840–1854. C. BECKER et J. H. von HEFNER-ALTENECK, *Kunstwerke und Geräthschaften des Mittelalters und der Renaissance*, Frankfurt am Main, Keller, 1852–1863. P. LACROIX, *Costumes historiques de la France d'après les monuments les plus authentiques, statues, bas-reliefs, tombeaux, sceaux, monnaies, peintures à fresque, tableaux, vitraux, miniatures, dessins, estampes. Histoire de la vie privée des français depuis l'origine de la monarchie jusqu'à nos jours*, Paris, Lacour et cie, 1852. VIOLLET-LE-DUC, *Dictionnaire raisonné du mobilier français de l'époque carlovingienne à la renaissance*, Paris, Morel, 1858–1875. H. WEISS, *Kostümkunde. Geschichte der Tracht und des Geräthes*, Stuttgart, Ebner und Seubert, 1860–1872. R. JACQUEMIN, *Iconographie générale et méthodique du costume du IVe au XIXe siècle (315–1815)*, Paris, published by the author, 1863–1869. Enlarged and revised editions: Nadaud, 1872, Delagrave, 1876, Nadaud, 1880. P. LACROIX, *Moeurs, usages et costumes au Moyen Âge et à l'époque de la Renaissance*. Paris, Firmin-Didot, 1872. Id., *XVIIIe siècle. Institutions, usages et costumes. France 1700–*

1789, Paris, Firmin-Didot, 1874. Id., *XVIIe siècle. Institutions, usages et costumes. France, 1590–1700*, Paris, Firmin-Didot, 1880. J. H. von HEFNER-ALTENECK, *Trachten, Kunstwerke und Geräthschaften vom frühen Mittelalter bis Ende des achtzehnten Jahrhunderts*, Frankfurt am Main, Keller, 1879–1889; French ed., 1880–1897. F. HOTTENROTH, *Trachten, Haus, Feld und Kriegsgeräthschaften der Völker alter und neuer Zeit*, Stuttgart, Weise, 1884–1891; French ed., Paris, Guérinet, 1898. L. ROGER-MILÈS, *Comment discerner les styles du VIIIe au XIXe siècle. Etudes sur les formes et les variations propres à déterminer les caractères du style dans le costume et la mode. La mode-les symboles-la tradition*, Paris, Rouveyre, c. 1906.

ACKNOWLEDGEMENTS

This reprint of Auguste Racinet's *Le Costume historique* of 1888 is based on a copy in the possession of Michael Whiteway in London and was made possible by the kind permission of the owner. The original volumes of *Le Costume historique* were digitally reproduced by the Digital-isierungsZentrum der Staats- und Universitätsbibliothek Göttingen. We wish to thank Martin Liebetruth of GDZ and the library of the Musée Galliera in Paris for their kind support.

**What Great
Paintings Say**

**Hieronymus Bosch.
Complete Works**

**Caravaggio.
Complete Works**

Gustav Klimt

**Vermeer.
Complete Works**

**Michelangelo.
Complete Paintings**

**Michelangelo.
The Graphic Work**

Dalí. The Paintings

Modern Art

Hiroshige

**Leonardo da Vinci.
Complete Paintings**

Bookworm's delight:
never bore, always excite!

TASCHEN
Bibliotheca Universalis

**Leonardo da Vinci.
The Graphic Work**

Impressionism

Monet

Van Gogh

Renoir

**Becker. Medieval &
Renaissance Art**

**Prisse d'Avennes.
Oriental Art**

**Prisse d'Avennes.
Egyptian Art**

**D'Hancarville.
Antiquities**

**Braun/Hogenberg.
Cities of the World**

**Mamerot. A Chronicle
of the Crusades**

The Book of Bibles

Encyclopaedia
Anatomica

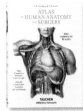

Bourgery. Atlas of
Anatomy & Surgery

Alchemy & Mysticism

Basilius Besler's
Florilegium

A Garden Eden

Martius.
The Book of Palms

Piranesi.
Complete Etchings

Seba. Cabinet of
Natural Curiosities

Bodoni. Manual of
Typography

Byrne. Six Books
of Euclid

The World
of Ornament

Racinet.
The Costume History

Karl Blossfeldt

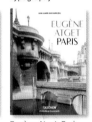

Eugène Atget. Paris

Curtis. The North
American Indian

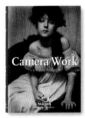

Stieglitz.
Camera Work

20th Century
Photography

New Deal
Photography

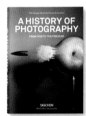

A History of
Photography

Eadweard Muybridge

Film Posters of the
Russian Avant-Garde

Bauhaus

Modern
Architecture A-Z

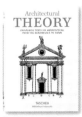

Architectural Theory

IMPRINT

EACH AND EVERY TASCHEN BOOK PLANTS A SEED!
TASCHEN is a carbon-neutral publisher. Each year, we offset
our annual carbon emissions with carbon credits at the Instituto Terra,
a reforestation programme in Minas Gerais, Brazil, founded by Lélia and Sebastião Salgado.
To find out more about this ecological partnership,
please check: www.taschen.com/zerocarbon
Inspiration: unlimited. Carbon footprint: zero.

To stay informed about TASCHEN and our upcoming titles,
please subscribe to our free magazine at www.taschen.com/magazine,
follow us on Instagram and Facebook, or e-mail your questions
to contact@taschen.com.

Endpapers: France, 1802: the promenade de Longchamp (plate 408/409)
Illustration page 2: title page of Racinet's *Le Costume historique*, 1888
Illustration page 4: detail from plate 9

Translation: Chris Miller, Oxford

Printed in China
ISBN 978-3-8365-5540-1